How Animals Affect Us

How Animals Affect Us

Examining the Influence of Human–Animal Interaction
on Child Development and Human Health

EDITED BY

Peggy McCardle, Sandra McCune,
James A. Griffin, and Valerie Maholmes

AMERICAN PSYCHOLOGICAL ASSOCIATION

WASHINGTON, DC

Published by
American Psychological Association
750 First Street, NE
Washington, DC 20002
www.apa.org

To order
APA Order Department
P.O. Box 92984
Washington, DC 20090-2984
Tel: (800) 374-2721; Direct: (202) 336-5510
Fax: (202) 336-5502; TDD/TTY: (202) 336-6123
Online: www.apa.org/pubs/books/
E-mail: order@apa.org

In the U.K., Europe, Africa, and the Middle East, copies may be ordered from
American Psychological Association
3 Henrietta Street
Covent Garden, London
WC2E 8LU England

Typeset in Goudy by Circle Graphics, Inc., Columbia, MD

Printer: Edwards Brothers, Inc., Ann Arbor, MI
Cover Designer: Berg Design, Albany, NY

The opinions and statements published are the responsibility of the authors, and such opinions and statements do not necessarily represent the policies of the American Psychological Association.

Library of Congress Cataloging-in-Publication Data

How animals affect us : examining the influence of human-animal interaction on child development and human health / edited by Peggy McCardle ... [et al.].—1st ed.
    p. cm.
 Includes bibliographical references and index.
 ISBN-13: 978-1-4338-0865-4
 ISBN-10: 1-4338-0865-X
 ISBN-13: 978-1-4338-0866-1 (e-book)
 ISBN-10: 1-4338-0866-8 (e-book)
 1. Pets—Therapeutic use. 2. Human-animal relationships. 3. Child development.
I. McCardle, Peggy D.

 RC489.P47H69 2011
 616.89'1658—dc22

                                                                    2010020978

British Library Cataloguing-in-Publication Data

A CIP record is available from the British Library.

Printed in the United States of America
First Edition

The pet, in a sense, becomes the mirror in which the child sees him(her)self wanted and loved not for what he (or she) should be or might be or might have been but for what he (or she) is.

—B. M. Levinson. *Pet-Oriented Child Psychotherapy* (2nd ed.)

CONTENTS

CONTRIBUTORS

Tim Adams, BVSc, Petcare Information and Advisory Service, Camberwell, Victoria, Australia

Karen M. Allen, PhD, State University of New York at Buffalo

Frank R. Ascione, PhD, University of Denver, Colorado

Sandra B. Barker, PhD, Virginia Commonwealth University, Richmond

Judy S. DeLoache, PhD, University of Virginia, Charlottesville

Nicole R. Dorey, PhD, University of Florida, Gainesville

Layla Esposito, PhD, *Eunice Kennedy Shriver* National Institute of Child Health and Human Development, Bethesda, MD

Lisa Freund, PhD, *Eunice Kennedy Shriver* National Institute of Child Health and Human Development, Bethesda, MD

Erika Friedmann, PhD, University of Maryland, Baltimore

Markus Grabka, PhD, German Institute for Economic Research, Berlin, Germany

Mark T. Greenberg, PhD, Pennsylvania State University, University Park

James A. Griffin, PhD, *Eunice Kennedy Shriver* National Institute of Child Health and Human Development, Bethesda, MD

Linda Handlin, University of Skövde, Skövde, Sweden

Bruce Headey, PhD, Melbourne Institute of Applied Economic and Social Research, Parkville, Australia

Karyl Hurley, DVM, Mars, Incorporated, McLean, VA

Rebecca A. Johnson, PhD, RN, FAAN, Missouri University College of Veterinary Medicine, Columbia

Alan E. Kazdin, PhD, ABPP, Yale University, New Haven, CT

Vanessa LoBue, New York University, New York, NY

Valerie Maholmes, PhD, CAS, *Eunice Kennedy Shriver* National Institute of Child Health and Human Development, Bethesda, MD

Mika Maruyama, PhD, Portland State University, Portland, OR

Peggy McCardle, PhD, MPH, *Eunice Kennedy Shriver* National Institute of Child Health and Human Development, Bethesda, MD

Sandra McCune, PhD, Waltham Centre for Pet Nutrition, Leicestershire, England

Gail F. Melson, PhD, Purdue University, West Lafayette, IN

Maria Petersson, Karolinska Institutet, Stockholm, Sweden

Megan Bloom Pickard, PhD, University of Virginia, Charlottesville

Jo Salmon, PhD, Deakin University, Burwood, Victoria, Australia

Anna Timperio, PhD, Deakin University, Burwood, Victoria, Australia

Monique A. R. Udell, PhD, University of Florida, Gainesville

Kerstin Uvnäs-Moberg, the Swedish University of Agricultural Sciences, Skara, Sweden

Clive D. L. Wynne, PhD, University of Florida, Gainesville

FOREWORD

MARK T. GREENBERG

This volume creates a landscape of new ideas on what we might consider both commonplace and yet mysterious—our relations with animals and their influences on children and developmental processes. The chapters collectively form a multilevel, ecological model from which to consider the social, emotional, physiological, and contextual effects of the growing child's relationship with other animals. How do we best characterize the nature of our relationships with our pets? What are the physiological and neural effects of human–animal touch across development? Can our fascination with, and love of, animals help to heal children or adults who have had trauma? These questions and many others are addressed by the research in this volume, as well as the possibility that child–animal interactions may help support children's coping and resilience. As with many areas of prevention research, carefully designed studies with well-characterized samples, well-designed interventions, and appropriate measures are necessary. We cannot rely on the claims of advocates or advertisers to know the answers to such questions.

The broad conceptual model introduced here is essential to our ability to move from personal experience to scientific discovery. A focus group with 10 teenagers might tell 10 different stories about their relationships with animals during childhood. A few would likely talk about their deep love for, and intimacy with, their pets and how important and meaningful these relationships were, including in times of stress. Others might talk about losing and grieving for their animals and the fond remembrances of them, or they might comment on how this loss, when young and with supportive parents, helped them learn to grieve and cope. Still others might talk about their fear of animals and tell stories of avoiding certain streets or certain friends' homes because of fear of their friends' pets. Like most aspects of developmental experience, children with different backgrounds and environments will have different experiences and outcomes from their encounters with animals. Thus, developing a scholarly understanding of the influence of animals on children's development will require understanding individual differences in children, their families, and their larger ecologies. All of these factors are likely to influence or moderate the effects of pet ownership and animal encounters.

As this book breaks new ground for developmental science, it also raises more questions than it can answer and thus provides a road map for future science. I look forward to the influence of this book in generating rigorous science that helps to test our deep intuitions about the importance of our relationships with other animals across the life span.

ACKNOWLEDGMENTS

This book is based in part on the workshop, Directions in Human–Animal Interaction Research: Child Development, Health and Therapeutic Interventions, which was held in the fall of 2008. This meeting served as a springboard for the more focused examination of human–animal interaction presented in the book and was sponsored through the public–private partnership between the Waltham Centre for Pet Nutrition, a division of Mars, Incorporated, and the *Eunice Kennedy Shriver* National Institute of Child Health and Human Development (NICHD), established to promote and support research on human–animal interaction (HAI). The editors acknowledge both partners for their support of the workshop and indirectly for making this volume possible.

The Waltham Centre for Pet Nutrition is located in the United Kingdom and is the hub of Mars, Incorporated's global research activities on animal nutrition and health, in support of their various brands of pet foods but also in support of science more generally. The Centre's scientists have pioneered important breakthroughs in pet nutrition and have shared their findings in more than 1,500 research publications. Their facility integrates office and research space for pets and people. Affiliated with the Centre is the Waltham

Foundation, formed in 2001, which is dedicated to scientific research on the nutrition and healthy longevity of companion animals. The foundation has funded research in more than 20 countries, providing research grants to improve the health and welfare of companion animals. Waltham–Mars have supported various conferences and meetings, as well as research studies examining various aspects of HAI, and in 2008, they initiated the current public–private partnership with the NICHD.

The *Eunice Kennedy Shriver* NICHD, one of the 27 institutes and centers comprised by the US National Institutes of Health, was established in 1962 to investigate the broad aspects of human development as a means of understanding developmental disabilities, including mental retardation, and the events that occur during pregnancy. Today, the Institute conducts and supports research on all stages of human development, from preconception to adulthood, to better understand the health of children, adults, families, and communities.

We also acknowledge several individuals who have been instrumental in making this volume a reality including John Lunde, Megan Sibole, Tiffany Ray, Wanda Hawkes, Fuambai Ahmadu, Sarah Wright, and Tim Adams. Also, for tracking chapters for the book, assisting with editing, and making sure the entire manuscript was delivered for publication, very special thanks go to Fuambai Ahmadu. And finally, for patiently assisting us in finalizing a book prospectus and for guiding us through the entire submission and production process at the American Psychological Association (APA), thanks to the APA in general and specifically to Maureen Adams, Shenny Wu, and Beth Hatch.

How Animals Affect Us

HUMAN–ANIMAL INTERACTION RESEARCH: AN INTRODUCTION TO ISSUES AND TOPICS

JAMES A. GRIFFIN, SANDRA McCUNE, VALERIE MAHOLMES, AND KARYL HURLEY

> It often happens that a man is more humanely related to a cat or dog than to any human being.
>
> —*Henry David Thoreau*

As humans evolved over the ages and interacted with other animals, they learned how to domesticate some of these animals, particularly dogs (Chapter 5, this volume). Over time, people brought companion animals into their homes, workplaces, and, more recently, therapeutic milieus. Yet, although human–animal interaction (HAI) is commonplace during childhood and throughout the life span, it was only recently recognized as an area of legitimate scientific inquiry, with the term *anthrozoology* introduced to describe the study of human–animal interactions.

A shortage of robust scientific research still limits our understanding of the effects of HAI on human health and development across the different stages of life, and there is confusion about which therapeutic practices involving companion animals have a solid evidentiary basis and which are merely anecdotal, yet appear promising. The need for additional rigorous research on HAI is clear, especially in light of (a) the changing role pets play throughout people's lives, (b) HAI's potential connection to a host of

The views expressed in this manuscript are those of the authors and do not necessarily represent those of the National Institutes of Health, *Eunice Kennedy Shriver* National Institute of Child Health and Human Development, the U.S. Department of Health and Human Service, or Mars, Incorporated.

d outcomes, and (c) the already increas-
nproven, HAI interventions by practi-
poses a framework for researching HAI
ginning of an evidence base for the ther-

OF HAI RESEARCH

mes include a pet (American Veterinary
07), with many people considering their
pets to be family members. Indeed, some people's earliest memories involve playing with a family pet. These interactions provide children with early mastery experiences, such as being able to pet a dog or cat, and they teach children that those around them have their own thoughts and feelings (e.g., when the dog or cat does not want to be petted and runs away). As children age, the bond between them and a companion animal tends to deepen, and many begin treating their pet as a best friend and confidant. Although these bonds may loosen in later adolescence or when the children leave home, there is often a renewed human–animal attachment when these children (now adults) acquire their own pet, either as a companion or in preparation for having children of their own. For the elderly, especially those living in isolation, a companion animal may be the most consistent source of social interaction and may serve as a surrogate for the now grown children.

Although the role of HAI at different stages of human growth and development is understudied (Chapter 1, this volume), exciting new research is providing insights into the role HAI plays in cognitive development in the earliest stages of life (Chapter 4, this volume). Psychopathology also can be expressed through the maltreatment of animals in childhood and adolescence, which is often predictive of later antisocial behaviors in adulthood (Chapter 6, this volume).

Perhaps the greatest contribution that HAI research has made to date is the exploration of the effects of HAI on human health. From preventing childhood obesity (Chapter 7, this volume), to promoting recovery after a heart attack (Chapter 9, this volume), to encouraging walking in the elderly (Chapter 10, this volume), interactions with companion animals are associated with a range of positive health behaviors and health outcomes. Although the exact mechanism by which these benefits accrue is not always clear (Chapter 8, this volume), new findings are emerging that provide fresh insights into the physiological underpinnings of the positive health effects associated with HAI (Chapter 3, this volume).

In addition to providing companionship in our homes, various animals are now also common visitors to schools, hospitals, nursing homes, prisons, and more, with an increasing number of animals involved in formal therapeutic interventions (Wells, 2009; Wilson, 2006). Examples of these activities include certified volunteers taking their dogs to visit classrooms, nursing homes, and cancer wards; the use of specially trained dogs working with children with autism spectrum disorders in classroom and home settings; and therapeutic horseback riding sessions by adolescents with emotional and behavioral difficulties. The common assumption underlying these activities is that the special relationship inherent in HAI has unique benefits.

CHALLENGES OF HAI RESEARCH

Given the popularity of pets and the promise of new HAI interventions to enhance human health, a single question comes to mind: Why don't we know more about this topic?

As described in this volume (Chapter 2, Chapter 10) and elsewhere (Griffin, McCune, Maholmes, & Hurley, 2010), more than any other reason, methodological limitations have slowed the accumulation of research knowledge in the field of HAI. In particular, HAI is difficult to study in a controlled fashion because HAI studies cannot be "blind" (i.e., people know whether they are interacting with an animal). As a result, many meta-analyses must exclude studies that fail to meet basic standards for methodological rigor. For example, two meta-analyses of animal-assisted activity and animal-assisted therapy research studies (Nimer & Lundahl, 2007; Souter & Miller, 2007) revealed moderate effect sizes for the interventions that met their inclusion criteria, but far more studies were excluded from the meta-analyses than were included. Nimer and Lundahl reviewed 250 studies and were able to use only 49 in their meta-analysis, whereas Souter and Miller reviewed 165 studies, of which only 5 met their inclusion criteria. Likewise, a recent Cochrane Collaboration meta-analysis of child educational dog-bite prevention programs (Duperrex, Blackhall, Burri, & Jeannot, 2009) reviewed information on 1,598 programs, finding 20 studies on such programs, 2 of which met their inclusion criterion. Of those two, neither used a measure of subsequent rate of dog bites as an outcome measure, making it impossible to say much about the efficacy of these interventions. Finally, a meta-analysis examining the relationship between exposure to furry pets and the risk of asthma and allergic rhinitis (Takkouche, Gonzalez-Barcala, Etminan, & Fitzgerald, 2008) reviewed 3,311 studies on this topic, but found that only 32 met their inclusion criteria.

The systematic study of HAI has proven elusive not only for methodological reasons but perhaps also because of a general bias in research circles against the subject. If HAI research demonstrates positive effects, it may be dismissed as being intuitively obvious or trivial. Conversely, if HAI research demonstrates negative effects, it may be dismissed as being flawed or failing to change the behavior in question. At the same time, the systematic study of HAI remains a challenge because of a possible bias among HAI researchers *toward* the subject. HAI research tends to be conducted by animal lovers, who may be biased toward finding positive HAI effects. Perhaps because of these perceived limitations, government and foundation funders of research have provided relatively little systematic support for studies in this area. A search of the National Institutes of Health database of funded research, the Computer Retrieval of Information on Scientific Projects, turned up few grants supporting studies on HAI, with most funded studies focusing on pets as a disease vector (e.g., as causes or carriers of allergies, asthma, and ticks), rather than as a household member.

Finally, one prominent challenge to HAI research is a lack of consistency in terminology. As demonstrated in the appendix of this volume, HAI studies are published in a plethora of journals representing such disparate fields as psychology, psychiatry, social work, sociology, public health, veterinary medicine, and special education, each of which has its own nomenclature. The literature lacks an agreed-upon set of index terms, making it difficult to locate the articles using modern search engines, or difficult to compare research across different fields. A common terminology is needed to unify this newly emerging field.

TERMINOLOGY

To fill the need for common terminology, this volume proposes the more consistent usage of the term *human–animal interaction*, or HAI. Although other terms may be more descriptive (e.g., human–companion animal bond), HAI is broad enough to cover both basic developmental and applied therapeutic research. In this volume, HAI refers to the mutual and dynamic interactions between people and animals and how these interactions may affect physical and psychological health and well-being.

Within the domain of HAI, various groups and subfields use different terminology. *Animal-assisted therapy* (AAT) describes the intentional inclusion of an animal in a treatment plan to facilitate healing and recovery of patients with acute or chronic conditions. AAT is goal directed based upon the individual's personalized treatment plan, is carried out by a trained professional, and should be evaluated to monitor progress. AAT is often used to enhance a variety of more traditional treatments, such as occupational therapy, speech therapy, physical rehabilitation, or even psychotherapy. The anticipated outcomes of AAT can include improvements in cognition, emotion regulation or affect, social competence, or physical abilities. On the other hand, animal-assisted activity (AAA) is the use of animals in a recreational or educational manner without specific treatment goals. AAA can be conducted without the direction of a professional, is less formal and structured than AAT, and typically does not involve the collection of outcome data (Delta Society, 2009). Together, AAT and AAA make up animal-assisted intervention (AAI). Of the two types of AAI, AAT may be particularly important in guiding and intervening in the lives of children and youth. Therefore, this volume pays particular attention to the need for AAT research.

SCOPE AND ORGANIZATION OF THIS BOOK

Despite the methodological and other limitations, efforts have been made to synthesize research findings in this new field. For example, in 1987, the National Institutes of Health (NIH) held the conference "The Health Benefits of Pets" to gather current research and provide a framework for future research on five topical areas: (a) the role of pets in cardiovascular health, (b) health correlates of pets in older persons, (c) the role of pets in social and therapeutic effects, (d) safety and risks in people–pet relationships, and (e) the role of pets in child development. The expert panel called for more research to determine the benefits and long-term consequences for the social, emotional, and cognitive development of children. Prospective longitudinal studies in home or neighborhood settings were recommended to add to our knowledge regarding the relationship between HAI and typical and atypical child development.

Of the five topics covered at the NIH 1987 conference, perhaps the one still in greatest need of systematic study is that of the role of pets in child development. In this volume, we broaden that topic to include not only pets but also animals that do not live with the individual. We also broaden the topic to include humans in all stages of development—childhood, adolescence, adulthood, and old age. The goals of this volume are to share some current research in HAI, highlight methods and approaches to move the field forward, and suggest an agenda for future research.

The first three chapters of this volume address methodological issues related to the study of HAI. First, Melson (Chapter 1) outlines how the study of child and adolescent development can enrich (and be enriched by) the study of HAI. She proposes six principles to guide future research. Then Kazdin (Chapter 2) focuses on the role of AAT in child and adolescent psychotherapy research. He points out the methodological weaknesses present in many of the research studies conducted to date and suggests steps that the field can take to strengthen research on AAI and AAT so that they can join the ranks of other evidence-based physical and mental health treatments. Next, Uvnäs-Moberg and colleagues (Chapter 3) explore HAI research at the neurotransmitter and hormone level—specifically, methodological concerns for studying both human and animal brain chemistries. This line of research sheds light on the biological basis of human–animal attachment (Nagasawa, Kikusui, Onaka, & Ohta, 2009).

The next three chapters address specific aspects of HAI in the context of typical child development. DeLoache, Pickard, and LoBue (Chapter 4) examine how very young infants exhibit a greater attentional and emotional attraction toward animals than toward other types of stimuli and the implications of such early preferences. Wynne, Dorey, and Udell (Chapter 5) then examine what we know about the development and behavior of dogs, including how domestication has shaped their human-like behaviors. These authors highlight the need for carefully controlled research to understand the behavioral cues between dogs and children. Finally, Ascione and Maruyama (Chapter 6) provide an overview of research on the relationship between the abuse of animals by children and adolescents and the development of psychopathology.

The final four chapters use four different approaches to examining how HAI may influence both child and adult health. Salmon and Timperio (Chapter 7) use targeted surveys to explore the relationship between HAI and obesity, noting that exercise associated with dog walking may promote a healthier adult lifestyle; however, data documenting this relationship for children are generally lacking. Headey and Grabka (Chapter 8) use large-scale national survey data to examine longitudinally the relationship between self-reports of pet ownership, health status, and health care use. Friedmann, Barker, and Allen (Chapter 9) discuss HAI research studies that employ physiological measures to examine the relationship between HAI and health indicators, including how the presence of a companion animal may moderate the stress response in children and adults. Finally, Johnson (Chapter 10) reviews research that has been conducted with child, adult, and elderly subjects to summarize what has been learned and what has yet to be explored regarding the use of AAI for a range of health conditions.

The Afterword by McCardle and colleagues outlines a research agenda for the field of HAI in relation to child development and human health, including topics of interest and methods that might be used in their exploration. Although not exhaustive, these recommendations, coupled with those made throughout the other chapters in this volume, can serve to guide researchers seeking to join this field of investigation.

With the increasing use of animals in therapeutic settings, research on HAI is increasingly important. We need an evidence base for advising parents on whether, how, and when to introduce pets to their families. We need to know how and why HAI affects human health and development and whether HAI can be used clinically from childhood onward. We hope that this volume helps advance these goals.

REFERENCES

American Veterinary Medicine Association. (2007). *US pet ownership and demographics sourcebook*. Schaumburg, IL: Author.

Delta Society. (2009). *Animal assisted activities & animal assisted therapy*. Retrieved November 3, 2009 from http://www.deltasociety.org/Page.aspx?pid=317

Duperrex, O., Blackhall, K., Burri, M., & Jeannot, E. (2009). Education of children and adolescents for the prevention of dog bite injuries. *Cochrane Database of Systematic Reviews*, Issue 2. Article No: CD004726. doi: 10.1002/14651858.CD004726.pub2

Griffin, J. A., McCune, S., Maholmes, V., & Hurley, K. (2010). Scientific research on human–animal interaction: A framework for future studies. In P. McCardle, M. McCune, J. A. Griffin, L. Esposito, & L. Freund (Eds.), *The role of pets in children's lives: Human–animal interaction in child development, health and therapeutic intervention* (pp. 227–236). Baltimore, MD: Brookes Publishing.

Nagasawa, M., Kikusui, T., Onaka, T., & Ohta, M. (2009). Dog's gaze at its owner increases urinary oxytocin during social interaction. *Hormones and Behavior, 55*, 434–441.

National Institutes of Health. (1987). *The health benefits of pets*. NIH Technology Assessment Statement Online 1987 September 10–11. Retrieved August 4, 2009, from http://consensus.nih.gov/1987/1987HealthBenefitsPetsta003html.htm

Nimer, J., & Lundahl, B. (2007). Animal-assisted therapy: A meta-analysis. *Anthrozoos, 20*, 225–238.

Souter, M. A., & Miller, M. D. (2007). Do animal-assisted activities effectively treat depression? A meta-analysis. *Anthrozoos, 20*(2), 167–180.

Takkouche, B., Gonzalez-Barcala, F. J., Etminan, M., & Fitzgerald, M. (2008). Exposure to furry pets and the risk of asthma and allergic rhinitis: A meta-analysis. *Allergy, 63*, 857–864.

Wells, D. L. (2009). The effects of animals on human health and well-being. *Journal of Social Issues, 65*(3), 523–543.

Wilson, C. C. (2006). The future of research, education, and clinical practice in the animal–human bond and animal-assisted therapy. In A. Fine (Ed.), *Handbook of animal-assisted therapy* (2nd ed., pp. 499–512). New York, NY: Academic Press.

I
METHODOLOGY

1

PRINCIPLES FOR H
INTERACTION

GAIL F. M

This chapter suggests a set of principles that should underlie a multi-disciplinary collaborative research agenda focused on human–animal inter-action (HAI) and child development. These principles approach HAI research from a contextual perspective. Such a perspective mandates the study of children within their naturally occurring contexts in all their complexity—including other humans, of course (family members, peers, neighbors, teachers, clergy, etc.), but also the physical, geographical, political, social, and cultural milieus within which these human relationships are experienced. This contextual perspective relies on the constructs of *developmental niche* (Super & Harkness, 2002, 2003) and *nested ecological systems* (Bronfenbrenner, 1979)—the family home; the neighborhood streets and alleys; the school yard, class-room, and gym; the church, mosque, or temple: the movie theater, restaurant, and park; the small screen worlds of computer and video game—in short, all the patterns of social organization from the most micro to the most macro level.

The human species evolved in codependence with myriad life forms that together form human niches, leading E. O. Wilson (1984) to posit as part of our evolutionary heritage *biophilia*, an innate human propensity to be attentive to other life forms (see Chapter 4, by DeLoache and Pickard). Indeed, every human culture suffuses its vocabulary with animal metaphors. We cannot study children in context without also considering their involvement with other life forms, particularly nonhuman animals.

Against this background, consider that pets are very common in North America and in other Western industrialized societies. Rates of pet ownership also are rising rapidly in Asia and in developing countries worldwide. A recent survey by the American Pet Products Manufacturers Association (APPMA, 2009) estimates that 62% of U.S. households had one or more animals in 2008, with dogs and cats in one of every three households. In 1988, 56% of U.S. households reported at least one resident animal, indicating that pet ownership has risen in the last 2 decades. An estimated 77.5 million dogs and 93.6 million cats were resident in U.S. households in 2008.

Families with children younger than 18 years of age account for 38% of all pet owners (APPMA, 2009). By some estimates, pets are most likely to be found in households with children, with rates as high as 75% of these households (Humane Society of the United States, 2006). But by other estimates, pets are just as common in households without children. For example, the APPMA (2008) found that dog ownership rates do not differ significantly between households with children younger than 18 (41%) compared with the general population (40%). There are varying estimates of pet ownership rates resulting from differences in surveying organizations, instruments, and response rates. Unlike estimates of human population conducted by the U.S. Census Bureau, there is no uniform population-wide assessment.

Based on surveys in the United States, the default response to a pet's role is "member of the family," although what respondents actually mean by this is far from clear (Albert & Bulcroft, 1986). The cultural trope considers pets to be especially beneficial to children or, at minimum, a desirable if not essential component of a child's optimal world. As I have noted elsewhere (Melson, 2001), children and animals are thought to "go together." This assumption is reflected ubiquitously in toys, children's books and games, and other cultural artifacts. In a recent study of seventy-two 7- to 15-year-old children in pet-owning families, parents overwhelmingly agreed that pets were beneficial to their children's development (Melson, Kahn, Beck, & Friedman, 2009). The parents' open-ended explanations centered on teaching responsibility, developing empathy, stimulating appreciation and respect for animals and other living beings, learning to care for others, and carrying on family traditions. Moreover, children themselves identify pets as important to their well-being. For example, when 8- to 12-year-old children took photographs to indicate sources of their well-being, the children (as compared with their parents or teachers) were more likely to include pets (Sixsmith, Gabhainn, Fleming, & O'Higgins, 2007).

Decreasing family size in the United States and other developed nations makes it less likely that children's homes will routinely include younger siblings, babies, and resident elderly individuals. This may make pets more salient as

emotional and social actors for the rema[...]
may be more likely to grow up with an [...]
grandparent in the home (Melson, 2[...]
small size of most companion animals n[...]
children may play out issues of powe[...]
Particularly important for boys, pets pr[...]
nurturance learning and practice (Mels[...]

Despite evidence that animals are [...]
an understudied and poorly understood [...]
stock of current HAI research in relat[...]
map out an agenda for the future, we [...]
gral part of developmental theory and research, rather than bracket HAI research as a specialized field of study and intervention. To that end, this chapter proposes the following six principles that might guide multidisciplinary research in the field of HAI and child development.

EMBED THE STUDY OF HAI WITHIN BROADER THEORETICAL FRAMEWORKS AND ISSUES AT THE CORE OF CHILD DEVELOPMENT STUDY

The study of HAI and its relation to child development must be informed by core issues and constructs in perceptual, cognitive, social–emotional, language, and moral development. The following selective, and by no means exhaustive, examples illustrate this principle.

Perceptual Development

Eleanor Gibson's (1988) construct of *perceptual affordances* is useful in asking what are the affordances (the "what can I do with this?") of animals that children encounter. Animals may be perceptually intriguing because their affordances are novel, unpredictable, and diverse. Thus, 7-month-old infants register a surprised expression if they see inanimate objects move without any force being applied to them, but not when people move (Spelke, Phillips, & Woodward, 1995). These differential reactions have been interpreted as evidence that a "naïve theory of physics"—what objects are like—and a "naïve theory of biology"—what living beings are like—are taking shape in the first year of life. Thus, even infants may respond to animals in distinctive ways. In support of this, infants and toddlers smile, follow, and make sounds more frequently toward their pet dogs and cats than to battery-operated, "lifelike" toy dogs and cats (Kidd & Kidd, 1987). In another observational study (Ricard & Allard, 1992), 9-month-old infants looked at, approached, and touched a live rabbit more frequently than a moving wooden turtle or an adult female stranger. The construct of "animal" as an ontologically basic category (Carey, 1985) appears in early childhood. In one study, 5-year-old children, when told that people had made a stuffed dog that looked and acted exactly like a real dog nevertheless insisted that the stuffed dog could not turn into a real dog (Dolgin & Behrend, 1984).

Evidence of differing responses to diverse species, indicating that children are responding to the distinct "affordances" of particular animals, comes from Nielsen and Delude's (1989) classroom observations of 2- to 6-year-old children as they encountered a tarantula, rabbit, cockatiel, and golden retriever dog, as well as two "realistic" stuffed animals—a dog and a bird. Whereas 10% of the children touched the tarantula, 74% touched the dog. More than two-thirds talked to the bird, as compared with 16% talking to the rabbit and none to the tarantula. Thus, each live animal (the children ignored the stuffed animals) evoked its own mix of looking, approaching, touching, and talking. Myers (1998) observed preschool children's responses to animals in their classroom over a 1-year period, concluding that each animal was approached and thought about as a distinct "subjective other."

Cognitive Development

Piaget's construct of moderate discrepancy from assimilated schema as the engine of conceptual growth (Piaget, 1950) prompts consideration of how an animal presents to the child elements both familiar and novel. If one assumes that cognitive growth is emotion laden and emotion driven, then children's interest in animals, children's motivation to attend to animal stimuli, and the emotions evoked in children by HAI are important areas of study because of implications for cognitive learning as well as emotional development. Thus, in a study by Hatano and Inagaki (1993), 5-year-old Japanese children who cared for goldfish at home, most for over a year, not only knew more about goldfish care than did their classmates without goldfish-care experience but also knew more about unobserved goldfish properties—for example, "Does a goldfish have a heart?" Furthermore, the experience of goldfish care allowed the children to reason accurately about unfamiliar animals using analogies from caring for the fish and to engage in accurate cause-effect reasoning. For example, half the children who had raised goldfish predicted correctly that feeding goldfish "10 times a day" would result in death, whereas none of the comparison children could explain the consequences of overfeeding or understood that 10 times a day would be excessive feeding. Thus, while empirical evidence is limited, animal care (and more broadly, contact) may contribute to children's understanding not only of the species cared for but also, through analogical reasoning (Gentner, 1989), of other species and other biological processes.

Social–Emotional Development

Perhaps no other developmental domain has received as much attention as socioemotional development, with respect to children's relationships with animals, particularly pets. As noted, children (and their parents) identify pets as "family members," and children report emotional bonds with their pets, sometimes calling them their "best friends" (Melson, 2001). When asked to name "most important" relationships, nearly half of 69 Scottish 9- to 12-year-old children identified a pet, a higher proportion than those naming a grandfather (42%), friend (41%), aunt/uncle (30%), teacher (28%), or neighbor/other adult (22%; Kosonen, 1996). In comparison to family and friends, elementary school children rated their pets as a relationship most likely to last "no matter what" and "even if you get mad at each other" (Furman, 1989). Adult pet owners show similar patterns: Adult dog owners turned to their pets as attachment figures in times of emotional distress more frequently than to family members (parents, siblings, or children) or best friends. Only romantic partners exceeded dogs as sources of comfort (Kurdek, 2009).

Like other close ties, relationships with pets can be complex, with multiple dimensions, both positive and negative. Thus, in interviews about their pets, children readily report what they dislike as well as what they like about the animal (Melson, 1991). In another study, children identified both benefits and costs—for example, distress and worry over pet safety, health, needs, and death (Bryant, 1990).

However, despite child and parental reports regarding the importance and complexity of the child–pet relationship, it remains unclear how this relationship is similar to and different from child–human relationships. Given many children's perception of their pet as a "friend," is the child–pet relationship comparable to a peer friendship? Close friendships between children are described as symmetrical or horizontal, with reciprocal exchanges (von Salisch, 2001). An empirical question is whether characteristics of close peer friendships appear in descriptions or observations of children with their pets. For example, a common assessment of peer friendship quality (Parker & Asher, 1993) identifies the following dimensions: conflict resolution, conflict/betrayal, companionship/recreation, intimate exchanges, help/guidance, and validation/caring. With the exception of the conflict dimensions, all of the dimensions listed have been identified in children's reports of their relationships with pets (Melson, 2001). Assessments of the child–pet relationship using a measure such as the Parker and Asher (1993) Friendship Quality Index would yield directly comparable data.

Is the child–pet relationship akin to a sibling tie, incorporating both horizontal and vertical elements? Specifically, one finds play, emotional expressiveness, and care-giving behaviors in both sibling and pet interactions (Dunn,

Having a pet sounds like having a friend or sibling without the shitty parts. As a youngest child, I probably played with our cats more than my siblings.

). On the other hand, the intensity, me sibling ties (Kretschmer & Pike, ptions of pet relationships. Does the ne children, as a conflict-free quasi-lder sibling role? Children without ngest children—engage in more play ning children who have younger sib-son & Fogel, 1996). Perhaps the rela-pecies merit consideration as unique, human–human relationship. Further of behavioral patterns and examination of children's "internal working models" of the child–pet relationship.

It also is important to describe the processes by which pet relationships form, are maintained, and end. A child's relationship with an animal begins with initial human–animal *interactions*, but the processes by which these interactions become a relationship remain unspecified. Research on the development of friendship among previously unacquainted children emphasizes conversational processes, such as establishing common ground and reciprocity (Gottman, 1983). Such processes do not appear applicable to relationship development with respect to an animal. Perhaps processes such as projection and scaffolding, as well as patterns of nonverbal communication and behavioral responsiveness, would be fruitful to explore.

The question of relationship development from interactions has implications for the fields of animal-assisted therapy (AAT) and animal-assisted education (AAE) because children generally receive these interventions with animals that are not their pets and with whom they have limited interaction. Nonetheless, AAT and AAE are based on the premise that social–emotional benefits, for typically developing children as well as for children with special needs, will flow from interactions with animals, even in the absence of pre-existing relationships with them (Melson & Fine, 2006). It remains unclear what the dose–response relation is; that is, how many interactions are needed and at what rate to yield measurable change in outcomes of interest.

Attachment theory (Bowlby, 1969) leads us to ask whether, for some children, the presence of their own or another animal might be reassuring in the face of activation of the attachment system (i.e., when the child feels insecure and unsafe). Can an animal provide a secure base to encourage exploration? Can a pet alleviate distress and serve as a source of support and comfort? Much AAT proceeds from the assumption that a friendly animal (usually not the child's own pet) reduces stress and allows the child to respond with less anxiety and defensiveness in the therapeutic milieu (Parish-Plass, 2008). As noted, these processes are thought to occur even when the animal is not the child's pet and the child has limited interaction with the animal.

Indirect evidence supports this hypothesis. One body of evidence shows the stress-reducing effects of friendly animal (usually dog) presence. The second body of evidence suggests that some children turn to their pets for feelings of comfort and support, particularly when feeling stress. Thus, under moderately stressful conditions (e.g., reading aloud) the presence of a friendly unfamiliar dog moderates the expected increase in blood pressure (Katcher, Friedman, Beck, & Lynon, 1983). Preschool children undergoing a simulated physical examination show reduced blood pressure (BP) and heart rate (HR) when in the presence of a friendly dog (Nagergost, Baun, Megel, & Leibowitz, 1997). Elementary school-age children waiting for dental surgery (actual, not simulated) showed less physiologic arousal when waiting with a friendly but unfamiliar dog (Havener et al., 2001).

There is considerable evidence that some children turn to their pets for support and comfort. Bryant (1985) found that 13% of the 10-year-old children she interviewed volunteered their pets in answer to the question: "To whom do you turn when you are feeling sad?" Melson and Schwarz (1994) reported that 42% of 5-year-old children who owned pets mentioned their pets as where they would turn when feeling emotions such as sadness, anger, happiness, or the need to share a secret. In a study of 10- to 14-year-old children with pets, 75% said they turned to their pets when upset (Covert, Whirren, Keith, & Nelson, 1985). Finally, 7- to 8-year-old children in the United Kingdom identified their pets more frequently than humans as providing comfort (McNicolas & Collis, 2001). In sum, there is converging evidence that some children find comfort and reassurance in their pets.

Language Development

Little is known about language development and HAI in children. Humans of all ages seem drawn to speak to their pets; in one study, 66% of adults who were dog owners and 95% of bird owners reported talking "frequently" to their animals (Katcher & Beck, 1986). Adult speech to pets bears some resemblance to "motherese," the conversational form of speech mothers (and other humans) use toward babies. People speak to their pets in a higher-pitched sing-song voice, often ending an utterance with a rising inflection and inserting pauses. Speech tempo and length of utterance are relatively short. However, unlike "motherese," speech to dogs, called "doggerel" in one study, is usually accompanied by close physical contact and mutual relaxation. Adults observed speaking to their dogs often place their heads close to the animal's head and stroke, nuzzle, and pet the animal (Hirsh-Pasek & Treiman, 1982). This suggests that "conversation" with dogs (and perhaps other species) functions to express intimacy and affirm the owner's bond with the animal (Melson, 2001).

Do children talk to dogs more than hamsters because its more common or is it because dogs respond more?

's speech to animals. In one study, play situation spoke to an unfamil- hands (61%), and questions (69%). use a motherese register and to with speech (Melson, Kahn, Beck, observations of preschool children few verbalizations to common wild " pets, such as hamsters, gerbils, and

content and structure of children's such as therapy animals. Tannen (2004) audiotaped conversations directed to and about pet dogs in two families over a 1-week period, examining the interpersonal functions of such speech. More descriptive studies are needed of what children understand and say about their pet animals, as well as unfamiliar companion animals, wild animals, and domestic farm animals.

Does language to or about animals reflect or contribute to the child's conversational skills with other partners, such as a parent, peer, or sibling? For example, between ages 2 and 4 years, children extend to peers conversational skills, such as maintaining dialogue through asking questions and calling attention, skills that they initially acquired in mother–child language exchanges (Martinez, 1987). One might investigate whether there is a relationship between children's language use with parents, siblings, or peers and with animals.

In addition to language directed at animals, language *about* animals is of interest because words for animals—dog, cat, horse—are among the first in young children's vocabularies (Melson, 2001). Given evidence of children's interest in animals, it is possible that verbal content, such as stories, might be more readily learned when it is about animals. In a study of 8- to 13-year-old Dutch children's Internet use, "seeking information about animals" was one of the four most common descriptions of positive experiences with the Internet (Valkenburg & Soeters, 2001).

Moral Development

Until recently, research on moral reasoning and moral behavior focused solely on children's ties to other humans. However, we now have evidence that children are reasoning about issues of justice, kindness, fairness, and right/wrong behavior with respect to animals and other living beings. Kahn's (1999) interviews with first-, third- and fifth-graders in several cultures show children's concern about animal welfare and their justifications for treatment that is morally "right." Similarly, in a recent study (Melson, Kahn, Beck, Friedman, Roberts, et al., 2009), 7- to 15-year-old children were interviewed about the moral claims and proper treatment of an unfamiliar but friendly dog with which the children had a brief play period. The children expressed strong and emotionally forceful condemnation of acts of omission (neglecting to immediately seek treatment for an injury to the animal's leg) or commission (destroying the animal if you no longer wanted it). Yet, nearly half the children gave qualified support to hitting the dog, as part of socializing its behavior. Analysis of justifications for these judgments showed that children were arguing for the inherent moral claims of the animal, as like a human, a family member, and themselves. One child, in a tone of outrage, asked: "What if *you* hurt your leg?"

Children justified their reasoning by analogies to treatment of humans and to broader principles of animal welfare and of right conduct. Such reasoning was not a generalized set of ideas toward any "plaything," since the same children judged a robotic dog to have significantly less claim to moral regard.

The development of moral reasoning with respect to animals and more broadly, nonhumans, is not well understood. Kellert (2002) describes developmental stages in thinking about natural systems, from a utilitarian, "dominionistic" perspective during the preschool years, to more abstract, conceptual and ethical reasoning during adolescence—a process that parallels Kohlberg's stages of moral reasoning (1976). Kellert's stages offer a useful framework for exploring developmental and other variations in moral reasoning about animals and HAI. Numerous questions await further research. How does engagement with animals—from wild bird feeding to zoo visits to caring for pets—affect children's moral reasoning about animals? What, if any, interventions (for example, humane education) may prompt development of animal-related moral reasoning? How is moral reasoning about animals related to behaviors such as meat eating, pet keeping, and involvement in animal welfare and conservation efforts? Is moral reasoning about animals related to moral reasoning about human–human relationships?

In sum, this abbreviated and selective set of theory-driven questions illustrates how we might integrate HAI research into broader core framing questions about children's development. Not only do we need to embed HAI hypotheses within developmental theories and constructs, we also need to show how interactions, feelings, and cognitions about animals may help us rethink generalizations based on human–human interaction research alone.

FOCUS ON INDIVIDUAL DIFFERENCES IN CHILD AND ANIMAL

This principle forces us to move away from thinking about companion animals or other animals in categorical generic terms. Instead, HAI research should take into account the diverse animal species that humans keep as pets and companions—from dogs to hamsters to goldfish. In addition to the human–companion animal relationship, there is wide variability in animal species encountered as domestic animals and wild animals. Obviously, species differences are reflected in diverse physical and behavioral attributes. As Udell and Wynne (2008) demonstrate, dogs, compared to other species, including nonhuman primates, are especially attuned to human social cues. Myers (1998) has shown that even preschool children are sensitive to the behavioral repertoire of different species and adapt their behaviors to different creatures.

Species differences may limit generalizability of findings. For example, in contrast to findings on the presence of a friendly dog, BP and HR reductions did not occur when individuals (not fearful of snakes) held or watched a snake (Friedmann & Tsai, 2006).

Within a single species, individual animals exhibit variation in behaviors, due to genetic history, rearing environments, and interaction history. Such individual variation has been shown to affect HAI. For example, the physical well-being of dogs is highest among pure breed dogs that belong to men and to people with strong preferences for dogs as pets (Marinelli, Adamelli, Normando, & Bono, 2007). Surveys of Australian adults concerning the "ideal" dog identify one who is medium-sized, short haired, desexed, house trained, friendly, obedient, healthy, and safe with children (King, Marston, & Bennett, 2009). However, animal-assisted interactions (AAI) and AAT currently lack a taxonomy (beyond basic health and safety concerns) of which animal species, and within species which behavioral and physical characteristics, are optimal for specified child outcomes. Despite this, therapists using AAT often find the child's choice of species (and of a particular individual animal) with which to interact, of diagnostic value (T. Axelrad-Levy, personal communication, 2009).

Just as individual differences among animals involved in HAI are important, so too are individual differences among children. For example, children with different psychiatric disorders (e.g., anorexia, bulimia, anxiety disorder, or autism) respond in distinct ways to the same therapy dog, such that a discriminant analysis of their behaviors can correctly assign 78% of the children to their correct diagnostic group (Prothmann et al., 2005). In general, research results that report mean differences obscure variability within a group of children. HAI research would benefit from studies that focus on the outliers of the distribution—those children, from among a group exhibiting high mean positive responses to some animal intervention or experience, who show no interest or negative responses, and at the other end, those children commonly called "animal lovers" who show very strong and sometimes preferential positive emotion toward some (or all) animals.

There is evidence that involvement and motivation mediate the impact of HAI. For example, adults with more positive attitudes toward dogs experi-

It makes sense that motivation an involvement effect the outcomes of HAI. Playing guitar would probably make me happier than someone who doesn't know how to play or isn't even interested in playing guitar.

ence significantly lower blood pressu[re] an unfamiliar dog than do adults wit[h] Tsai, 2006). Similarly, the presence o[f] gram resulted in lower depression ar *only* among elderly men who sought not (Holcomb, Jendro, Weber, & Na effectiveness of an AAT program to by the motivation level and involve & Wilkins, 2000). Similarly, pediat rapport with an unfamiliar dog durin in respiratory rate during play and ph dren who failed to develop rapport with the animal (Wu, Niedra, Pendergast, & McCrindle, 2002).

Person and context variables also may be important. With respect to relationships with pets, gender or developmental differences in animal preferences, attachment to pets, or interaction with animals are limited and inconsistent (Melson, 2001). By contrast, there is some evidence that children with varying levels of empathy (Daly, 2006; Melson, Peet, & Sparks, 1992), altruism and nurturance (Zhou, Zheng, & Fu, 2007), or moral reasoning (Melson, Kahn, Beck, & Friedman, 2009), to use a few examples, think about and interact with animals differently. To date, associations of such variables with pet ownership or pet attachment have been interpreted as suggesting the beneficial role of animals in promoting such outcomes (Dizon, Butler, & Koopman, 2007). In the absence of experimental research, however, one also might interpret such findings as evidence of individual-difference child variables affecting aspects of HAI.

A truism often neglected in practice is that every interaction requires at least two individuals who are mutually influencing each other. For example, Kurdek (2009) found that *both* person characteristics (being male, widowed, and uncomfortable with self-disclosure) and perceived dog characteristics (strongly meeting the owner's relatedness needs) together predicted adults' use of their pet dog as an attachment figure in times of emotional distress. Similarly, among adult dog owners, level of pet care was predicted by the combination of person variables (being single, male) and animal variables (age of dog; Marinelli et al., 2007). Another example of the interaction between animal and person characteristics comes from an evaluation of assistance dogs with children with autism spectrum disorder: Child behaviors toward the dog that resulted in lack of predictable routines, prodding and poking, and lack of recovery and recreation time adversely affected dog behavior, which in turn negatively affected parental satisfaction with the therapy dog (Burrows, Adams, & Millman, 2008).

In sum, we must incorporate into research a deeper understanding of species-specific characteristics and behavior, as well as the appearance and behaviors of the individual animals and characteristics of individual children in an interaction. As the Kurdek (2009) study illustrates, human perceptions of animal characteristics and behaviors are important because the adult's or child's "construction" of animal may mediate outcomes. To better understand these issues requires collaborative research between animal behavior experts and child development scholars. Even when the outcome variables of interest are child health or development, HAI should be operationalized interactively. Microanalytic case studies of dynamic change in interactive variables, such as latency to respond to an interaction bid, are appropriate for capturing the dynamics of mutual influence over time.

The concept of *environmental specificity* is helpful here (Wachs & Gruen, 1982). This concept poses questions of the following type: *Which* interventions with *which* animals are helpful with *which* children in *which* contexts? Each of these "whiches" implies that individual differences interact with one another. The challenge is to develop research designs that allow us to tease out such differential predictions, rather than group main effects.

COMBINE MULTIPLE LEVELS OF ANALYSIS

HAI focuses on behavioral measures of interaction, but cognitive representations, emotions, and culturally conditioned attitudes mutually influence behavior. Research designs are strengthened when they incorporate behavioral, cognitive, affective, and where possible, physiologic measures. As an example, Kaminski, Pellino, and Wish (2002) measured child mood (in both self- and parent-report) and observed affect and touch, heart rate, and salivary cortisol in hospitalized children participating in play therapy (without animals) or pet therapy. Pet therapy was superior in terms of lowered heart rate, observed affect, and parental report of child's mood. Thus, the use of multiple levels of analysis (and multiple informants) provided convergent evidence of pet therapy effects and discriminated among variables showing such effects.

STUDY HAI WITHIN THE CONTEXT OF CHILD–HUMAN INTERACTIONS AND RELATIONSHIPS

Children encounter animals in their homes or outside in contexts that almost always include other humans. AAI and AAT are mediated by human service providers; pets are part of a human family; and school pets share the classroom with teachers and students. If pets can provide a sense of security or a feeling of social support for children, or are cognitively compelling objects of attention (and there is evidence for all three of these assertions), these effects

likely are mediated through hum
catalyst" effect, whereby the pres
approaches and conversation from
strates that HAI and child–hum
(Mader, Hart, & Bergin, 1989).

Another body of evidence i
between violence toward animals a
children from families where dome
witness or commit animal abuse
2008). Retrospective evidence fro
who committed or witnessed anim
treatment or domestic violence during that period (DeGue & Dilillo, 2009).

Links between child–animal interactions and CHI patterns should not be surprising because children's multiple human relationships mutually influence one another. For example, children's peer and sibling relations mutually enhance one another; the quality of the mother–child relationship predicts the quality of peer friendships; and interparental relationship quality affects parent–child interactions (Lewis, 2005). Within a dynamic systems perspective on development, one would expect children's diverse relationships to mutually affect one another (Melson, 2007). To the extent that pets become incorporated into the family, they could become part of complex dynamics. Thus, Tannen (2004) documented the role that dogs played in interpersonal interactions within families. In speaking to and about their dogs, parents and children used the dogs to effect a "frame shift" in conversation, introducing humor, buffering criticism, delivering praise, teaching values, resolving conflict, and creating a family identity that included the dog.

A research agenda focused on links between HAI and CHI would be helpful. For example, how do therapists' experiences with animals, attitudes toward their own pets, and relationship with a therapy animal affect therapist behavior with the child and the therapy animal? What human behaviors facilitate the "bridge" effect spoken of by many therapists using AAT? That is, what do therapists do that helps a child who establishes positive responsiveness to an animal transfer that to the therapist or to another human? How do social catalyst effects of friendly animal presence affect peer interaction variables, such as peer acceptance, group cohesion, or friendship formation?

Moreover, pets are only one among many other sources of attachment, support, and interest. Crucial questions of generalization, compartmentalization, and discrimination require data on both HAI and CHI from the same children:

- To what extent do pets function as compensatory mechanisms when human attachment or support figures are insufficient?

ns with animals generalize
r therapists, educators, or
be maintained when the
no longer present? (Aaron
ations suggest a lag time of
occur from intervention
nduct disorder [Katcher &

er humans a necessary con-
es to companion animals?

benefit from application of Bronfenbrenner's (1979) concept of the *mesosystem*, the connections (or lack thereof) among contexts of development (for example, how family patterns and school expectations mutually influence one another). With respect to HAI research, mesosystem questions might include the following question: How does pet ownership or a child's bond with a pet relate to the child's responsiveness to a therapy animal, interest in a classroom pet, or engagement in animal-related activities, such as wild bird feeding? As an example of a mesosystem hypothesis, in a recent study, we examined children's attachment to their pets in relation to their reasoning about characteristics of an unfamiliar, friendly dog with whom they had a short play session. Children who were more attached to their pets at home (most had a dog, a cat, or both) were more likely to view the unfamiliar dog as having mental states (intentions, emotions, and ideas) as well as moral claims to just, fair, and kind treatment. In addition, children more attached to their pets behaved differently toward the unfamiliar dog, using more verbalizations (greetings, commands, questions) than did less pet-attached children (Melson, Kahn, Beck, & Friedman, 2009).

ASSESS THE MULTIDIMENSIONALITY OF CHILD–ANIMAL RELATIONSHIPS

Study of children's relationships with animals until recently has tended to focus either on positive developmental outcomes (empathy, feelings of support) or on negative outcomes (cruelty toward animals). If for most children, a relationship with a companion animal is more like that with a human sibling— containing both positive and negative elements, a mix of love, caring, empathy, anger, neglect, even cruelty—research designs need to incorporate the full range of emotions and behaviors. Underlying AAI and AAT is the hypothesis that HAI may be stress reducing. Without minimizing this possibility, we should also measure components of HAI that may be stress producing or have neutral effects. For example, taken as a whole, the evidence on the physiologic stress-reducing effects of animal presence is mixed, with some situations causing increases in BP and HR (Friedmann & Tsai, 2006).

When addressing the potential of HAI to reduce stress in children, it is important to develop research designs that can test the "main effects hypothesis" versus the "buffering hypothesis." The "main effects hypothesis" posits that a specific type of HAI would be associated with positive outcomes for children, regardless of their initial stress levels. By contrast, the "buffering hypothesis" holds that the stress-reduction benefits of HAI would occur only for children who initially experience high levels of stress (i.e., levels that would impede adaptive functioning). Research designs should test HAI predictors of a wide range of outcomes with mediating and moderating variables as part of the model.

CONSIDER THE CULTURAL MEANINGS OF HAI

Child development is a long apprenticeship in the specific cultural norms and values of the ecological niche. Every culture has a complex set of codes or tropes about other species—animals to keep, animals to shun, animals to destroy as pests, animals to eat, animals forbidden to eat, animals to protect, animals to love. These codes, themselves in dynamic flux, contain cultural messages, sometimes contradictory, about the treatment and welfare of animals. This cultural variability would suggest that children's interactions with animals, their relationships with pets, and the impact of animal contact on development would all vary by culture and historical time.

Cross-cultural investigations are still in their infancy in this field. There is evidence of both continuity and cultural difference. For example, Japanese children, compared with British youngsters, have fewer pets and few animal-related experiences such as visiting farms, and as university students have less positive attitudes toward animals and less concern for animal welfare issues. However, for both cultures, childhood experiences with animals, recalled retrospectively, were related to young adult attitudes toward animals and their welfare (Miura, Bradshaw, & Tanida, 2002). Similarly, patterns of deriving comfort and support from pets, as well as nurturing and care-giving directed at animals, found in studies of U.S. children, are similar to studies of children in the United Kingdom (McNicolas & Collis, 2001), Japan (Kurumisawa, Fukumoto, & Iwatate, 2009), and China (Zhou et al., 2007). Links between animal abuse and family violence, first documented in U.S. samples (Ascione, 1993), have been replicated in Australian samples (Volant et al., 2008).

Generalizations about cultural differences and similarities are difficult for numerous reasons: (a) the lack of systematic cross-cultural replication, using uniform measurements; (b) the lack of research on the sometimes subtle variations in cultural meanings of animal contact and relationships; and (c) the lack of theoretical frameworks that might guide the search for cultural differences and similarities. Collaborative research with anthropologists and geographers might help answer questions such as the following: Do children from cultures in which children help with domestic animal production (herding goats, for example) differ in their attitudes toward animals and their experiences with pets? How do children in societies that rely on hunting and fishing for subsistence differ in HAI from children in societies where hunting and fishing are largely recreational?

Children's acquisition of societal attitudes about animals and HAI is an important topic to be investigated cross-culturally. Alongside and not independent of the morality of human–human relations is the morality of human–animal relations. Children are learning about and taking stands on current hot button issues of vegetarianism, animal rights, medical and other research using animal models, conservation of animal habitats, endangered species, and related concerns. How children learn, understand, and in turn influence these cultural codes is itself an important topic for research and future social policy.

The cultural vocabulary of animals in children's stories, books, and games is not fully explicated. Nor do we understand its function in development. There are assumptions and some empirical support that young children are more responsive to content when presented in animal form, but this interest decreases with advancing age (Melson, 2001). To what extent do children's experiences with living animals affect the understanding of this cultural vocabulary, or their responsiveness to animal symbols? And conversely, how do cultural norms color a child's behavior, cognitions, and emotions toward a pet or an unfamiliar therapy animal?

CONCLUSION

The study of child development is now beginning to incorporate children's relationships with nonhumans, particularly animals, in understanding not only children's important relationships, but also their development, broadly encompassing perceptual, cognitive, language, and moral development. This brief sketch of principles that might guide future research in HAI and child development remains incomplete and will be subject to revision. However, taken together, such principles aim to capture the complexity and multidisciplinary nature of this important area of inquiry, while moving the study of HAI from the periphery to the center of child development theory and research.

REFERENCES

Albert, A., & Bulcroft, K. (1986). Pets and urban life. *Anthrozoos, 1*, 9–23.

American Pet Products Manufacturers Association (APPMA). (2008). *Industry statistics and trends*. Retrieved April 24, 2008, from http://www.appma.org

American Pet Products Manufacturers Association (APPMA). (2009). *2008–2009 APPMA national pet owners survey*. APPMA. Retrieved November 12, 2009, from http://americanpetproducts.org/press_industrytrends.asp

Ascione, F. R. (1993). Children who are cruel to animals: A review of research and implications for developmental psychopathology. *Anthrozoos, 6*, 226–247.

Bowlby, J. (1969). *Attachment and loss: Vol. 1. Attachment*. New York, NY: Basic Books.

Bronfenbrenner, U. (1979). *The ecology of human development*. Cambridge, MA: Harvard University Press.

Bryant, B. (1985). The neighborhood walk: Sources of support in middle childhood. *Monographs of the Society for Research in Child Development, 50*, 1–114.

Bryant, B. K. (1990). The richness of the child-pet relationship: A consideration of both benefits and costs of pets to children. *Anthrozoos, 3*, 253–261.

Burrows, K. E., Adams, C. L., & Millman, S. T. (2008). Factors affecting the behavior and welfare of service dogs for children with autism spectrum disorder. *Journal of Applied Animal Welfare Science, 11*, 42–62.

Carey, S. (1985). *Conceptual change in childhood*. Cambridge, MA: MIT Press.

Covert, A. M., Whirren, A. P., Keith, J., & Nelson, C. (1985). Pets, early adolescents and families. *Marriage and Family Review, 8*, 95–108.

Daly, B. (2006). An investigation of human–animal interactions and empathy as related to pet preference, ownership, attachment, and attitudes in children. *Anthrozoos, 19*, 113–127.

DeGue, S., & Dilillo, D. (2009). Is animal cruelty a "red flag" for family violence? Investigating co-occurring violence toward children, partners and pets. *Journal of Interpersonal Violence, 24*, 1036–1056.

Dizon, M., Butler, L. D., & Koopman, C. (2007). Befriending man's best friends: Does altruism toward animals promote psychological and physical health? In S. G. Post (Ed.), *Altruism and health: Perspectives from empirical research* (pp. 277–291). New York, NY: Oxford University Press.

Dolgin, K. G., & Behrend, D. A. (1984). Children's knowledge about animates and inanimates. *Child Development, 55*, 1646–1650.

Dunn, J., Creps, C., & Brown, J. (1996). Children's family relationships between two and five: Developmental changes and individual differences. *Social Development, 5*, 230–250.

Friedmann, E., & Tsai, C. C. (2006). The animal–human bond: Health and wellness. In A. H. Fine (Ed.), *Handbook on animal-assisted therapy* (2nd ed., pp. 95–117). New York, NY: Academic Press.

Furman, W. (1989). The development of children's social networks. In D. Belle (Ed.), *Children's social networks and social supports*. (pp. 151–172). New York, NY: Wiley.

Gentner, D. (1989). The mechanisms of analogical reasoning. In S. Vosniadou & A. Ortony (Eds.), *Similarity and analogical reasoning* (pp. 199–241). Cambridge, England: Cambridge University Press.

Gibson, E. (1988). Exploratory behavior in the development of perceiving, acting and the acquiring of knowledge. *Annual Review of Psychology, 39*, 1–41.

Gottman, J. M. (1983). How children become friends. *Monographs of the Society for Research in Child Development, 48*(203).

Hatano, G., & Inagaki, K. (1993). Desituating cognition through the construction of conceptual knowledge. In G. Salomon (Ed.), *Distributed cognitions* (pp. 115–133). New York, NY: Cambridge University Press.

Havener, L., Gentes, L., Thaler, B., Megel, M. E., Baun, M. M., Driscoll, F. A., … Agrawal, S. (2001). The effects of a companion animal on distress in children undergoing dental procedures. *Issues in Comprehensive Pediatric Nursing, 24*, 137–152.

Hirsh-Pasek, K., & Treiman, R. (1982). Doggerel: Motherese in a new context. *Journal of Child Language, 9*, 229–237.

Holcomb, R., Jendro, C., Weber, B., & Nahan, U. (1997). Use of an aviary to relieve depression in elderly males. *Anthrozoos, 10*, 32–36.

Humane Society of the United States. (2006). *U.S. pet ownership statistics*. Available from: http://www.hsus.org/pets/issues_affecting_our_pets/pet_overpopulation_and_ownership_statistics/us_pet_ownership_statistics.html

Kahn, P. H. Jr. (1999). *The human relationship with nature: Development and culture*. Cambridge, MA: MIT Press.

Kaminski, M., Pellino, T., & Wish, J. (2002). Play and pets: The physical and emotional impact of child-life and pet therapy on hospitalized children. *Children's Health Care, 31*, 321–335.

Katcher, A. H., & Beck, A. M. (1986). Dialogue with animals. *Transactions and Studies of the College of Physicians of Philadelphia, 8*, 105–112.

Katcher, A. H., Friedman, E., Beck, A. M., & Lynch, J. J. (1983). Talking, looking and blood pressure: Physiological consequences of interaction with the living environment. In A. H. Katcher & A. M. Beck (Eds.), *New perspectives on our lives with companion animals* (pp. 351–359). Philadelphia: University of Pennsylvania Press.

Katcher, A. H., & Wilkins, G. G. (2000). The centaur's lessons: Therapeutic education through care of animals and nature study. In A. Fine (Ed.), *Handbook on animal assisted therapies* (pp. 153–177). New York, NY: Academic Press.

Kellert, S. R. (2002). Experiencing nature: Affective, cognitive and evaluative development in children. In P. H. Kahn Jr. & S. R. Kellert (Eds.), *Children and nature: Psychological, sociocultural, and evolutionary investigations* (pp. 117–152). Cambridge, MA: MIT Press.

Kidd, A. H., & Kidd, R. M. (1987). Reactions of infants and toddlers to live and toy animals. *Psychological Reports, 61*, 455–464.

King, T., Marston, L. C., & Bennett, P. C. (2009). Describing the ideal Australian companion dog. *Applied Animal Behaviour Science, 120,* 84–93.

Kohlberg, L. (1976). Moral stages and moralization: The cognitive/developmental approach. In T. Lickona (Ed.), *Moral development and behavior*. New York, NY: Holt, Rinehart & Winston.

Kosonen, M. (1996). Siblings as providers of support and care during middle childhood: Children's perceptions. *Children and Society, 10,* 267–279.

Kretschmer, T., & Pike, A. (2009). Young children's sibling relationship quality: Distal and proximal; correlates. *Journal of Child Psychology & Psychiatry, 50,* 581–589.

Kurdek, L. A. (2009). Pet dogs as attachment figures for adult family owners. *Journal of Family Psychology, 23,* 439–446.

Kurumisawa, R., Fukumoto, S., & Iwatate, S. (2009). Influence of being nurtured and past nurturing experiences on university students' current levels of nurturance. *Japanese Journal of Educational Psychology, 57,* 168–179.

Lewis, M. (2005). The child and its family: The social network model. *Human Development, 48,* 8–27.

Mader, B., Hart, L. A., & Bergin, B. (1989). Social acknowledgments for children with disabilities: Effects of service dogs. *Child Development, 60,* 1529–1534.

Marinelli, L., Adamelli, S., Normando, S., & Bono, G. (2007). Quality of life of the pet dog: Influence of owner and dog's characteristics. *Applied Animal Behaviour Science, 108,* 143–156.

Martinez, M. A. (1987). Dialogues among children and between children and their mothers. *Child Development, 58,* 1035–1043.

McNicolas, J., & Collis, G. (2001). Children's representations of pets in their social networks. *Child Care, Health & Development, 27,* 279–294.

Melson, G. F. (1991). Studying children's attachment to their pets: A conceptual and methodological review. *Anthrozoos, 4,* 91–99.

Melson, G. F. (2001). *Why the wild things are: Animals in the lives of children.* Cambridge, MA: Harvard University Press.

Melson, G. F. (2007). Children in the living world: Why animals matter for children's development. In A. Fogel & S. Shanker (Eds.), *Human development in the 21st century: Visionary ideas from systems scientists.* New York, NY: Cambridge University Press.

Melson, G. F. (2010). Play between children and domestic animals. In E. Enwokah (Ed.), *Play as engagement and communication.* New York, NY: University Press of America.

Melson, G. F., & Fine, A. H. (2006). Animals in the lives of children. In A. H. Fine (Ed.), *Handbook of animal-assisted therapy* (2nd ed., pp. 207–226). New York, NY: Academic Press.

Melson, G. F., & Fogel, A. (1996). Parental perceptions of their children's involvement with household pets: A test of a specificity model of nurturance. *Anthrozoos, 9,* 95–105.

Melson, G. F., Kahn, P. H. Jr., Beck, A., & Friedman, B. (2009). Robotic pets in human lives: Implications for the human–animal bond and for human relationships with personified technologies. *Journal of Social Issues, 65,* 545–567.

Melson, G. F., Kahn, P. H. Jr., Beck, A., Friedman, B., Roberts, T., Garrett, E., & Gill, B. (2009). Children's behavior toward and understanding of robotic and living dogs. *Journal of Applied Developmental Psychology, 30,* 92–102.

Melson, G. F., Peet, S., & Sparks, C. (1992). Children's attachment to their pets: Links to socio-emotional development. *Children's Environments Quarterly, 8,* 55–65.

Melson, G. F., & Schwarz, R. (1994). *Pets as social supports for families with young children.* Paper presented to the Delta Society, New York, NY.

Miura, A., Bradshaw, J. W. S., & Tanida, H. (2002). Childhood experiences and attitudes toward animal issues: A comparison of young adults in Japan and the UK. *Animal Welfare, 11,* 437–448.

Myers, G. (1998). *Children and animals: Social development and our connection to other species.* Boulder, CO: Westview Press.

Nagergost, S. L., Baun, M. M., Megel, M., & Leibowitz, J. M. (1997). The effects of the presence of a companion animal on physiologic arousal and behavioral distress in children during a physical examination. *Journal of Pediatric Nursing, 12,* 323–330.

Nielsen, J. A., & Delude, L. A. (1989). Behavior of young children in the presence of different kinds of animals. *Anthrozoos, 3,* 119–129.

Parish-Plass, N. (2008). Animal-assisted therapy with children suffering from insecure attachment due to abuse and neglect: A method to lower the risk of intergenerational transmission of abuse? *Clinical Child Psychology and Psychiatry, 13,* 7–30.

Parker, J. G., & Asher, S. R. (1993). Friendship and friendship quality in middle childhood: Links with peer group acceptance and feelings of loneliness and social distress. *Developmental Psychology, 29,* 611–621.

Piaget, J. (1950). *The psychology of intelligence.* New York, NY: Harcourt.

Prothmann, A., Albrecht, K., Dietrich, S., Hornfeck, U., Stieber, S., & Ettrich, C. (2005). Analysis of child–dog play behavior in child psychiatry. *Anthrozoos, 18,* 43–58.

Ricard, M., & Allard, L. (1992). The reaction of 9- to-10-month-old infants to an unfamiliar animal. *Journal of Genetic Psychology, 154,* 14.

Sixsmith, J., Gabhainn, S., Fleming, C., & O'Higgins, S. (2007). Children's, parents', and teachers' perceptions of wellbeing. *Health Education, 107,* 511–523.

Spelke, E. S., Phillips, A., & Woodward, A. L. (1995). Infants' knowledge of object motion and human action. In D. Sperber, D. Premack, & A. J. Premack (Eds.), *Causal cognition: A multidisciplinary debate* (pp. 48–78). Oxford, England: Clarendon Press.

Super, C., & Harkness, S. (2002). Culture structures the environment for development. *Human Development, 45,* 270–274.

Super, C., & Harkness, S. (2003). The metaphors of development. *Human Development, 46,* 3–23.

Tannen, D. (2004). Talking the dog: Framing pets as interactional resources in family discourse. *Research on Language and Social Interaction, 37,* 399–420.

Udell, M. A., & Wynne, C. D. (2008). A review of domestic dogs' (*canis familiaris*) human-like behaviors: Or why behavior analysts should stop worrying and love their dogs. *Journal of Experimental Analysis of Behavior, 89,* 247–261.

von Salisch, M. (2001). Children's emotional development: Challenges in their relations to parents, peers and friends. *International Journal of Behavioural Development, 25,* 310–319.

Valkenburg, P. M., & Soeters, K. E. (2001). Children's positive and negative experiences with the Internet: An exploratory survey. *Communication Research, 28,* 652–675.

Volant, A. M., Johnson, J. A., Gullone, E., & Coleman, G. J. (2008). The relation between domestic violence and animal abuse: An Australian study. *Journal of Interpersonal Violence, 23,* 1277–1295.

Wachs, T. E., & Gruen, G. E. (1982). *Early experience and human development.* New York, NY: Plenum Press.

Wilson, E. O. (1984). *Biophilia.* Cambridge, MA: Harvard University Press.

Wu, A. S., Niedra, R., Pendergast, L., & McCrindle, B. W. (2002). Acceptability and impact of pet visitation on a pediatric cardiology inpatient unit. *Journal of Pediatric Nursing, 17,* 354–362.

Zhou, X., Zheng, R., & Fu, N. (2007). Pet ownership and socio-emotion of school children. *Chinese Mental Health Journal, 21,* 804–880.

2

ESTABLISHING THE EFFECTIVENESS OF ANIMAL-ASSISTED THERAPIES: METHODOLOGICAL STANDARDS, ISSUES, AND STRATEGIES

ALAN E. KAZDIN

Animal-assisted therapies (AATs) with children[1] gain their immediate credibility from everyday experience. The reciprocity, friendship, and mutual support of the human–pet relationship are obvious to those who have a pet or have seen others interact with their pets. Relationship, friendship, and support are among key concepts in the context of psychotherapy (e.g., Schofield, 1986). Consequently, there is no conceptual leap in considering the promising role of animals in assisting humans through a range of social, emotional, and behavioral problems.

The credibility of AATs as a means of helping is a strength, because once we learn to harness their impact, the treatments might be more easily disseminated to children and families than more traditional interventions that have emerged from a mental health/illness perspective. However, the credibility can be a liability as well. The intuitive appeal and widespread belief that animals have therapeutic effects can detract from rigorous scientific scrutiny of AAT. After all, is it not obvious that animals and people help each other? Do we need research if it is obvious? That animals are subjectively

---

[1]"Children" in this chapter refers to children and adolescents, unless a specific distinction is required.

valued and improve the quality of life are easily evaluated by just asking people. It is quite another matter to raise the empirical question of whether AATs can ameliorate social, emotional, or behavioral adjustment problems and diagnosable psychiatric disorders (e.g., anxiety, depression, conduct disorders). The requirements for addressing the question include programmatic research and meticulous scientific scrutiny.

The goal of this chapter is to foster further scientific evaluation of AATs in contexts in which the goal is to improve the social, emotional, or behavioral adjustment or adaptive functioning, or to ameliorate some psychological or psychiatric condition among children. This chapter highlights the current status of psychosocial interventions for children as a context to convey current methodological standards for intervention research. Common methodological flaws that interfere with drawing conclusions about the effects of treatment, and the range of questions relevant to establishing AATs as effective interventions, are discussed in this chapter.

OVERVIEW OF PROGRESS IN CHILD PSYCHOTHERAPY

AATs are often designed to improve adjustment and functioning of children and to decrease various psychological conditions. Child psychotherapies without the use of animals share these goals and thus provide a relevant backdrop and context for research on AATs. There has been enormous progress in child therapy research in the past few decades (Kazdin, 2000b; Weisz & Kazdin, 2010). First, the quantity of controlled therapy outcome studies is remarkable. The last formal estimate of such studies in 1999 placed the number at 1,500 (Kazdin, 2000a). It is difficult to evaluate that number without some comparison, so it is useful to mention in passing that a recent review of AATs identified six studies of children and adolescents in which there were control or comparison groups (Nimer & Lundahl, 2007).

Second, the quality of child psychotherapy research has improved over the years. Several methodological practices have become standard, including:

- Random assignment of participants to conditions;
- Careful specification of the client sample and the inclusion and exclusion criteria required for participation;
- Use of strong control or comparison groups (e.g., treatment as usual or another viable treatment);
- Use of treatment manuals to codify procedures and practices to permit replication of treatment;
- Assessment of treatment integrity (i.e., the extent to which the intervention was carried out as intended);

- Use of multiple outcome measures with multiple assessment methods (e.g., self-report, parent report, direct observation) and measures of multiple domains of functioning (e.g., symptoms, prosocial functioning);
- Evaluation of the clinical significance of change (i.e., whether the changes at the end of treatment make a difference in returning individuals to adaptive functioning); and
- Evaluation of follow-up weeks, months, or years after posttreatment assessment of child functioning.

Not all studies include all of these practices, but it is difficult to obtain funding for treatment research or to publish the results of a psychotherapy outcome study in the scientific literature without including most of these features.

Third, quantitative (meta-analytic) reviews of the research consistently conclude that many forms of psychotherapy for children are effective (Weisz, 2004). Improvements among children in treatment groups surpass the changes made by children in control group conditions. Moreover, the magnitude of the effects of treatment is reasonably large (effect size > .70).

Fourth and related, there are now several evidence-based psychotherapies. These refer to psychotherapies that have controlled studies to support them, where the effects of treatment have been replicated, and where several of the characteristics noted above (bulleted) have been included (Christophersen & Mortweet, 2001; Weisz & Kazdin, 2010). As an illustration, aggressive and antisocial behavior is the most commonly referred clinical problem to child outpatient services and constitutes 33% to 50% of all referrals. There are now at least seven evidence-based treatments, and they encompass young children through adolescents and mildly oppositional and aggressive behavior to severe and repetitive antisocial behavior that has led to adjudication.[2]

Child psychotherapy is not all a bed of roses. There are more than 550 techniques in use for children and adolescents (Kazdin, 2000b). Most treatments in use have never been investigated empirically; many effective treatments are *not* in widespread use; some treatments in widespread use are not effective; and well-intentioned efforts to help children (e.g., horticulture therapy, smudge art therapy, wilderness camps) still have no empirical evidence to support them. It is relevant to refer to a large and actively used set of treatments in clinical work that have little evidence to support them. Historically, unevaluated psychotherapies have had little scrutiny or accountability. However, the absence of evidence for a given intervention provides

---

[2]The seven treatments include: parent management training, multisystemic therapy, multidimensional treatment foster care, cognitive problem-solving skills training, anger control training, brief strategic family therapy, and functional family therapy. For a description and review of these treatments, other sources are available (Kazdin, 2007; Weisz & Kazdin, 2010).

a sharp contrast to many other interventions now available. Scrutiny by agencies, third-party payers, and perhaps eventually by consumers will influence what interventions are administered and reimbursed.

In many ways, the progress in child psychotherapy research can be explained as part of a broader movement in intervention research in the area of health care. The standards for clinical trials across many disciplines have become higher and more explicit. As a prominent illustration, standards for reporting clinical trials, referred to as Consolidated Standards of Reporting Trials (or CONSORT), have emerged to guide how clinical trials are reported. A checklist for investigators is available to address critical facets of the trial, such as how the sample was identified, how participants were allocated to conditions, how many started in the trial and completed treatment, whether they received the intended treatment, and more (see http://www.consort-statement.org). The standards have been adopted by hundreds of journals from many disciplines and countries (see http://www.consort-statement.org/about-consort/supporters/consort-endorsers—journals) in an effort not only to improve reporting of trials but also to increase their overall quality.

The implications of progress in child psychotherapy research and explicit standards (e.g., CONSORT) for conducting intervention trials are clear. For AATs we have to go beyond saying more empirical research is needed. Methodological standards are in place and evolving; these standards convey what study is suitable to evaluate any intervention. Any newly proposed treatment, or treatment that has been available for some time but has not undergone careful empirical evaluation, has a methodological template to follow to gain the attention of the scientific community.

Establishing the effectiveness of an AAT requires comparison with some other treatment or viable control condition. It is still appropriate to compare treatment versus no treatment in a randomized controlled trial (RCT). More often, a treatment of interest (e.g., AAT) would need to be compared to another treatment, such as the care that is routinely provided (often called "treatment as usual"), if one is available. "No-treatment" is not a strong test of the effects of an AAT because virtually any treatment is likely to appear to be more effective. Thus, an AAT is likely to be more effective than no treatment, but the same treatment (e.g., just talking) without the animal present is also likely to surpass the effects of no treatment. There is a separate and fascinating body of evidence in psychotherapy research related to various control and comparison groups and their credibility to clients. The more credible (plausible, believable) the control condition to the clients and the higher expectations for change that treatment generates, the greater the clients' improvements (e.g., Baskin, Tierney, Minami, & Wampold, 2003; Grissom, 1996). This effect occurs even if a "fake" treatment condition is constructed that is intended only to mobilize expectations that it will work. Thus, it is essential in current work to show that treatment is better than some alternative.

COMMON METHODOLOGICAL PROBLEMS

A more concrete way to convey current methodological standards is to identify numerous practices that interfere with providing the needed evidence for AATs. Several are listed, but do not assume the list is comprehensive.[3]

Single-Group Pre-to-Post–Only Design

Occasionally reports include one group in which the children's presenting problems (e.g., anxiety, disruptive behavior) are assessed before and after completion of an AAT. There is no control or comparison group. The children are likely to show improvements from the beginning to the end of the program, and the improvements are attributed by the investigator to the AAT. Yet, change from pre- to posttreatment can occur for many reasons that are well codified in methodology, including the effects of repeated testing, history, maturation, and statistical regression. Pre-to-post change of one group allows the researcher to say there was a change, but from a methodological standpoint, one cannot attribute that change to the intervention. There are other interpretations that are more parsimonious and plausible to account for the change.

Heterogeneous Samples

In conducting an outcome study, one would like to begin with a relatively homogeneous sample, that is, children who are similar in age and who present roughly similar problems. Often the opposite strategy is selected with the rationale that one wants a diverse sample (e.g., all comers or all the clients seen at a facility) so the results are generalizable. However, the initial task of research is to evaluate unambiguously if there is an effect and whether the AAT in the study makes a difference. The more diverse the study sample, the greater the variability (individual differences) shown on any outcome measure. The greater the variability, the more difficult it can be to demonstrate a treatment effect. The high variability resulting from a diverse sample usually

---

[3]There may be a "Minute Waltz" (Waltz in D flat major, opus 64, No. 1 by Chopin) in music, but there is no "minute methodology" for intervention research. The discussion of common methodological flaws is brief and cannot convey in detail the rationale as to why these are flaws and how they can be circumvented (see Kazdin, 2003).

requires a much larger sample size to ensure that there is sufficient statistical power to detect an intervention effect. Even with that increased power, the success and failure of the intervention for multiple subgroups within the study could obscure genuine treatment effects.

As a place to begin, it is usually advisable to establish the effectiveness of the intervention with a relatively homogeneous sample. Once treatment is established as effective, the next steps can include evaluating the effects with various samples (e.g., types of clinical, social, or educational problems), conditions of administration (e.g., individual, group; daily, weekly), and other variables (e.g., therapist or animal characteristics, matching animals to children) that might influence outcome.

Ambiguous Samples and Treatment Foci

AAT studies occasionally focus on "at risk" individuals. This can be problematic in two ways. First, it often is unclear for what the children are at risk. Second, the outcome measures of a study ought to focus on the domain or outcomes for which the children are at risk. If the youth are at risk for delinquency or academic failure, it is important to evaluate the extent to which the treatment reduced risk for these specific outcomes and, even better, if they reduced the actual outcomes themselves. The generic use of "at risk" without much further specification is likely to generate a heterogeneous sample for the study and raises the prior concern about variability that obscures identifying significant intervention effects.

If "at risk" children are identified for inclusion, another issue is the need to specify what makes them at risk (what characteristics or variables) and how those variables were measured. Sometimes the measures are easily obtained or available (e.g., age, family socioeconomic standing) and sometimes they are described but not systematically measured (e.g., psychiatric diagnosis). Interpretation and replication of the results require knowing who was studied, their key characteristics, and how these characteristics were assessed.

Questionable or Unsupported Assumptions

Therapy studies occasionally focus on constructs that are presumed to relate to an outcome of interest. In many instances, the very premise can threaten the credibility of the study. As an example, a youth might be identified because of behavior problems or apparent lack of impulse control. The rationale for using a particular AAT may be that the treatment will build self-esteem. Improving self-esteem becomes the focus or goal of treatment and also serves as a means to change the behavioral problems. Yet, self-esteem has no strong connection to behavioral or other mental health problems (Baumeister,

Campbell, Krueger, & Vohs, 2003). (An exception is that low self-esteem can accompany and be part of clinical depression.) There is no strong reason to focus on self-esteem to change disruptive behavior, anxiety, poor academic performance, or social skills deficits, and, indeed, empirical reasons to avoid this focus. One might focus on self-esteem as an end in itself. That is, if the problem is low self-esteem and the goal is to build self-esteem, obviously the means and ends are aligned. It is the notion that self-esteem is an important target to accomplish some other goal that is difficult to support.

My comments are not about self-esteem per se. Rather, the target of treatment or what the treatment is trying to change must have a connection to the outcomes that are measured. Many studies begin with the premise that if the children had a better understanding, if they showed more empathy, if they knew better, if they developed caring for an animal, or if they took responsibility for an animal, they would no longer have the problems or would be significantly improved in some specific domain (e.g., symptoms, academic performance, social skills). Each of these views has little empirical support. Three lines of evidence are needed: (a) that children with clinical dysfunction or social, emotional, and behavioral problems have deficits of some kind (e.g., in understanding, self-esteem, or empathy); (b) that changing understanding (or one of the other constructs) leads to change in the target focus (e.g., disruptive behavior, anxiety); and (c) that working with animals changes that specific focus (understanding or other constructs), which then leads to improvement in clinical outcomes. Evidence for (a) is available for many clinical problems. Children with clinical problems (e.g., conduct disorder, autistic spectrum disorder) often have deficits in multiple domains. However, evidence for (b) is rare; I could not find evidence for (c), but of course that does not mean it does not exist.

If the goal of an AAT is to teach knowledge about animals, build self-esteem, develop empathy, develop responsibility, overcome loneliness, provide social support, improve human–animal relations and bonding, and reduce cruelty to animals, then an AAT may be a reasonable means of accomplishing these goals. However, if the goal is to reduce violence, aggression, or anxiety or to improve interpersonal relations and academic performance, the connection is less clear. I am not asserting AATs could not achieve these latter goals and am hopeful that they can. If research has one of these latter goals, it is critical that the outcome measures focus on these goals and that the rationale for the study convey the connection of the means and these goals. More generally, it is valuable to begin a study with a conceptual view that links the problem (e.g., anxiety, disruptive behavior, or risk status in relation to a specific outcome) and treatment. The overarching question is why would one expect the addition of animals in treatment to make a difference in a particular outcome domain?

Conceptual Issues

In specifying the rationale for AATs, it is important to distinguish theory of etiology and theory of change. Etiology refers to the causes or origins of the problems the child is experiencing. Change refers to what can be done to overcome or alleviate the problems. A common view is that one must get at the "putative" root of the problem and that unless one undoes the cause, there will be no improvement or amelioration of the problem. There are many examples in which this is quite true (e.g., rabies, strep throat). Whether in medicine, psychology, or counseling, we always want to know the cause(s), and once we do, effective preventive efforts become so much more feasible. However, we do not have to know the cause to have effective interventions. For example, in medicine, headaches, childhood leukemia, and many cancers can be effectively treated; in clinical psychology, anxiety, depression, and sexual dysfunction, to mention a few areas, can be effectively treated. In each instance, we do not know the causes—indeed there are likely to be many causes. Researchers are working on identifying subtypes and on causal factors; in the meantime we have effective interventions.

I mention this in the context of AAT research because more attention is needed on articulating why and how the presence of animals can enhance or lead to change. That is, we would profit from a theory of change for AATs or theories of change for various problem domains (e.g., anxiety or depression). The articulation of how change comes about will provide hypotheses about the change process, and these can be tested by assessing the critical intervening process. If supported, the hypotheses can guide us on how to make AATs more effective. For example, for a child diagnosed with anxiety, one might propose the calming effect of an animal and the ability of that calming effect to help with graduated exposure of the child to anxiety-provoking situations. The focus is on how change can occur, even though we do not know how or why the child's anxiety emerged.

Single Therapists, Single Animals

As a general rule, evaluation of an AAT requires at least two therapists administering the intervention and at least two different animals (of the same species). For example, if an AAT is compared with no treatment and a dog is the animal of choice, it is important to have at least two therapists administer treatment and at least two dogs. The dogs can be similar, and so can the therapists! (It would be helpful to pair each therapist with each dog as they treat different children, but we can ignore that nuance for the moment.) The reason for at least two is not the obvious one of testing whether the results are generalizable. More nuanced is that the effects of treatment must be separable (statistically) from the conditions of administration (which therapist, which dog). If only one therapist (therapist A) and only one dog (dog A) were used and the AAT were effective, a conclusion cannot be reached that the AAT was responsible for the effects. Rather the conclusion has to be discussed as the combination of AAT + therapist A + dog A. It might be that this special combination was responsible for the change, and concluding that it was the AAT is not appropriate. Adding one more therapist and one more dog to the study allows one to separate the impact of these influences statistically and reach a clearer conclusion. For example, one could then conclude that the AAT works independently of which of the two (or more) therapists and which of the two (or more) dogs. Perhaps treatment is more effective with one of the therapists or one of the dogs. That is not necessarily a problem. That is different from the fundamental methodological problem raised by using only one therapist or one dog (or other animal).

Codifying the Intervention

Treatment manuals are used in research to codify treatment procedures and how they were implemented. The manuals permit replication by others. The manuals vary from a list of general principles with illustrations of how these are applied (e.g., Henggeler, Schoenwald, Borduin, Rowland, & Cunningham, 1998) to word-for-word, session-by-session scripts to guide therapists (e.g., Kazdin, 2005). Codifying treatment does not mean that treatment is rigidly applied or that we ignore individual differences in the children or the animals. Bypass surgery and appendectomies have some standard features, even though every operation varies as a function of the patient. Here too in AATs, a study should codify key procedures, such as what kinds of interactions are important among the therapist, child, and animal; what is likely to be discussed; what activities will be performed; and what the role of the animal will be. The task of developing a treatment manual for an AAT is slightly greater than for a similar treatment without an animal. The role of the animal (e.g., any activity, any contact with the child, approximately how much) ought to be described. Also, there may be different species used for similar AATs, and the manual might change as a function of the animal. Guidelines describing the activities and role of the animal, apart from describing the equivalent for the therapist, are essential.

Treatment manuals become odious to ponder if one views them as recipe books with ingredients and their amounts precisely specified. Treatments are not rigid recipes. However, for therapy research, the other extreme is not permissible either, namely, freewheeling, idiosyncratic therapist delivery of an intervention in which we have no way of knowing what was done and no way of replicating treatment. Those days are long past in light of the progress of therapy research highlighted previously. The details of treatment procedures, as the treatment allows, are critical from a scientific standpoint to train therapists participating in a study, help evaluate whether they are adhering to treatment, and replicate the effects of treatment in subsequent studies.

Multiple Measures of Outcome

Outcome measures refer to those indices that assess the effects of the intervention. The measures are connected closely to the reasons the children were selected to participate. For example, if the children have behavioral problems, the measures are selected to reflect these problems. In any given study, it is important to have more than one measure of the outcome and more than one method of assessment. We are interested in the construct (or domain), such as behavioral problems (or anxiety or depression, for examples) rather than the measure. The measure is one index to operationalize the construct, but the construct is better represented by more than one measure. As a common example, parent and teacher ratings on standardized and well-validated measures such as the Child Behavior Checklist are commonly used to evaluate psychotherapy for children. They both sample multiple domains of functioning (e.g., symptoms of many types, positive social behavior) and yield different perspectives on how well the child is doing. Sometimes direct observations of behavior or samples of child behavior in the treatment setting are assessed as well. The point here is that more than one measure and use of more than one rater or method of assessment are advisable. Multiple measures and methods of assessment strengthen the conclusion that the domain of interest was altered.

The use of more measures or many measures does not always need to be onerous. Not all outcome measures are time consuming or client unfriendly. There are validated measures that have been used with adults and children in clinical settings to evaluate progress of ongoing treatment. A prominent example is a family of measures referred to as Outcome Questionnaires with versions that vary by age group (see http://www.oqmeasures.com/site). For each version, patients (or for children, their parents) can rate several items that assess several symptom domains (e.g., depression, anxiety, interpersonal problems, and others). The measure can be completed weekly, takes approximately 5 minutes to complete, and provides information on multiple domains of functioning. Some of the versions have been well-tested and validated (e.g., > 10,000 patients) and shown to be useful in evaluating and predicting response to treatment (e.g., Lambert et al., 2003). I write not to lobby for any particular measure but rather to convey that valid assessments are available that are compatible with the exigencies of clinical work and research.

Scope of Assessment

Emphasis is on assessing the problem domains that serve as the impetus for providing AATs in a given study, yet we might also want to evaluate more domains than the primary problem. As an illustration, at Yale Child Conduct Clinic, where I work, our treatments (parent management training, cognitive problem-solving skills training) lead to reductions in aggressive and antisocial child behaviors. Interestingly, treatment also is associated with reductions in mother depression and stress in the home and improved family relations (Kazdin & Wassell, 2000). We do not specifically focus on these, but it is helpful to document broader effects beyond the treatment goals.

For a given application, it might well be that an AAT is equally effective as some other treatment in improving child functioning, yet an AAT might be viewed as more acceptable to children and parents, have less stigma associated with it, or have lower rates of dropping out, when compared with a more traditional form of therapy. The benefits of treatment and the relative benefits in relation to alternatives do not necessarily derive from the effect on the clinical problem alone. For example, medications for depression or anxiety in any given comparison might not differ in their effect on the disorder, but vary in some other feature (e.g., side effects) that influences their use. It is likely that an AAT would have broad as well as specific effects, and including measures of these, to the extent feasible, could be useful.

RESEARCH DESIGN OPTIONS BRIEFLY NOTED

Quantitative research refers to the methods in which most researchers are trained. Familiar features of the methodology include null hypothesis testing, comparison of groups that are exposed to separate conditions or interventions, and use of statistical significance testing to draw inferences about the impact of an intervention or experimental condition. Within this research tradition, RCTs are considered to be the "gold standard" for intervention research, whether those interventions are medical (e.g., chemotherapy), educational (e.g., special curriculum), or psychosocial (e.g., psychotherapy, AAT). The key characteristic, of course, is identifying a set of participants and assigning them randomly to groups (e.g., treatment and control conditions) within the study. The progress in therapy research and development of evidence-based treatments highlighted previously was based primarily on RCTs. RCTs are the Esperanto of the sciences and therefore a language with which AAT research ought to be fluent, even though such trials can be difficult and expensive to mount in light of many requirements (e.g., administering, collecting, coding assessments; protecting client rights through informed consent and procedures to assure privacy and confidentiality of the clients and their data; monitoring the delivery and integrity of treatment; and entering, checking, and analyzing the data).

In addition to RCTs, three other strategies could play a pivotal role in developing the research base of AATs. First, within the quantitative research tradition there are more options than just the RCT. *Quasi-experiments* include studies in which individuals cannot be assigned randomly to conditions (Shadish, Cook, & Campbell, 2002). Individuals from different groups in an institution or from different institutions can be exposed to different treatments (e.g., an AAT) or control conditions (e.g., a waiting list that serves as a temporary no-treatment control group). There are ways to draw inferences about the impact of treatment by taking into account characteristics of the sample and by matching samples using statistical techniques (e.g., propensity score matching, instrumental variable techniques, trajectory modeling). Quasi-experiments often are much more feasible than RCTs, and their yield can be important.

Second, beyond the quantitative tradition, other design strategies are available and feasible. *Single-case experimental designs* can readily permit drawing valid inferences about the impact of an intervention (Kazdin, 2010). The designs are infrequently taught but are just as powerful in demonstrating causal relations as are RCTs. Among the key characteristics of these designs is assessment of functioning on multiple occasions over time under different conditions (e.g., pretreatment baseline and then during the intervention). For example, in one of the designs, an AAT could be introduced to different children or different programs or groups at different points. The staggering of when the intervention is introduced, against a backdrop of continuous assessment (e.g., daily or several times per week), permits causal statements to be drawn about the impact of the interventions. Single-case designs could be useful in establishing the efficacy of AATs, because they can be used in a single facility (clinic, institution) where such programs are already ongoing and do not require random assignment or withholding treatment from those in need.

Third, *qualitative research* would be quite useful as well. In clinical work, the term "qualitative" is occasionally misused to refer to case material or anecdotal descriptions. Yet qualitative research is a rigorous method of study that meets the desiderata of science; the methods are systematic, replicable, and cumulative (e.g., Denzin & Lincoln, 2005). The unique feature is the in-depth evaluation and richly detailed information about how individuals represent (perceive, feel) and react to their situations and contexts. The methods provide a rigorous way to codify experience and analyze the resulting data. For example, qualitative research can examine the experiences of those who go through an AAT and thematic ways in which their lives are changed. The information could be useful for understanding how treatment works and the changes that are produced and in generating hypotheses to be tested in other types of studies.

I have highlighted methodological approaches with broad strokes and in the process might have unwittingly understated the options available to researchers. First, I may have implied that one approach rather than another must be selected for an investigation. Different approaches can be combined in the same study, including quantitative and qualitative research (e.g., Yoshikawa, Weisner, Kalil, & Way, 2008) and quantitative and single-case research (e.g., Azrin & Peterson, 1990). There are advantages in such combinations because how different types of information and data relate to each other in a single study is likely to be more informative than two separate studies each using a different approach. In a single study that combines strategies, the convergence, overlap, and complementary nature of the yield is better illustrated because many conditions (e.g., participant characteristics, institution) that would vary between separate studies are constant. Second, I may have incorrectly implied that methods within a given approach are static and fixed to a small number of options. New methodologies continue to emerge for evaluation of clinical trials and for comparing groups when randomization is not possible (e.g., Foster & Kalil, 2008; Jennison & Turnbull, 2000). Thus, the range of research options and opportunities is enormous.

Knowledge blooms where several methods converge on a topic and at once reveal different facets of the phenomenon of interest as well as replicate common features. Consequently, no one research approach must be followed exclusively to build the empirical base of AATs. RCTs are essential, but so many questions, including the efficacy of treatment, can be addressed in multiple ways. We should foster a broad portfolio of methods as this field continues to develop. Therefore, we need basic research establishing that AAT is an evidence-based treatment. The assessment and design criteria are clear if AATs are to enter mainstream intervention research and practice for children.

QUESTIONS TO GUIDE ANIMAL-ASSISTED TREATMENTS

There are many questions to ask about AATs in relation to treatment of children. Exhibit 2.1 lists several questions that dominate intervention research and apply to AATs. The first and most fundamental question is whether treatment is effective and surpasses changes over time without treatment. Although this is not easy to do in many situations because of ethical issues alone (withholding treatment from those in need), from a methodological standpoint, this is the easiest of the studies to show that treatment is effective. An alternative would be to compare an AAT to another viable treatment. At some point that is important. However, a much larger difference

EXHIBIT 2.1
Questions That Guide Psychotherapy Research

1. What is the impact of treatment relative to no-treatment?
2. What components contribute to change?
3. What treatments can be added (combined treatments) to optimize change?
4. What parameters can be varied to influence (improve) outcome?
5. How effective is this treatment relative to other treatments for this problem?
6. What patient, therapist, treatment, and contextual factors influence (moderate) outcome?
7. What processes within or during treatment influence, cause, and are responsible for outcome (therapeutic change)?
8. To what extent are treatment effects generalizable across problem areas, settings, and other domains?

(treatment effect) between groups is likely when one of the groups includes no treatment than when one of the groups includes another treatment or a control condition in which sessions are provided. In this latter study, a much larger sample size is needed for statistical power.[4] Consequently, clear evidence that addresses the first question is usually a place to begin. In the case of AATs, even that question is a lengthy agenda based on different goals of treatment, child populations of interest, and options for animals that can assist in treatment.

The second question in the exhibit, what components contribute to change, may be of special relevance to AATs. In evaluating and establishing the effectiveness of AATs, we take almost as a given that use of an animal in therapy contributes to therapeutic change. A study in which an AAT is compared to no treatment does not provide specific evidence for that assumption. There is strong evidence that meeting with a client and establishing a relationship contributes to therapeutic change when no animal is present. Thus, when an AAT shows an effect that surpasses no treatment, the most parsimonious interpretation is that the effect was due to the treatment provided with a therapist; no evidence is available in this demonstration as I have described it to establish that the presence of an animal increased the impact of treatment from the same or similar procedures without an animal present. Moreover, I mentioned previously that any treatment that appears credible can lead to greater changes than those associated with no treatment. Thus, the first question in the exhibit is a preliminary albeit important focus.

Question two asks whether the animal makes a contribution to therapeutic change. To test that requires that one group receive an AAT and

---

[4]Statistical power refers to the extent to which a study can detect a difference between groups when a genuine difference exists. It is quite possible that treatments have different effects and that one is in fact superior to the other but no differences are obtained on statistical evaluation. Such studies are likely to have insufficient power.

another group receive a similar treatment but without the animal present. Of all the questions, from my perspective, question two is the highest priority. There is a firm belief that presence of the animal makes a difference. I am not challenging that. However, I do not believe there is a strong body of empirical research in the context of child treatment to make the case persuasively.

The questions in this exhibit provide a broad portfolio, and a well-designed study addressing any of the questions would be an excellent contribution. I have favored question two; other questions might be equally compelling. For example, the question about moderators refers to what type of children or what type of child–animal matching maximizes therapeutic change. Such questions obviously are important. As the questions move down the list, they tend to be slightly more complex or demanding in terms of what is needed in the assessment, design, and data analyses.

CLOSING COMMENTS

Evidence-based psychotherapies for children are developing very well, and now many disorders and other domains of functioning can be treated effectively. It would be excellent to add AATs to this list. AATs encompass many different treatments, applied to many different disorders or areas of child functioning, and in many different settings. Also, diverse species of animals are in use, and these can readily vary in the roles they play and perhaps in relation to the goals of treatment. AATs are a rich area of work that can apply to children, adolescents, and adults, to a broad range of physical and mental health conditions, and to the quality of life more generally. The broad relevance is an impetus for ensuring that there is a prioritization of foci in research.

Progress might be accelerated if we could begin in an area or two where AATs are believed to be especially likely to have therapeutic impact with children. What youth, with what problems or areas in need of care are most likely to respond to treatment? And what variation of AAT is likely to be the most effective? We are building a literature empirically, but it is useful to draw on our strongest clinical experience as the focus of our research.

This chapter conveys the need for rigorous studies of AAT, a message that is not new (see Fine, 2006; Nimer & Lundahl, 2007). The message is worth repeating in the context of non-AATs (i.e., therapies in which animals are not involved). Research on many forms of psychotherapy that share the goals with many AATs continues and often with rigorous studies that show changes on significant clinical problems, including children with multiple problems and psychiatric diagnoses.

The methodology for intervention research is well worked out and has a continuous set of exemplars that are published regularly. Not all research needs to be based on RCTs. As I have listed, several research questions can be asked about the effects of therapy and the factors that contribute to outcome. Many design options are available that do not require RCTs, yet research is needed to test AATs in a rigorous way. We need programs of research where one or two variations of AATs are examined to ensure that the methodology is worked out (e.g., treatment manuals) and that treatment delivery and outcomes can be replicated. A few such programs would provide a model on which we could build. The public is likely to be sympathetic to AATs; many therapists are enthusiastic already. To bring others on board (e.g., practitioners trained in more traditional therapy, researchers, third-party payers, and grant funding agencies), we need to build a strong evidence base. The challenges I have outlined in this chapter are not rocket science, but they are science. The goals of treatment are clear, the methods are available, and we can and ought to move vigorously to the next step.

REFERENCES

Azrin, N. H., & Peterson, A. L. (1990). Treatment of Tourette's syndrome by habit reversal: A waiting-list control group. *Behavior Therapy, 21*, 305–318.

Baskin, T. W., Tierney, S. C., Minami, T., & Wampold, B. E. (2003). Establishing specificity in psychotherapy: A meta-analysis of structural equivalence of placebo controls. *Journal of Consulting and Clinical Psychology, 71*, 973–979.

Baumeister, R. F., Campbell, J. D., Krueger, J. I., & Vohs, K. D. (2003). Psychological science in the public interest: Does high self-esteem cause better performance, interpersonal success, happiness, or healthier lifestyles? *Psychological Science in the Public Interest, 4*, 1–44.

Christophersen, E. R., & Mortweet, S. L. (2001). *Treatments that work with children: Empirically supported strategies for managing childhood problems*. Washington, DC: American Psychological Association.

Denzin, N. K., & Lincoln, Y. S. (Eds.). (2005). *The SAGE handbook of qualitative research* (3rd ed.). Thousand Oaks, CA: Sage.

Fine, A. H. (Ed.). (2006). *Handbook on animal-assisted therapy: Theoretical foundations and guidelines for practice*. (2nd ed.). San Diego, CA: Academic Press.

Foster, E. M., & Kalil, A. (2008). New methods for new questions: Obstacles and opportunities. *Developmental Psychology, 44*, 301–304.

Grissom, R. J. (1996). The magical number .7 +/− .2: Meta-meta-analysis of the probability of superior outcome in comparisons involving therapy, placebo, and control. *Journal of Consulting and Clinical Psychology, 64*, 973–982.

Henggeler, S. W., Schoenwald, S. K., Borduin, C. M., Rowland, M. D., & Cunningham, P. B. (1998). *Multisystemic treatment of antisocial behavior in children and adolescents*. New York, NY: Guilford.

Jennison, C., & Turnbull, B. W. (2000). *Group sequential methods with applications to clinical trials*. Boca Raton, FL: CRC Press.

Kazdin, A. E. (2000a). Developing a research agenda for child and adolescent psychotherapy research. *Archives of General Psychiatry, 57*, 829–835.

Kazdin, A. E. (2000b). *Psychotherapy for children and adolescents: Directions for research and practice*. New York, NY: Oxford University Press.

Kazdin, A. E. (2003). *Research design in clinical psychology* (4th ed.). Needham Heights, MA: Allyn & Bacon.

Kazdin, A. E. (2005). *Parent management training: Treatment for oppositional, aggressive, and antisocial behavior in children and adolescents*. New York, NY: Oxford University Press.

Kazdin, A. E. (2007). Psychosocial treatments for conduct disorder in children and adolescents. In P. E. Nathan & J. M. Gorman (Eds.), *A guide to treatments that work* (3rd ed., pp. 71–104). New York, NY: Oxford University Press.

Kazdin, A. E. (2010). *Single-case research designs: Methods for clinical and applied settings* (2nd ed.). New York, NY: Oxford University Press.

Kazdin, A. E., & Wassell, G. (2000). Therapeutic changes in children, parents, and families resulting from treatment of children with conduct problems. *Journal of the American Academy of Child and Adolescent Psychiatry, 39*, 414–420.

Lambert, M. J., Whipple, J. L., Hawkins, E. J., Vermeersch, D. A., Nielsen, S. L., & Smart, D. W. (2003). Is it time for clinicians to routinely track patient outcome? A meta-analysis. *Clinical Psychology: Science and Practice, 10*, 288–301.

Nimer, J., & Lundahl, B. (2007). Animal-assisted therapy: A meta-analysis. *Anthrozoos, 20*, 225–238.

Schofield, W. (1986). *Psychotherapy: The purchase of friendship*. Piscataway, NJ: Transaction Publishers.

Shadish, W. R., Cook, T. D., & Campbell, D. T. (2002). *Experimental and quasi-experimental designs for generalized causal inference*. Boston, MA: Houghton Mifflin.

Weisz, J. R. (2004). *Psychotherapy for children and adolescents: Evidence-based treatments and case examples*. Cambridge, England: Cambridge University Press.

Weisz, J. R., & Kazdin, A. E. (Eds.). (2010). *Evidence-based psychotherapies for children and adolescents* (2nd ed.). New York, NY: Guilford Press.

Yoshikawa, H., Weisner, T. S., Kalil, A., & Way, N. (2008). Mixing qualitative and quantitative research in developmental science: Uses and methodological choices. *Developmental Psychology, 44*, 344–354.

3

PROMISES AND PITFALLS OF HORMONE RESEARCH IN HUMAN–ANIMAL INTERACTION

KERSTIN UVNÄS-MOBERG, LINDA HANDLIN,
AND MARIA PETERSSON

INTRODUCTION

An abundant literature suggests that interaction between humans and animals can be of great value for human health. In general, this literature shows that a human–dog interaction has a positive influence on human social interaction and also acts as a stress reducer in humans (Olmert, 2009; Serpell, 1986, 2000). These two effects are also induced when humans are in close contact with each other (e.g., interaction between mother and child). The hormone oxytocin is released in response to this type of interaction. Because administration of oxytocin gives rise to the above-mentioned effects, it might be assumed that oxytocin released both during mother–infant interaction and during human–animal interaction (HAI) causes the increased social interaction and the stress buffering effect (Uvnäs-Moberg, 1998b). It may therefore be of interest to study physiological, endocrine, and behavior variables that reflect oxytocin release and oxytocin-mediated activity/functions during HAI.

One important function of oxytocin is to lower the levels of the stress hormone cortisol. Cortisol is a hormone that is active during physiological responses to emotional and physical stressors. These responses are necessary for supporting survival in life-threatening situations and during physical exercise, as well as supporting problem solving in everyday, commonplace situations. Increased cortisol levels have been associated with decreased immune function; increased cholesterol levels; increased stress reactions resulting from pain or mental stress, depression, other mental illnesses or brain injury, sexual or physical abuse; and psychosocial stressors, such as separation from an attachment figure or performance anxiety (Brand et al., 2010; Gunnar, Talge, & Herrera, 2009; Knorr, Vinberg, Kessing, & Wetterslev, 2010; Mondelli et al., 2010). Because oxytocin can lower cortisol levels, studying the relation between cortisol and HAI is important because it may be a reflection of oxytocin release and oxytocin-mediating effects, such as stress reactivity and social behavior.

Conducting endocrinologic research requires not only a well-designed study (randomized, controlled, etc.) but also adequate techniques for physiological and endocrine measures. This chapter focuses on techniques for measuring hormones, particularly oxytocin and cortisol. First it provides an overview of hormone chemistry, including how oxytocin and cortisol function and interact with sensory stimulation. Studies on animals and studies on humans are described. The chapter also explores how to use oxytocin, cortisol, and other endocrinologic research to determine the effects of HAI on both humans and animals. Methodological considerations for measuring hormones are discussed, such as whether to measure from blood samples or urine samples. Finally, the chapter discusses results of published studies involving HAI and endocrine measurement.

OVERVIEW OF HORMONE CHEMISTRY

Most hormones studied in experimental conditions are either steroids or peptides. The stress hormone cortisol (and the less abundant corticosterone in humans) and the sex hormones testosterone, estrogen, and progesterone are all steroids. In contrast, the pituitary hormones (such as adrenocorticotrophic hormone, oxytocin, and vasopressin), the pancreatic hormone insulin, and gastrointestinal hormones (such as gastrin and cholecystokinin) are examples of peptide hormones.

Steroid Hormones

The steroid hormones (such as cortisol) are all derivatives of the cholesterol molecule, which is a lipid. Because of their chemical property, steroids easily pass through most cell membranes, the gastrointestinal mucosa, and the blood–brain barrier. For the same reasons, they easily pass into saliva, milk, and urine, where they can be detected. Most steroids are degraded in the liver, and the half-life is relatively long. The effect caused by steroids occurs after a certain delay because it acts on intracellular cytoplasmic or nuclear receptors. These facts affect how and when the steroids should be measured for most accurate results.

Peptide Hormones

The peptide hormones (such as oxytocin) are built up by chains of amino acids. At one end of the peptide hormone, an amino acid with an exposed amino group (slightly alkaline) is situated, and on the other side is a carboxyl group (slightly acidic). The peptide hormones are polar substances, and unlike steroids, they do not readily pass through membranes. That is, they are not well absorbed from the gastrointestinal tract, and only small amounts cross the blood–brain barrier. Peptide hormones are degraded in circulation, in the liver, and in the kidneys. The peptides often activate receptors in the cell membranes. Many peptides are produced in endocrine cells and act as endocrine or hormonal substances, in addition to being released from neurons in the central nervous system, where they act as neurotransmitters or neuromodulators.

OVERVIEW OF OXYTOCIN

A Hormone and a Neurotransmitter

Oxytocin is a peptide that is produced in the paraventricular nuclei (PVN) and the supraoptic nuclei (SON) of the hypothalamus, an important regulation center of the brain, located just above the brain stem, which controls the function of the major endocrine gland—the pituitary—and also the activity of the autonomic nervous system. Oxytocin from both these hypothalamic nuclei is released into the circulation via the posterior pituitary to stimulate uterine contractions and excretion of milk (Ludwig & Leng, 2006) during childbearing. In addition, oxytocin serves as a neurotransmitter, when released from neurons originating in the PVN that project to many important regulatory areas in the brain. Oxytocin-containing nerve fibers reach many brain and other central nervous system areas that control various functions (Buijs, De Vries, & Van Leeuwen, 1985):

- amygdala—social interaction and fear
- hippocampus—memory and learning
- PVN—for example, the hypothalamic–pituitary–adrenal (HPA axis)
- anterior pituitary—control of hormone secretion, including the HPA-axis

gression and wakefulness, noradrener-

otonergic neurons
accumbens (NA)—motor functions,
opaminergic neurons
G)—pain
y nuclei (e.g., dorsal motor nucleus
e tractus solitaries [NTS])—autonomic
gic neurons
l

Effects and Functions

Oxytocin increases social interactive behavior, including maternal behavior, increases bonding between mother and offspring (Kendrick, Keverne, & Baldwin, 1987; Keverne & Kendrick, 1992, 1994; Pedersen & Prange, 1979), and stimulates pair bonding in some nonhuman species. The dopaminergic neurons of the NA are involved in the latter effect (Insel, 2003; Young, 2009). Vasopressin, a hormone and neurotransmitter that is related to oxytocin, also plays an important role in pair bonding (Caldwell, Lee, Macbeth, & Young, 2008).

Oxytocin has several behavioral and physiological effects. It decreases anxiety by affecting the amygdala (Amico, Mantella, Vollmer, & Li, 2004; Uvnäs-Moberg, Ahlenius, Hillegaart, & Alster, 1994). It decreases pain sensation by an effect in the PAG and spinal cord involving endogenous opioid effects as well (Petersson, Alster, Lundeberg, & Uvnäs-Moberg, 1996; Petersson, Eklund, & Uvnäs-Moberg, 2005). Oxytocin counteracts aggression and arousal by effects in the LC, an effect in which alpha-2 adrenoceptors are involved (Petersson, Uvnäs-Moberg, Erhardt, & Engberg, 1998). Oxytocin counteracts the activity of the HPA-axis by inhibiting the secretion of corticotrophin-releasing factor (CRF) and of adrenocorticotrophic hormone (ACTH) in the PVN and anterior pituitary, respectively. As a consequence, the secretion of corticosterone (in rats) or cortisol (in humans) is decreased (Legros, Chiodera, & Geenen, 1988; Neumann, Wigger, Torner, Holsboer, & Landgraf, 2000; Petersson, Hulting, & Uvnäs-Moberg, 1999). It also decreases the activity of some important aspects of the sympathetic nervous system regulating the cardiovascular system, which leads to lowering of blood pressure and increased peripheral cutaneous circulation and increased skin temperature (Petersson, Lundeberg, & Uvnäs-Moberg, 1999). Oxytocin also increases the function in some aspects of the parasympathetic nervous system controlling the endocrine system function of the gastrointestinal tract, which leads to an enhanced digestive function and use of nutrients for storing, growth, and restoration (Eriksson et al., 1994; Uvnäs-Moberg, 1989, 1994; Widstrom et al., 1988).

If oxytocin is administered repeatedly, the effects become long lasting (up to several weeks) because the function of various signaling systems (e.g., the opioidergic, [nor]adrenergic, serotonergic, dopaminergic, and cholinergic signaling systems) is reinforced (Uvnäs-Moberg, 1998a). In humans, intranasal administration of oxytocin is associated with effects similar to those seen in the animal experiments described social interaction and competence are increased; anxiety and stress levels (cortisol) are decreased (Domes et al., 2007; Domes, Heinrichs, Michel, Berger, & Herpertz, 2007; Guastella, Mitchell, & Dadds, 2008; Guastella, Mitchell, & Mathews, 2008; Heinrichs, Baumgartner, Kirschbaum, & Ehlert, 2003; Hollander et al., 2007; Jonas, Nissen, Ransjo-Arvidson, Matthiesen, & Uvnäs-Moberg, 2008; Kirsch et al., 2005); and trust in others is enhanced (Kosfeld, Heinrichs, Zak, Fischbacher, & Fehr, 2005).

Role of Sensory Stimulation in the Release of Oxytocin

Findings From Animal Experiments

It is well known that oxytocin is released during parturition (giving birth), in response to suckling in lactating animals, and in response to sexual interaction. Oxytocin can also be released in response to other types of non-noxious (i.e., not unpleasant, or nonirritating) and pleasant sensory stimulation.

When anesthetized rats were exposed to gentle stroking on their backs or afferent electrical stimulation of the sciatic or the vagal nerves, oxytocin levels in plasma increased more than twofold (Stock & Uvnäs-Moberg, 1988), and when they were exposed to electroacupuncture, thermal stimulation, or vibration, oxytocin levels increased both in plasma and cerebrospinal fluid (Uvnäs-Moberg, Bruzelius, Alster, & Lundeberg, 1993). Such gentle stimulation mainly activates sensory nerves that are thicker and more rapidly conducting than those activated by pain.

Five minutes of stroking on the front side of the rat (40 strokes per minute) induces a multitude of behavioral and physiological effects. Oxytocin is released by this type of stimulation, so the effects of stroking may involve a mechanism causing the release of oxytocin. The effects of non-noxious sensory stimulation are stronger if applied on the ventral side of the body than if applied to the back. The presence of "vagal" afferent nerves in the skin on the ventral side, which via the NTS reach the oxytocin-producing cells in the PVN, may explain this difference because more oxytocin may be released in response to stroking of the ventral side.

The elevation of the pain threshold (meaning that the individual can better tolerate pain) and the calming and anxiolytic (anxiety-reducing) effects caused by stroking on the front side are probably exerted in the PAG, amygdala, and LC, by oxytocin released from oxytocinergic fibers originating in the PVN. The connection between oxytocin and the effects induced by stroking is supported by findings that some of the effects (e.g., the elevation of pain threshold caused by the stroking treatment) are blocked if the animals are given an oxytocin antagonist before the treatment. (An antagonist is a chemical that inhibits or limits the effect of the hormone, in this case, oxytocin). In further support of a role for oxytocin in the increase in pain threshold caused by stroking is the fact that increased oxytocin levels have been demonstrated in the PAG, an area in the brain that is of central importance for nociception (the perception of pain; Lund et al., 2002).

Stroking on the front side of female and male rats also lowers tail skin temperature (a way of saving energy), pulse rate, and blood pressure for several hours (Kurosawa, Lundeberg, Agren, Lund, & Uvnäs-Moberg, 1995; Lund, Lundeberg, Kurosawa, & Uvnäs-Moberg, 1999). The effect on pulse rate and blood pressure in response to stroking may be due to a direct effect of the stroking in the NTS in combination with effects of oxytocin released from nerves projecting to the NTS from the PVN. In this way the activity of relevant aspects of the sympathetic nervous system is decreased and the parasympathetic system is increased, with consequent changes in cardiovascular function. More simply stated, stroking the rat's front side (what we would call the abdomen) lowers tail skin temperature, pulse rate, and blood pressure by causing oxytocin to be released in the brain, affecting parts of the brain that control these bodily functions.

As has been demonstrated, the effect pattern induced by oxytocin exhibits clear similarities to the effect pattern induced by non-noxious sensory stimulation. This similarity, together with the finding that some of the effects induced by non-noxious sensory stimulation are blocked by oxytocin antagonists (Uvnäs-Moberg et al., 1993), supports the assumption that oxytocinergic transmission in the brain may play an important regulatory function at the hypothalamic level on the effect spectrum induced by non-noxious sensory stimulation. In other words, there is support from the studies of oxytocin that these pleasant (or not unpleasant) actions such as stroking set in motion brain activity that regulates how the body responds by releasing oxytocin in the brain.

It is important to note that we cannot simply measure blood levels of oxytocin when studying these effects. The effects induced by oxytocin on physiological and behavioral function in response to sensory stimulation are exerted in the brain. Oxytocin may be released into the brain in many situations without a concomitant release of oxytocin into the blood circulation. Therefore, circulating levels of oxytocin are not always a relevant marker for the release of oxytocin in the brain. However, a parallel secretion of oxytocin into both the brain and the circulation has been shown during suckling, feeding, parturition, and vaginocervical stimulation (Kendrick, Keverne, Baldwin, & Sharman, 1986). In rats, electroacupuncture, vibration, and thermal stimuli significantly increase oxytocin levels in both the circulation and the cerebrospinal fluid (Uvnäs-Moberg et al., 1993). For a more detailed description of the effects induced by non-noxious sensory stimulation, see Uvnäs-Moberg and Petersson (2010).

Findings From Human Experiments

Touching and stimulation of cutaneous nerves is an integral part of close human relationships, regardless of age and sex. In particular, research on breast-feeding shows that behavioral and physiological effects are induced by closeness in humans.

Breast-feeding is associated with a pulsatile release of oxytocin into the circulation, aimed at stimulating milk ejection. At the same time, oxytocin is released within the brain from oxytocinergic neurons, dendrites, and nerve fibers to induce behavioral and physiological adaptations in the breast-feeding mothers (Jonas, Nissen, Ransjo-Arvidson, Matthiesen, et al., 2008). The release of oxytocin, ACTH, and cortisol in response to breast-feeding is demonstrated in Figures 3.1, 3.2, and 3.3. Figures 3.1 and 3.2 are based on data presented in Jonas et al. (2009), and the data in Figure 3.3 is taken from Nissen et al. (1996).

During breast-feeding, the mother experiences pleasure and a sense of well-being. In addition, her level of anxiety is decreased, and her social skills are increased. The well-being may be related to a release of dopamine in the NA induced by oxytocin, and the decrease in anxiety and increase in social skills may be related to the effects of oxytocin induced in the amygdala and other areas in the brain related to social behavior. The close relationship between oxytocin and these behavioral and physiological adaptations is illustrated by the fact that plasma levels of oxytocin, which here probably reflect oxytocin levels in the brain, correlate negatively with the mother's levels of anxiety and positively with her social skills (Nissen, Gustavsson, Widstrom, & Uvnäs-Moberg, 1998). An antistress pattern is induced, as reflected by a fall in cortisol levels and in blood pressure, indicating a suckling-related decrease of the activity in the HPA-axis and in the sympathoadrenal system (SAM; Amico, Johnston, & Vagnucci, 1994; Handlin et al., 2009; Jonas, Nissen, Ransjo-Arvidson, Matthiesen, et al., 2008; Jonas, Nissen, Ransjo-Arvidson, Wiklund, et al., 2008; Nissen et al., 1996). Suckling is also accompanied by increased levels of gastrointestinal hormones (Uvnäs-Moberg, Eriksson, Blomquist, Kunavongkrit, & Einarsson, 1984). These effects are induced by oxytocin released within the hypothalamus, the pituitary, and in areas in the brain stem involved in the control of the autonomic nervous tone, such as the NTS and DMX.

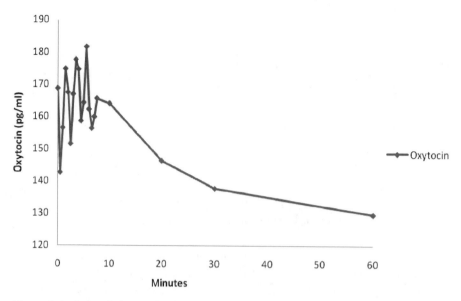

Figure 3.1. Oxytocin levels (pg/ml) during a breast-feeding session in 61 mothers. The first sample was drawn immediately after the infant had latched on to the breast (sample 0). The next samples followed at 30-second intervals during the first 7.5 minutes. Thereafter, the samples were collected at 10, 20, 30, and 60 minutes after breast-feeding had started. Samples were analyzed by enzyme immunoassay (EIA). Data from Jonas et al., 2009.

During breast-feeding the mother receives sensory stimulation, not only when the infant suckles but also when the infant is lying in skin-to-skin contact with her. Interestingly, most of the adaptive effects previously observed during breast-feeding and ascribed to the suckling stimulus are indeed also triggered by touch and closeness. Cortisol levels and blood pressure fall, and the mother becomes less anxious and more interactive by skin-to-skin contact (Handlin et al., 2009), and oxytocin levels are increased, particularly in response to hand massage performed by the infant (Matthiesen, Ransjo-Arvidson, Nissen, & Uvnäs-Moberg, 2001; Nissen et al., 1996). In contrast, milk ejection requires suckling and the intensively pulsatile oxytocin release to occur. The infant also reacts to skin-to-skin contact with oxytocin-related effects, such as calming, relaxation, and an activation of the gastrointestinal tract (Christensson, Cabrera, Christensson, Uvnäs-Moberg, & Winberg, 1995; Jonas, Wiklund, Nissen, Ransjo-Arvidson, & Uvnäs-Moberg, 2007; Tornhage, Serenius, Uvnäs-Moberg, & Lindberg, 1998).

Oxytocin is also released in response to warm contact in adults (Light, Grewen, & Amico, 2005) and probably in response to social support (Heinrichs & Domes, 2008). Altogether these data suggest that oxytocin released during social interaction has important modulatory effects on social behavior and stress coping.

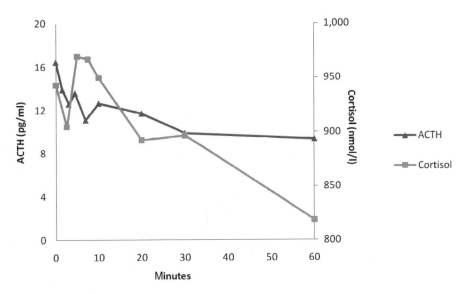

Figure 3.2. ACTH (pg/ml) and cortisol (nmol/l) levels during a breast-feeding session in 61 mothers. The first sample was drawn immediately after the infant had latched on to the breast (sample 0). The next samples followed at 30-second intervals during the first 7.5 minutes. Thereafter, the samples were collected at 10, 20, 30, and 60 minutes after breast-feeding had started. Samples were analyzed by enzyme immunoassay (EIA). Data from Jonas et al., 2009.

BRIEF OVERVIEW OF CORTISOL

Cortisol is a steroid hormone produced in the cortex of the adrenal gland. It is regulated by ACTH from the pituitary and CRF from the hypothalamus (HPA axis). Cortisol is released in response to stress (for example, it increases blood pressure and glucose levels and has immunomodulatory effects). Oxytocin reduces cortisol levels in both humans and rats (corticosterone; Legros et al., 1988; Petersson, Hulting, & Uvnäs-Moberg, 1999).

METHODOLOGICAL CONSIDERATIONS
FOR ENDOCRINOLOGIC MEASUREMENT

Hormone levels can also be measured to describe the consequences of an interaction between humans and animals. For example, oxytocin and cortisol levels obtained before, during, and after a 3-minute interaction period between a dog and its owner are shown in Figures 3.4 and 3.5 (Handlin et al., 2010). It is important to measure oxytocin because it is involved in social interaction and bonding interactions. The stress hormone cortisol is important because cortisol is released in response to physical activity and stress and is inhibited

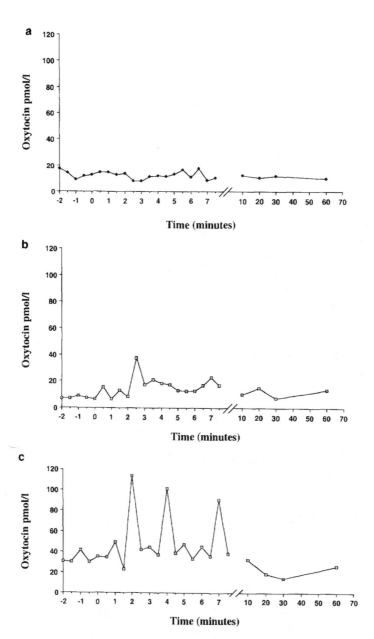

Figure 3.3. Oxytocin levels (pmol/l) in response to breast-feeding in individual women. **(A)** A woman with emergency caesarean section, and **(B)** and **(C)** Women with vaginal delivery. The first sample was drawn immediately after the infant had latched on to the breast (sample 0). Samples were analyzed by radioimmunoassay (RIA). From "Different Patterns of Oxytocin, Prolactin But Not Ccortisol Release During Breastfeeding in Women Delivered by Caesarean Section or by the Vaginal Route," by E. Nissen, K. Uvnäs-Moberg, K. Svensson, S. Stock, A. M. Widstrom, and J. Winberg,1996, *Early Human Development, 45*[1–2], 103–118. Copyright 1996 by Elsevier. Reprinted with permission.

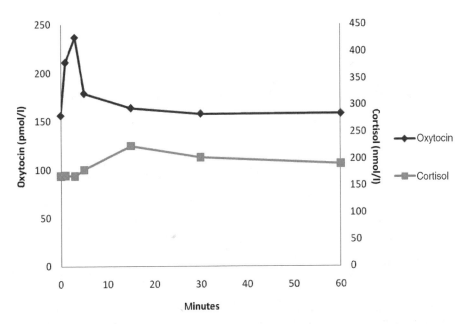

Figure 3.4. Oxytocin (pmol/l) and cortisol (nmol/l) levels in 10 dogs during an inter-action experiment. The owner interacted with her dog during the first 3 minutes. The first blood sample was taken immediately before the owner started to interact with her dog (0 min). The remaining samples were collected 1, 3, 5, 15, 30, and 60 minutes after the first sample was taken. Samples were analyzed by enzyme immunoassay (EIA). Data from Handlin et al., 2009.

by oxytocin via its effects on CRF in the hypothalamus and on ACTH in the anterior pituitary. Vasopressin levels are also be important because vasopressin too is related to social interaction and bonding experiences. In addition, the levels of some gastrointestinal hormones are important because oxytocinergic neurons projecting to the NTS and DMX influence their release. In particular, gastrin, cholecystokinin, and insulin are influenced by oxytocin via the vagal nerve and may even reflect the level of physical closeness between humans and possibly also between human and animal (Petersson, Hulting, Andersson, & Uvnäs-Moberg, 1999; Widstrom et al., 1988).

If one chooses to use endocrinological measures to demonstrate effects of HAI (e.g., oxytocin release and oxytocin-mediated effects), several methodological aspects should be considered to avoid false-positive and false-negative results.

Where Should Hormones Be Measured—in Blood, Saliva, or Urine?

As described, steroid hormones such as cortisol are lipids and therefore pass through membranes easily. It is therefore possible to detect cortisol in saliva

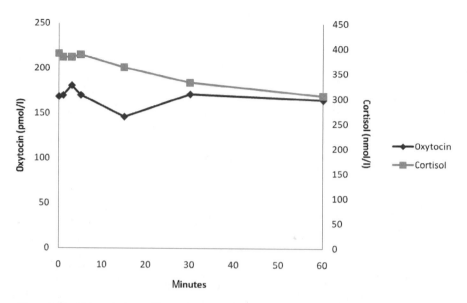

Figure 3.5. Oxytocin (pmol/l) and cortisol (nmol/l) levels in 10 dog owners during an interaction experiment. The owner interacted with her dog during the first 3 minutes. The first blood sample was taken immediately before the owner started to interact with her dog (0 min). The remaining samples were collected 1, 3, 5, 15, 30, and 60 minutes after the first sample was taken. Samples were analyzed by enzyme immunoassay (EIA). Data from Handlin et al., 2009.

because it passes from the blood vessels into saliva. Cortisol is not degraded in the kidney but can be inactivated by conversion to another substance, for example, corticosterone. It easily passes into urine and is not degraded in urine. Thus cortisol and other steroids can be measured in urine, as a reflection of the release of hormone into the circulation. By contrast, oxytocin and other peptides from the circulation are not likely to be secreted into the saliva in measurable amounts. Nor should they be analyzed in urine because peptides are rapidly degraded in plasma and in the kidney.

Almost all cortisol is produced in the adrenal glands; therefore, circulating cortisol levels reflect cortisol being released from the adrenal cortex. As mentioned, cortisol is a lipophilic structure, which easily passes across biological membranes. This is the reason cortisol can be measured in saliva and in urine. The fact that steroids are metabolized in the liver and not in the kidney contributes to the recovery of cortisol in urine.

Oxytocin, as mentioned, is produced in the SON and PVN and is released via oxytocinergic nerves into many important regulatory areas in the brain and also to the neurohypophysis, and from there it is released into the circulation. The oxytocin released within the brain does not contribute to the circulating levels, and circulating oxytocin does not readily enter the brain because of the blood–brain barrier (Jones & Robinson, 1982). Nonetheless, there is sometimes a strong parallel between the effects of oxytocin induced in the brain and circulating oxytocin levels (Keverne & Kendrick, 1994). It is therefore likely that oxytocin is released in parallel into the circulation and into the brain in response to some stimuli. This seems in particular to be the case when oxytocin release is stimulated by high levels of estrogen and during the intense stimulation occurring during labor and suckling. In the case of labor and suckling, oxytocin exerts effects in the periphery by stimulating uterine contractions or milk ejection in parallel with inducing effects in the brain (Nissen et al., 1998).

Oxytocin is also produced in and released from many different organs in the body. For example, oxytocin is produced in the gastrointestinal tract and in the cardiovascular system. Oxytocin is produced in the testes, adrenal gland, pancreas, ovaries, uterus, and thymus (Amico, Finn, & Haldar, 1988; Geenen et al., 1986; Jankowski et al., 1998; Lefebvre, Giaid, Bennett, Lariviere, & Zingg, 1992; Nicholson et al., 1984; Wathes & Swann, 1982). There is also production of oxytocin in endothelial cells (Wang, Gutkowska, Marcinkiewicz, Rachelska, & Jankowski, 2003). This widespread production of oxytocin means that circulating oxytocin may not reflect oxytocin of only hypothalamic origin.

As noted, oxytocin (a peptide) does not easily cross biological membranes; it also circulates in very low levels. It is therefore unlikely that oxytocin that is circulating in the body or oxytocin released within the brain will be reflected by increasing levels in saliva. On the other hand, because oxytocin is produced in many peripheral organs and cells, oxytocin of local origin may be detected in saliva. Whether oxytocin produced in peripheral organs and cells is under neurogenic control (that is, whether it is controlled at the level of brain structures) is not known.

For the same reason, it is highly unlikely that oxytocin released from the hypothalamus in response to physiological stimuli can be detected in urine because oxytocin, like other peptides, is degraded in the plasma and the kidney. Urine levels of oxytocin may instead reflect oxytocin release from a more proximal site. Of course, this does not exclude the possibility that the oxytocin content of urine parallels that of circulating oxytocin because oxytocin levels in urine also may be controlled by neurogenic activity. Until it has been proven by proper experimental techniques that oxytocin from the circulation is transferred to saliva or urine during physiological conditions, data suggesting that salivary and urinary oxytocin levels can be used as a reflection of circulating levels should not be accepted (for further discussion, see below).

...Collected?

...n be obtained with a simple finger-stick (in ...ust be used. After the catheter has been ...least 30 minutes before starting to collect ...e stress reaction induced by the insertion of ...tant that catheter insertion and sampling of ...throughout the experiment for consistency ...umans, blood draws should be performed by ...giver and experienced nurse, respectively, ...t. If repeated samples are collected, blood should be drawn in a similar way (i.e., with the same force and speed).

At What Time Should Samples Be Collected?

Hormones can be measured under basal conditions or in response to some kind of stimulation. It is sometimes necessary to perform some kind of provocation test to be able to record differences in hormone levels between experimental groups. Whether hormone levels are measured under basal conditions or in response to some kind of stimulation, the timing of sampling is of great importance because many hormones have a diurnal or time-of-day rhythm. This is particularly important in the case of cortisol because its diurnal rhythm is prominent, and cortisol levels are much higher in the morning. Therefore, if cortisol levels are going to be measured, single or multiple samples have to be collected at the same time of day (Van Cauter & Turek, 1995). Oxytocin levels are not subject to any particular form of diurnal variation. Many hormone analyses are performed after fasting because previous food intake also may influence the hormone levels measured. For example, insulin and many gastrointestinal hormones are released when food is present in the gastrointestinal tract. Thus, oxytocin blood samples are best obtained before a meal is eaten or a period of time after a meal.

At What Intervals Should Samples Be Collected?

It is important for researchers to understand the pathways through which hormones are released within the body and to be aware of when hormones are released into the blood. The release profiles of hormones vary, and different release curves can be obtained in response to different stimuli, such as interaction, stress, or feeding. In response to stress, the signaling peptide CRF is released within the PVN of the hypothalamus. CRF reaches the anterior pituitary via the hypophyseal portal blood vessels to release adrenocorticotrophic hormone (ACTH). ACTH is then released into the circulation, mediating the release of cortisol from the adrenal cortex. Due to this cascade of events that precedes the release of cortisol, the levels of cortisol rise after a delay of 15 to 30 minutes. In contrast, peptides, including oxytocin, are often released (or the release is inhibited) more quickly, often within minutes in response to a stimulus. This initial peak is sometimes, but not always, followed by a more protracted rise of hormone levels.

To capture the release of oxytocin and cortisol in response to a certain stimulus, it is necessary to collect repeated samples over at least a 1-hour period. Samples have to be collected within minutes after the stimulus to detect the release of oxytocin and after 15 to 30 minutes to capture the rise of cortisol. Due to the short half-life of oxytocin in plasma, it is often necessary to collect several samples with 30- or 60-second intervals in response to the stimulus. The different profiles of oxytocin and cortisol release in response to breast-feeding and HAI are shown in Figures 3.1 to 3.5.

How Should Researchers Account for Differences Between the Sexes?

Sex differences always have to be considered when hormone levels are analyzed. Obviously the level of testosterone is higher in males and the level of estrogen and sometimes of progesterone higher in females. In addition, the release of some hormones is under the control of sex steroids. Cortisol levels are often higher in women than in men.

Oxytocin levels are strongly influenced by estrogen. In fact, the release of oxytocin is stimulated by estrogen via the estrogen beta receptor (Bodo & Rissman, 2006). This complicates analyses of oxytocin levels because the levels of estrogen vary (for example, during the estrus cycle). Oxytocin levels are higher during the follicular phase than in the luteal phase in humans (Amico, Seif, & Robinson, 1981). In addition, oxytocin levels are higher during puberty and extremely high during pregnancy in response to the increase of endogenous estrogen. In contrast, oxytocin levels decrease after menopause as a consequence of falling estrogen production. In addition, ingestion of oral estrogens, such as oral contraceptives and hormone replacement therapy, may be followed by increased levels of oxytocin (Silber, Almkvist, Larsson, Stock, & Uvnäs-Moberg, 1987).

In dogs there is also a strong effect of estrogen/progesterone on oxytocin levels along the estrus cycle. After heat, the ovarian follicles continue to produce estrogen and progesterone for weeks and even months. This long-lasting ovarian hormone production may even result in pseudopregnancy. As a consequence of the rising estrogen levels, oxytocin levels rise. This rise is strongly and inversely correlated to a decrease in cortisol levels and also to falling levels of the gastrointestinal hormone somatostatin (indicating increased function of the digestive tract and increased storing of nutrients). The behavior of the dog shifts from an aggressive response to a defensive response to a stress test during this period (Tapper et al., unpublished observations). Unless controlled for the cycle, hormonal values in female dogs may be difficult to evaluate and compare.

How Should Researchers Account for Differences Between Species?

It is important to consider that, even if the basal structure of the neuroendocrine system is very similar among different mammalian species, there are differences with regard to release patterns that have to be considered to obtain accurate measurements. For example, dogs more often react with increased oxytocin levels in the circulation than do humans. Dogs, like cows, react with a clear peak of oxytocin in response to feeding, whereas such a peak has not been demonstrated in humans (Uvnäs-Moberg et al., 1985). In addition, calves react with a clear rise of oxytocin levels in response to suckling, whereas no such peak can be observed in the human infant (Svennersten, Gorewit, Sjaunja, & Uvnäs-Moberg, 1995; Svennersten, Nelson, & Uvnäs-Moberg, 1992). However, this does not mean that oxytocin is not released in human infants in response to suckling but that the amount of oxytocin released into the brain and into the circulation, respectively, is different. As mentioned, oxytocin release into the circulation of humans mainly occurs in situations when oxytocin exerts peripheral effects (e.g., with milk ejection during suckling/breast-feeding and during labor).

By Which Methods Should Steroids and Peptides Be Measured?

Several types of analyses exist to determine the levels of steroids and peptides. In the case of steroids such as cortisol, radioimmunoassay (RIA) or enzyme immunoassay (EIA) is used. Provided the samples are collected properly, the values obtained through these analytic methods are valid. The steroids are not broken down in blood or plasma, and if samples are stored frozen, they survive for a very long time. Because the concentration of steroids is within the nanograms-per-milliliter (ng/ml) range, relatively little material is needed for the assays.

Peptides such as oxytocin are usually present in plasma in much lower concentrations than steroids (picograms per milliliter [pg/ml] vs. ng/ml). Because of this difference, more blood may be needed for analysis of peptides than for steroids. Actual measurement of levels of peptides is also more difficult. Many peptides are easily broken down, even in blood samples or plasma, due to the presence of degrading enzymes. Therefore, it is sometimes necessary to add substances such as Trasylol to the samples to block the activity of such enzymes. Even after Trasylol is added, it is important to keep any remaining enzymatic activity to a minimum; this is achieved by immediately putting the collected blood samples on ice and keeping them on ice until it is time to separate blood corpuscles from plasma. This separation should be done under cold conditions (4°C), and the plasma samples should be frozen immediately to avoid degradation. If properly frozen and not thawed, peptides may survive in plasma for several years.

The levels of peptides are most often measured with RIA or EIA/ELISA (enzyme-linked immunosorbent assay). Both techniques are indirect and represent changes in the degree of binding to a tracer (in the case of RIA to iodinated hormone, and in the case of oxytocin-EIA to an alkaline phosphatase molecule to which oxytocin is covalently attached) and to an antibody, which binds the substance to be measured. The amount of binding between tracer and antibody can be reduced depending on the level of oxytocin in the blood sample being assayed. Plasma samples often have to be extracted or purified before analysis with EIA or RIA to avoid material that may interfere with the assay.

In the case of oxytocin, the levels obtained by RIA are much lower than those obtained by EIA. Because standard curves give valid results with EIA, it must be assumed that something more than oxytocin is measured with this technique. Whether this is because the antibodies used not only recognize oxytocin but also bind to substances that are similar to oxytocin (e.g., precursors, fragments, and metabolites of oxytocin) or something completely different is not known. Therefore, EIA measurements do not give rise to correct basal levels. These measurements can sometimes be used to demonstrate changes in response to a certain stimulus, but care must always be taken regarding the interpretation of levels obtained with EIA.

Oxytocin levels were measured with EIA in the experiments shown in Figures 3.1 and 3.2 and with RIA in the experiment demonstrated in Figure 3.3. Note that basal oxytocin levels are almost 0 in the experiment demonstrated in Figure 3.3 but more than 150 pg/ml in the experiments illustrated in Figures 3.1 and 3.2. These basal levels are most likely due to a nonspecific interference with the binding in the assay. Still, the effect in response to breast-feeding (repeated peaks with 30-second intervals) was demonstrated by both techniques, as was the rise of oxytocin in dogs in response to interaction. It should also be stated that different RIAs may give rise to different values, depending on the specificity of the antibody used. Some antibodies recognize precursor molecules of oxytocin and possibly also some fragments; consequently, different results are obtained when such antibodies are used. As an example, not all RIAs detect variations of oxytocin levels during the menstrual cycle, whereas some do.

There are other techniques based on electrical detection of substances and high performance liquid chromatography (HPLC). These techniques are not as well established as the RIA and EIA. Very different levels and results are often obtained with these techniques, and it is difficult to evaluate whether these differences are due to the detection technique per se or to the schedule for sampling of blood or other experimental reasons.

METHODS USED FOR OXYTOCIN DETERMINATION
IN SOME RELEVANT PUBLICATIONS

Oxytocin in Blood

Two studies have been published in which oxytocin levels in blood have been recorded in humans in response to interaction with dogs (Miller et al., 2009; Odendaal & Meintjes, 2003). In both studies, single samples were collected before and after the interaction. In the study by Miller et al., oxytocin levels rose in women but not in men. If several blood samples had been collected and they had been collected closer to the interaction, a different result might have been obtained. In the study performed by Odendaal and Meintjes, oxytocin levels were measured both in humans and in the dogs, and a reciprocal response was found. However, the second sample was collected between 5 and 24 minutes after the interaction and was linked to falling blood pressure (i.e., at the time when the level of some peptides might already have fallen back to basal levels). Statistically significant changes for a broad spectrum of endocrine variables were found. The levels are difficult to compare with those obtained in other studies because an HPLC technique was used. However, together these studies suggest that oxytocin is released into the circulation and also into the brain in response to HAI, but clearly additional studies with more precise timing and additional samples would be useful to increase our confidence in these findings.

Oxytocin in Urine

As stated, the half-life of oxytocin is only a few minutes in blood, and oxytocin, like other peptides, is broken down to fragments in the circulation and in the kidney. Nonetheless, some published studies claim that oxytocin can be measured in urine.

Urinary excretion of oxytocin was studied in three different mice models. Oxytocin levels were measured in urine from mice that lack the ability to produce oxytocin, in mice that produce oxytocin and received oxytocin infusions, and in mice allowed consumption of 2% sodium chloride, causing physical stimulation. No urinary oxytocin was found in the animals that could not produce oxytocin, but in the animals that do produce oxytocin, basal urinary oxytocin levels were around 250 pg/ml, suggesting that oxytocin can be recovered in urine. In contrast, enormously increased urinary oxytocin levels were found in animals receiving intravenous oxytocin either 5 or 20 pmol/minute for 2 hours (i.e., 5,000 or 20,000 pg/minute), which gave rise to levels of 89 and 844 ng/ml, respectively. The mice stimulated by increased sodium chloride ingestion showed no increase of oxytocin. These data suggest that oxytocin can be recovered in urine after infusion of large amounts of the peptide (Polito, Goldstein, Sanchez, Cool, & Morris, 2006).

These data clearly show that oxytocin can be recovered in the urine of mice when they are exposed to high amounts of intravenous oxytocin. In these cases, the degrading systems might have been overloaded, allowing oxytocin to pass into urine. Whether the oxytocin found in urine under basal conditions reflects oxytocin levels in plasma is not known.

Seltzer and Ziegler (2007) recovered some tritium-labeled oxytocin in the urine of small marmosets after injection into the peripheral blood during a 48-hour collection time. These data indicate that labeled oxytocin, probably with changed molecular characteristics, is secreted into urine. The researchers also found greater amounts of oxytocin and vasopressin in animals that had social contact than in those that were isolated. It is difficult to understand why both oxytocin and vasopressin levels should be higher after social contact; based on these data, it may be that the peptides reached urine by local release in the urogenital tract or that both oxytocin and vasopressin levels in urine were affected by some other common mechanism not necessarily related to kidney function.

In a study by Amico, Ulbrecht, and Robinson (1987), three different doses of synthetic oxytocin were infused in each of four men. Oxytocin was measured in plasma and in urine after extraction. Amico and colleagues found that urinary oxytocin excretion during infusion of synthetic oxytocin was linearly correlated with plasma oxytocin concentration. However, less than 1% of the administered oxytocin was cleared in urine (Amico et al., 1987). Jonas et al. (2009) measured plasma oxytocin in second-day postpartum women who had received oxytocin infusion to stimulate labor. Jonas and colleagues found that, when patients were infused with the same amounts as used in the study by Amico et al., by the second postpartum day, the secretion of endogenous oxytocin was down-regulated in a dose-dependent manner, indicating that oxytocin levels were uncharacteristically high. These data suggest that infusion of oxytocin in nonphysiological amounts may result in some, but very little, excretion of the peptide into urine. White-Traut, Powlesland, Gelhar, Chatterton, and Morris (1998) tried to measure oxytocin levels in human infants and found that less oxytocin was excreted into urine in crying infants. Again, this may be due to stress and unspecific vasoconstriction in the urogenital tract.

It has been suggested that early experience in humans is associated with changes in neuropeptides critical for regulating social behavior. In a research article that generated much interest, both the urinary excretion of oxytocin and of vasopressin was reported to be reduced in the urine of children with adverse social experiences (Fries, Ziegler, Kurian, Jacoris, & Pollak, 2005). In a later study, Anderson (2006) pointed out that the HPLC technique used by Fries et al. was not sensitive enough to pick up urinary oxytocin and vasopressin levels and that, in fact, the levels reported were a million-fold higher than oxytocin levels reported in several previous studies of oxytocin levels in human urine. Anderson suggests that the results of Fries et al. be considered a methodological artifact and additional, more rigorous studies on the role of oxytocin in human social behavior are needed.

Of particular interest in the context of HAI is the article by Nagasawa, Kikusui, Onaka, and Ohta (2009) showing that a dog's gaze at and touch by its owner increases the owner's oxytocin levels in urine during the social interaction. The data are supportive of a relationship between oxytocin levels in human urine and this type of interaction between dogs and their owners. The authors have interpreted these data as indicating that urinary oxytocin reflects oxytocin in plasma. However, this interpretation is not likely to be correct because very little oxytocin is released into the plasma from the pituitary in response to interaction between humans and dogs. Considering that only 1% of oxytocin infused in low doses is recovered in urine, the small amounts of oxytocin released into plasma during HAI are unlikely to influence urinary oxytocin levels. It is possible that the oxytocin levels in urine are secondary to some other indirect mechanism influencing urine production or oxytocin levels. As pointed out, close contact and warmth causes peripheral vasodilation in infants, which parallels mental calm (Bystrova et al., 2003; Christensson et al., 1995). Perhaps oxytocin is released from another source in the kidneys or the bladder, or perhaps metabolic or excretory processes are influenced in a way that results in increased urinary levels of oxytocin during close contact. Because oxytocin has a natriuretic effect, urine production may have been influenced.

Taken together, the data from these various studies show that oxytocin or vasopressin may be found in urine and that the urinary levels of the peptides may be influenced by long-term infusion of the peptide, in particular at high doses or in response to extreme nonphysiological long-term stimulation. It is highly unlikely that oxytocin released from the hypothalamus in response to touch, breast-feeding, massage, or other physiological stimuli that cause subtle changes in plasma levels can be detected by changes in urinary oxytocin levels.

Whether changes in oxytocin levels in urine (increase during relaxation and decrease during stress) result from completely different physiological effects on the circulation in the urogenital tract or from local release of oxytocin in this area or whether they reflect differences in the rate of degradation or excretion, is not known but remains a possibility that should be investigated.

Oxytocin in Saliva

Because oxytocin is a highly polar molecule that does not easily cross biological membranes, it is not likely to be secreted into saliva. In addition, saliva is full of enzymes that degrade peptides. In an extensive, elegant, and comprehensive series of experiments, it was shown that saliva does not contain oxytocin in measurable amounts and that oxytocin is not a valid salivary biomarker, when measured by currently available immunological methods (Horvat-Gordon, Granger, Schwartz, Nelson, & Kivlighan, 2005). Horvat-Gordon et al. concluded that levels of immunoreactive oxytocin in saliva are primarily due to non-specific interference with antibody–antigen binding; they stated with a high degree of certainty that measurement of oxytocin in saliva does not yield meaningful indices of individual differences or intra-individual change.

Despite this evidence, Carter et al. (2007) and White-Traut et al. (2009) claim that oxytocin in saliva can be used as a biomarker for oxytocin release during breast-feeding and even massage. These authors found (using EIA, a technique that yields too high basal levels due to unspecific binding in the assay) salivary oxytocin levels ranging between 6 and 60 pg/ml. Levels in the 6- to 60-pg/ml range, in fact, approximate the basal levels in the circulation found when measured with RIA (i.e., much more than can be expected to be found in saliva). They also stated that oxytocin values in saliva varied significantly as a function of the time of breast-feeding; oxytocin levels were highest before breast-feeding, followed by a decrease at the time of breast-feeding and by an increase 30 minutes after breast-feeding. Based on these findings, the authors suggest that oxytocin release into saliva increases in anticipation of breast-feeding. A more reasonable conclusion is that their oxytocin levels, both basal and breast-feeding related, obtained with EIA represent, as suggested by Horvat-Gordon et al. (2005), unspecific interference with antibody–antigen binding. No further chemical characterization was performed of the immunoreactive material found in saliva, and the basal values are (as mentioned) too high. Furthermore, the profile of oxytocin release into the circulation in response to breast-feeding (see Figs. 3.1 and 3.3) and massage has no resemblance with that suggested to occur in saliva. It therefore seems unlikely that the oxytocin reactivity obtained by EIA in saliva corresponds to oxytocin.

CONCLUSION

In order to study physiological and endocrine correlates to HAI, it is important to have a well-designed study (randomized, controlled, etc.) and equally important to use adequate techniques for physiological and endocrine measurements. Cortisol levels can be measured in plasma, saliva, and urine due to cortisol's chemical properties. In contrast, if one wants to use the most accurate and precise indicators, measuring oxytocin in blood would be the best approach, despite the challenges of needing to draw blood and to do so repeatedly to sample optimally.

There is no proof that it is possible to measure oxytocin in saliva. In some studies, oxytocin levels in urine have been shown to rise in response to nonendogenous increases of plasma levels of oxytocin (e.g., in response to infusions of oxytocin). Oxytocin levels in urine have been demonstrated to change in response to some behavioral interventions, but whether these changes in urinary levels really reflect modest changes in plasma levels or are due to other parallel physiological effects, such as circulatory changes in the urogenital tract or altered patterns of degradation or metabolism or local release of oxytocin, is not known. Studies in which oxytocin levels are measured in parallel in the circulation and urine are needed to shed additional light on this question.

Because the majority of the effects of oxytocin during HAI are exerted in the brain and because circulating oxytocin levels only partly reflect oxytocin levels in the brain, it is often advantageous to record the secondary effects of oxytocin at the same time. Determination of ACTH and cortisol levels may be a way of demonstrating the antistress effects of oxytocin. Cardiovascular parameters (such as blood pressure) or peripheral skin temperature as an expression of the level of circulation in the skin represent indirect ways of recording the inhibitory effects of oxytocin on the sympathetic nervous system. The level of gastrointestinal hormones as well as heart rate and heart rate variability may help to measure the effects of oxytocin linked to vagal/parasympathetic nerve activity. In addition, behavioral effects may be noted in companion animals and in humans separately but also during their interaction. In particular the amount of interactive sensory stimulation (touch, stroking, sound, gazing, etc.) may give important information and may even correlate with endocrine and other physiological variables.

REFERENCES

Amico, J. A., Finn, F. M., & Haldar, J. (1988). Oxytocin and vasopressin are present in human and rat pancreas. *American Journal of the Medical Sciences, 296*(5), 303–307.

Amico, J. A., Johnston, J. M., & Vagnucci, A. H. (1994). Suckling-induced attenuation of plasma cortisol concentrations in postpartum lactating women. *Endocrine Research, 20*(1), 79–87.

Amico, J. A., Mantella, R. C., Vollmer, R. R., & Li, X. (2004). Anxiety and stress responses in female oxytocin deficient mice. *Journal of Neuroendocrinology*, 16(4), 319–324.

Amico, J. A., Seif, S. M., & Robinson, A. G. (1981). Elevation of oxytocin and the oxytocin-associated neurophysin in the plasma of normal women during mid-cycle. *Journal of Clinical Endocrinology and Metabolism*, 53(6), 1229–1232.

Amico, J. A., Ulbrecht, J. S., & Robinson, A. G. (1987). Clearance studies of oxytocin in humans using radioimmunoassay measurements of the hormone in plasma and urine. *Journal of Clinical Endocrinology and Metabolism*, 64(2), 340–345.

Anderson, G. M. (2006). Report of altered urinary oxytocin and AVP excretion in neglected orphans should be reconsidered. *Journal of Autism and Developmental Disorders*, 36(6), 829–830.

Bodo, C., & Rissman, E. F. (2006). New roles for estrogen receptor beta in behavior and neuroendocrinology. *Frontiers in Neuroendocrinology*, 27(2), 217–232.

Brand, S. R., Brennan, P. A., Newport, D. J., Smith, A. K., Weiss, T., & Stowe, Z. N. (2010). The impact of maternal childhood abuse on maternal and infant HPA axis function in the postpartum period. *Psychoneuroendocrinology*, 35(5), 686–693.

Buijs, R. M., De Vries, G. J., & Van Leeuwen, F. W. (1985). *The distribution and synaptic release of oxytocin in the central nervous system*. Amsterdam, the Netherlands: Elsevier Science Publishers BV.

Bystrova, K., Widstrom, A. M., Matthiesen, A. S., Ransjo-Arvidson, A. B., Welles-Nystrom, B., Wassberg, C., ... Uvnäs-Moberg, K. (2003). Skin-to-skin contact may reduce negative consequences of "the stress of being born": a study on temperature in newborn infants, subjected to different ward routines in St. Petersburg. *Acta Paediatrica*, 92(3), 320–326.

Caldwell, H. K., Lee, H. J., Macbeth, A. H., & Young, W. S., III. (2008). Vasopressin: behavioral roles of an "original" neuropeptide. *Progress in Neurobiology*, 84(1), 1–24.

Carter, C. S., Pournajafi-Nazarloo, H., Kramer, K. M., Ziegler, T. E., White-Traut, R., Bello, D., & Schwertz, D. (2007). Oxytocin: behavioral associations and potential as a salivary biomarker. *Annals of the New York Academy of Sciences*, 1098, 312–322.

Christensson, K., Cabrera, T., Christensson, E., Uvnäs-Moberg, K., & Winberg, J. (1995). Separation distress call in the human neonate in the absence of maternal body contact. *Acta Paediatrica*, 84(5), 468–473.

Domes, G., Heinrichs, M., Glascher, J., Buchel, C., Braus, D. F., & Herpertz, S. C. (2007). Oxytocin attenuates amygdala responses to emotional faces regardless of valence. *Biological Psychiatry*, 62(10), 1187–1190.

Domes, G., Heinrichs, M., Michel, A., Berger, C., & Herpertz, S. C. (2007). Oxytocin improves "mind-reading" in humans. *Biological Psychiatry*, 61(6), 731–733.

Eriksson, M., Bjorkstrand, E., Smedh, U., Alster, P., Matthiesen, A. S., & Uvnäs-Moberg, K. (1994). Role of vagal nerve activity during suckling. Effects on plasma levels of oxytocin, prolactin, VIP, somatostatin, insulin, glucagon, glucose and of milk secretion in lactating rats. *Acta Physiologica Scandinavica, 151*(4), 453–459.

Fries, A. B., Ziegler, T. E., Kurian, J. R., Jacoris, S., & Pollak, S. D. (2005). Early experience in humans is associated with changes in neuropeptides critical for regulating social behavior. *Proceedings of the National Academy of Sciences of the United States of America, 102*(47), 17,237–17,240.

Geenen, V., Legros, J. J., Franchimont, P., Baudrihaye, M., Defresne, M. P., & Boniver, J. (1986). The neuroendocrine thymus: Coexistence of oxytocin and neurophysin in the human thymus. *Science, 232*(4749), 508–511.

Guastella, A. J., Mitchell, P. B., & Dadds, M. R. (2008). Oxytocin increases gaze to the eye region of human faces. *Biological Psychiatry, 63*(1), 3–5.

Guastella, A. J., Mitchell, P. B., & Mathews, F. (2008). Oxytocin enhances the encoding of positive social memories in humans. *Biological Psychiatry, 64*(3), 256–258.

Gunnar, M. R., Talge, N. M., & Herrera, A. (2009). Stressor paradigms in developmental studies: What does and does not work to produce mean increases in salivary cortisol. *Psychoneuroendocrinology, 34*(7), 953–967.

Handlin, L., Hydbring-Sandberg, E., Nilsson, A., Ejdebäck, M., Jansson, A., & Uvnäs-Moberg, K. (2010). *Short-term interaction between dogs and their owners—effects on oxytocin, cortisol, insulin and heart rate*. Unpublished manuscript.

Handlin, L., Jonas, W., Petersson, M., Ejdeback, M., Ransjo-Arvidson, A. B., Nissen, E., & Uvnäs-Moberg, K. (2009). Effects of sucking and skin-to-skin contact on maternal ACTH and cortisol levels during the second day postpartum—influence of epidural analgesia and oxytocin in the perinatal period. *Breastfeeding Medicine, 4*(4), 207–220.

Heinrichs, M., Baumgartner, T., Kirschbaum, C., & Ehlert, U. (2003). Social support and oxytocin interact to suppress cortisol and subjective responses to psychosocial stress. *Biological Psychiatry, 54*(12), 1389–1398.

Heinrichs, M., & Domes, G. (2008). Neuropeptides and social behaviour: effects of oxytocin and vasopressin in humans. *Progress in Brain Research, 170*, 337–350.

Hollander, E., Bartz, J., Chaplin, W., Phillips, A., Sumner, J., Soorya, L., ... Wasserman, S. (2007). Oxytocin increases retention of social cognition in autism. *Biological Psychiatry, 61*(4), 498–503.

Horvat-Gordon, M., Granger, D. A., Schwartz, E. B., Nelson, V. J., & Kivlighan, K. T. (2005). Oxytocin is not a valid biomarker when measured in saliva by immunoassay. *Physiology and Behavior, 84*(3), 445–448.

Insel, T. R. (2003). Is social attachment an addictive disorder? *Physiology and Behavior, 79*(3), 351–357.

Jankowski, M., Hajjar, F., Kawas, S. A., Mukaddam-Daher, S., Hoffman, G., McCann, S. M., & Gutkowska, J. (1998). Rat heart: A site of oxytocin production and action. *Proceedings of the National Academy of Sciences of the United States of America, 95*(24), 14,558–14,563.

Jonas, W., Johansson, L. M., Nissen, E., Ejdeback, M., Ransjo-Arvidson, A. B., & Uvnäs-Moberg, K. (2009). Effects of intrapartum oxytocin administration and epidural analgesia on the concentration of plasma oxytocin and prolactin, in response to suckling during the second day postpartum. *Breastfeeding Medicine, 4*(2), 71–82.

Jonas, W., Nissen, E., Ransjo-Arvidson, A. B., Matthiesen, A. S., & Uvnäs-Moberg, K. (2008). Influence of oxytocin or epidural analgesia on personality profile in breastfeeding women: a comparative study. *Archives of Women's Mental Health, 11*(5–6), 335–345.

Jonas, W., Nissen, E., Ransjo-Arvidson, A. B., Wiklund, I., Henriksson, P., & Uvnäs-Moberg, K. (2008). Short- and long-term decrease of blood pressure in women during breastfeeding. *Breastfeeding Medicine, 3*(2), 103–109.

Jonas, W., Wiklund, I., Nissen, E., Ransjo-Arvidson, A. B., & Uvnäs-Moberg, K. (2007). Newborn skin temperature two days postpartum during breastfeeding related to different labour ward practices. *Early Human Development, 83*(1), 55–62.

Jones, P. M., & Robinson, I. C. (1982). Differential clearance of neurophysin and neurohypophysial peptides from the cerebrospinal fluid in conscious guinea pigs. *Neuroendocrinology, 34*(4), 297–302.

Kendrick, K. M., Keverne, E. B., & Baldwin, B. A. (1987). Intracerebroventricular oxytocin stimulates maternal behaviour in the sheep. *Neuroendocrinology, 46*(1), 56–61.

Kendrick, K. M., Keverne, E. B., Baldwin, B. A., & Sharman, D. F. (1986). Cerebrospinal fluid levels of acetylcholinesterase, monoamines and oxytocin during labour, parturition, vaginocervical stimulation, lamb separation and suckling in sheep. *Neuroendocrinology, 44*(2), 149–156.

Keverne, E. B., & Kendrick, K. M. (1992). Oxytocin facilitation of maternal behavior in sheep. *Annals of the New York Academy of Sciences, 652*, 83–101.

Keverne, E. B., & Kendrick, K. M. (1994). Maternal behaviour in sheep and its neuroendocrine regulation. *Acta Paediatrica (Suppl), 397*, 47–56.

Kirsch, P., Esslinger, C., Chen, Q., Mier, D., Lis, S., Siddhanti, S., … Gallhofer, B. (2005). Oxytocin modulates neural circuitry for social cognition and fear in humans. *Journal of Neuroscience, 25*(49), 11489–11493.

Knorr, U., Vinberg, M., Kessing, L. V., & Wetterslev, J. (2010). Salivary cortisol in depressed patients versus control persons: A systematic review and meta-analysis. *Psychoneuroendocrinology.* Advance online publication. doi:10.1016/j.psyneuen.2010.04.001

Kosfeld, M., Heinrichs, M., Zak, P. J., Fischbacher, U., & Fehr, E. (2005). Oxytocin increases trust in humans. *Nature, 435*(7042), 673–676.

Kurosawa, M., Lundeberg, T., Agren, G., Lund, I., & Uvnäs-Moberg, K. (1995). Massage-like stroking of the abdomen lowers blood pressure in anesthetized rats: Influence of oxytocin. *Journal of the Autonomic Nervous System, 56*(1–2), 26–30.

Lefebvre, D. L., Giaid, A., Bennett, H., Lariviere, R., & Zingg, H. H. (1992). Oxytocin gene expression in rat uterus. *Science, 256*(5063), 1553–1555.

Legros, J. J., Chiodera, P., & Geenen, V. (1988). Inhibitory action of exogenous oxytocin on plasma cortisol in normal human subjects: Evidence of action at the adrenal gland. *Neuroendocrinology, 48,* 204–206.

Light, K. C., Grewen, K. M., & Amico, J. A. (2005). More frequent partner hugs and higher oxytocin levels are linked to lower blood pressure and heart rate in premenopausal women. *Biological Psychology, 69*(1), 5–21.

Ludwig, M., & Leng, G. (2006). Dendritic peptide release and peptide-dependent behaviours. *Nature reviews: Neuroscience, 7*(2), 126–136.

Lund, I., Ge, Y., Yu, L. C., Uvnäs-Moberg, K., Wang, J., Yu, C., ... Lundeberg, T. (2002). Repeated massage-like stimulation induces long-term effects on nociception: Contribution of oxytocinergic mechanisms. *European Journal of Neuroscience, 16*(2), 330–338.

Lund, I., Lundeberg, T., Kurosawa, M., & Uvnäs-Moberg, K. (1999). Sensory stimulation (massage) reduces blood pressure in unanaesthetized rats. *Journal of the Autonomic Nervous System, 78*(1), 30–37.

Matthiesen, A. S., Ransjo-Arvidson, A. B., Nissen, E., & Uvnäs-Moberg, K. (2001). Postpartum maternal oxytocin release by newborns: Effects of infant hand massage and sucking. *Birth, 28*(1), 13–19.

Miller, S. C., Kennedy, C., DeVoe, D., Hickey, M., Nelson, T., & Kogan, L. (2009). An examination of changes in oxytocin levels in men and women before and after interaction with a bonded dog. *Anthrozoos, 22*(1), 31–42.

Mondelli, V., Dazzan, P., Hepgul, N., Di Forti, M., Aas, M., D'Albenzio, A., ... Pariante, C. M. (2010). Abnormal cortisol levels during the day and cortisol awakening response in first-episode psychosis: The role of stress and of antipsychotic treatment. *Schizophrenic Research, 116*(2-3), 234–242.

Nagasawa, M., Kikusui, T., Onaka, T., & Ohta, M. (2009). Dog's gaze at its owner increases owner's urinary oxytocin during social interaction. *Hormones and Behavior, 55*(3), 434–441.

Neumann, I. D., Wigger, A., Torner, L., Holsboer, F., & Landgraf, R. (2000). Brain oxytocin inhibits basal and stress-induced activity of the hypothalamo–pituitary–adrenal axis in male and female rats: Partial action within the paraventricular nucleus. *Journal of Neuroendocrinology, 12*(3), 235–243.

Nicholson, H. D., Swann, R. W., Burford, G. D., Wathes, D. C., Porter, D. G., & Pickering, B. T. (1984). Identification of oxytocin and vasopressin in the testis and in adrenal tissue. *Regulatory Peptides, 8*(2), 141–146.

Nissen, E., Gustavsson, P., Widstrom, A. M., & Uvnäs-Moberg, K. (1998). Oxytocin, prolactin, milk production and their relationship with personality traits in women after vaginal delivery or Cesarean section. *Journal of Psychosomatic Obstetrics and Gynaecology, 19*(1), 49–58.

Nissen, E., Uvnäs-Moberg, K., Svensson, K., Stock, S., Widstrom, A. M., & Winberg, J. (1996). Different patterns of oxytocin, prolactin but not cortisol release during breastfeeding in women delivered by caesarean section or by the vaginal route. *Early Human Development, 45*(1–2), 103–118.

Odendaal, J. S., & Meintjes, R. A. (2003). Neurophysiological correlates of affiliative behaviour between humans and dogs. *Veterinary Journal, 165*(3), 296–301.

Olmert, M. (2009). *Made for each other—The biology of the human animal bond.* Cambridge, MA: The Perseus Books Group.

Pedersen, C. A., & Prange, A. J., Jr. (1979). Induction of maternal behavior in virgin rats after intracerebroventricular administration of oxytocin. *Proceedings of the National Academy of Sciences of the United States of America, 76*(12), 6661–6665.

Petersson, M., Alster, P., Lundeberg, T., & Uvnäs-Moberg, K. (1996). Oxytocin increases nociceptive thresholds in a long-term perspective in female and male rats. *Neuroscience Letters, 212*(2), 87–90.

Petersson, M., Eklund, M., & Uvnäs-Moberg, K. (2005). Oxytocin decreases corticosterone and nociception and increases motor activity in OVX rats. *Maturitas, 51*(4), 426–433.

Petersson, M., Hulting, A., Andersson, R., & Uvnäs-Moberg, K. (1999). Long-term changes in gastrin, cholecystokinin and insulin in response to oxytocin treatment. *Neuroendocrinology, 69*(3), 202–208.

Petersson, M., Hulting, A. L., & Uvnäs-Moberg, K. (1999). Oxytocin causes a sustained decrease in plasma levels of corticosterone in rats. *Neuroscience Letters, 264*(1–3), 41–44.

Petersson, M., Lundeberg, T., & Uvnäs-Moberg, K. (1999). Short-term increase and long-term decrease of blood pressure in response to oxytocin-potentiating effect of female steroid hormones. *Journal of Cardiovascular Pharmacology, 33*(1), 102–108.

Petersson, M., Uvnäs-Moberg, K., Erhardt, S., & Engberg, G. (1998). Oxytocin increases locus coeruleus alpha 2-adrenoreceptor responsiveness in rats. *Neuroscience Letters, 255*(2), 115–118.

Polito, A. B., III, Goldstein, D. L., Sanchez, L., Cool, D. R., & Morris, M. (2006). Urinary oxytocin as a non-invasive biomarker for neurohypophyseal hormone secretion. *Peptides, 27*(11), 2877–2884.

Seltzer, L. J., & Ziegler, T. E. (2007). Non-invasive measurement of small peptides in the common marmoset (Callithrix jacchus): A radiolabeled clearance study and endogenous excretion under varying social conditions. *Hormones and Behavior, 51*(3), 436–442.

Serpell, J. A. (1986). *In the company of animals.* Oxford, England: Basil Blackwell.

Serpell, J. A. (2000). Creatures of the unconscious: Companion animals as mediators. In A. L. Podberscek, E. S. Paul, & J. A. Serpell (Eds.), *Companion animals and us: Exploring the relationships between people and pets* (pp. 108–124). Cambridge, England: Cambridge University Press.

Silber, M., Almkvist, O., Larsson, B., Stock, S., & Uvnäs-Moberg, K. (1987). The effect of oral contraceptive pills on levels of oxytocin in plasma and on cognitive functions. *Contraception, 36*(6), 641–650.

Stock, S., & Uvnäs-Moberg, K. (1988). Increased plasma levels of oxytocin in response to afferent electrical stimulation of the sciatic and vagal nerves and in response to touch and pinch in anaesthetized rats. *Acta Physiologica Scandinavica, 132*(1), 29–34.

Svennersten, K., Gorewit, R. C., Sjaunja, L. O., & Uvnäs-Moberg, K. (1995). Feeding during milking enhances milking-related oxytocin secretion and milk production in dairy cows whereas food deprivation decreases it. *Acta Physiologica Scandinavica, 153*(3), 309–310.

Svennersten, K., Nelson, L., & Uvnäs-Moberg, K. (1992). Atropinization decreases oxytocin secretion in dairy cows. *Acta Physiologica Scandinavica, 145*(2), 193–194.

Tornhage, C. J., Serenius, F., Uvnäs-Moberg, K., & Lindberg, T. (1998). Plasma somatostatin and cholecystokinin levels in response to feeding in preterm infants. *Journal of Pediatric Gastroenterology and Nutrition, 27*(2), 199–205.

Uvnäs-Moberg, K. (1989). The gastrointestinal tract in growth and reproduction. *Scientific American, 261*(1), 78–83.

Uvnäs-Moberg, K. (1994). Role of efferent and afferent vagal nerve activity during reproduction: Integrating function of oxytocin on metabolism and behaviour. *Psychoneuroendocrinology, 19*(5-7), 687–695.

Uvnäs-Moberg, K. (1998a). Antistress pattern induced by oxytocin. *News in Physiological Sciences, 13*, 22–25.

Uvnäs-Moberg, K. (1998b). Oxytocin may mediate the benefits of positive social interaction and emotions. *Psychoneuroendocrinology, 23*(8), 819–835.

Uvnäs-Moberg, K., Ahlenius, S., Hillegaart, V., & Alster, P. (1994). High doses of oxytocin cause sedation and low doses cause an anxiolytic-like effect in male rats. *Pharmacology, Biochemistry, and Behavior, 49*(1), 101–106.

Uvnäs-Moberg, K., Bruzelius, G., Alster, P., & Lundeberg, T. (1993). The antinociceptive effect of non-noxious sensory stimulation is mediated partly through oxytocinergic mechanisms. *Acta Physiologica Scandinavica, 149*(2), 199–204.

Uvnäs-Moberg, K., Eriksson, M., Blomquist, L. E., Kunavongkrit, A., & Einarsson, S. (1984). Influence of suckling and feeding on insulin, gastrin, somatostatin and VIP levels in peripheral venous blood of lactating sows. *Acta Physiologica Scandinavica, 121*(1), 31–38.

Uvnäs-Moberg, K., Stock, S., Eriksson, M., Linden, A., Einarsson, S., & Kunavongkrit, A. (1985). Plasma levels of oxytocin increase in response to suckling and feeding in dogs and sows. *Acta Physiologica Scandinavica, 124*(3), 391–398.

Uvnäs-Moberg, K., & Petersson, M. (2010). Role of oxytocin and oxytocin related effects in manual therapies. In H. H. King, W. Jänig, & M. M. Patterson (Eds.), *The science and clinical application of manual therapy* (pp. 147–161). Amsterdam, The Netherlands: Elsevier.

Van Cauter, E., & Turek, F. W. (1995). Endocrine and other biological rhythms. In L. J. DeGroot (Ed.), *Endocrinology* (3rd ed., pp. 2497–2548). Philadelphia, PA: WB Saunders.

Wang, D., Gutkowska, J., Marcinkiewicz, M., Rachelska, G., & Jankowski, M. (2003). Genistein supplementation stimulates the oxytocin system in the aorta of ovariectomized rats. *Cardiovascular Research, 57*(1), 186–194.

Wathes, D. C., & Swann, R. W. (1982). Is oxytocin an ovarian hormone? *Nature, 297*(5863), 225–227.

White-Traut, R., Powlesland, J., Gelhar, D., Chatterton, R., & Morris, M. (1998). Methodologic issues in the measurement of oxytocin in human neonates. *Journal of Nursing Measurement, 6*(2), 155–174.

White-Traut, R., Watanabe, K., Pournajafi-Nazarloo, H., Schwertz, D., Bell, A., & Carter, C. S. (2009). Detection of salivary oxytocin levels in lactating women. *Developmental Psychobiology, 51*(4), 367–373.

Widstrom, A. M., Winberg, J., Werner, S., Svensson, K., Posloncec, B., & Uvnäs-Moberg, K. (1988). Breast feeding-induced effects on plasma gastrin and somatostatin levels and their correlation with milk yield in lactating females. *Early Human Development, 16*(2–3), 293–301.

Young, L. J. (2009). Being human: Love: Neuroscience reveals all. *Nature, 457*(7226), 148.

II

HUMAN–ANIMAL INTERACTION AND CHILD DEVELOPMENT

4

HOW VERY YOUNG CHILDREN THINK ABOUT ANIMALS

JUDY S. DeLOACHE, MEGAN BLOOM PICKARD,
AND VANESSA LoBUE

Throughout human history, people have lived in proximity to animals. For early humans and their primate ancestors, avoiding predation by animals, scavenging or hunting animals to eat, and recognizing conspecifics constituted crucial elements of survival. Those who were more successful at meeting these challenges enjoyed a survival advantage (Barton, Briggs, Eisen, Goldstein, & Patel, 2007; Hart & Sussman, 2005; Stiner, 1994).

Archaeological excavations of prehistoric settlements have unearthed a wealth of evidence of direct human–animal interaction (HAI) and of the importance of other animals to early humans and of direct HAI (Curtis, 2006). Depictions of animals abound in some of the earliest known art, from the famous Pleistocene paintings of horses and buffaloes on the walls of European caves to ancient aboriginal rock paintings of wallabies, turtles, and fish in Australia. Egyptian effigies of animal gods date as far back as 5500 BC.

Early people made tools and weapons from animal bones, dressed in animal skins, and adorned themselves with jewelry fashioned from animal bones

The research summarized in this chapter was supported by research grant 0819508 from the National Science Foundation and a MERIT Award from the National Institutes of Health.

and teeth. Eventually, some types of animals were drafted to play a variety of vital roles in early human societies—such as lookout, guard, beast of burden, mode of transportation, source of power—all of which they continue to fulfill in various parts of the world today.

In addition, and more to the point of this volume, some types of animals came to serve as human companions and targets of affection: Some animals became pets. Very early evidence of the existence of pets—and of their importance to their masters—comes from ancient Egypt, where various animals were often embalmed, put in sarcophagi, and entombed with their masters.

Today, 60% of American households have at least one pet in residence. There are even more—70%—in homes with children (Weise, 2007). Children pay attention to these animals, as shown by the fact that some of the most frequently occurring words in infants' early vocabularies are "cat," "dog," and the names of family pets (Nelson, 1973; Tardif et al., 2008). Many children develop extremely important relationships with their family pets.

This chapter examines how and why infants exhibit a greater attentional and emotional attraction toward animals than toward other types of stimuli and the implications of such early preferences. The chapter begins with an overview of biophilia theory and the animate-monitoring hypothesis. Next, it describes four experiments conducted regarding infants' visual attention to animals.

BIOPHILIA

Several decades ago, E. O. Wilson (1984) introduced the concept of "biophilia," proposing that a fundamental aspect of human nature is our innate affinity for life and lifelike processes. He proposed that humans possess an affinity for nature and life as a result of our evolutionary past—the landscapes we inhabited and the animals with which we shared them. Wilson's original contention was that biophilia encompasses not only positive affiliations that humans have with nature and animals, but also negative orientations, such as the common fear of snakes. The research that has been conducted in the biophilia tradition has focused primarily on the positive bonds humans have with animals, particularly the benefits from animal interaction.

Given the history of close interaction and mutual dependence of humans and other animals, might humans have an inherent affinity for animals? According to Wilson's (1984) concept of biophilia, the answer is yes. Wilson proposed that we have an evolved tendency to pay attention to animals, arguing that such an inclination would have had adaptive value in our evolutionary history. A high degree of attention to other species would have facilitated the rapid detection of dangerous predators, delicious prey, and conspecifics—all of which are important regarding survival and passing on one's genes.

Much of the research to date in the biophilia tradition has focused on the appeal and benefits of natural landscapes for adults. For example, simply looking through a window increases subjective well-being and productivity in the workplace (Kahn et al., 2007) and promotes healing in hospitalized patients (Ulrich, 1984). Adults report a strong preference for natural landscapes over built ones (Kaplan & Kaplan, 1989). Perhaps biophilia contributes to the frequency with which people build and rebuild beach-front residences, despite the high likelihood of further danger from hurricanes and flooding.

ANIMATE-MONITORING HYPOTHESIS

Recently, the animate-monitoring hypothesis was proposed by New, Cosmides, and Tooby (2007). Their claim is that an important aspect of the human visual attention system is an evolved tendency to monitor the environment for the presence and location of animals and other humans, two categories that have always constituted both opportunities and dangers with respect to our survival. Consequently, our attention is more readily recruited by other humans and animals than by inanimate entities.

In support of their hypothesis, New et al. (2007) reported a set of studies in which adults participated in a change–detection task. The participants were presented with a series of brief exposures of photographs of natural scenes. Their task was to respond as quickly as they could whenever they detected a change from one picture to the next. Some of the time, the pictures in a sequence were identical. Other times, there was some difference in the position of either an animal or an inanimate object.

The participants more rapidly and more reliably detected changes in the animal location than changes in the object location. For example, they were faster to detect when an elephant appeared in a new place than when a truck did. This result was interpreted by the authors as evidence for an evolved attentional priority for the detection of animate over inanimate stimuli.

In related research, LoBue and DeLoache (LoBue, 2010; LoBue & DeLoache, 2008, 2010) reported results for very young children that are consistent with the findings of New et al. (2007). LoBue and DeLoache established that preschool children detect the presence of snakes and spiders more rapidly than a variety of other stimuli. In these studies, 3-year-old children and their accompanying parents were shown a series of highly realistic color photographs, arranged in 3 × 3 matrices. The task is to find and touch as quickly as possible a single target stimulus among the other eight nontargets. For example, there may be one snake photo among eight frog photos. In a series of studies, 3-year-old children and adults reliably detected snakes more rapidly than a variety of different distracters. These results offer evidence for a priority in the visual system for the detection of threat-relevant stimuli.

VISUAL ATTENTION TO ANIMALS IN INFANCY

Biological Motion Preference in Newborns

Recent evidence that humans are particularly attuned to animals right from the start comes from research conducted with newborns. Simion, Regolin, and Buff (2008) recently reported that newborns have a preference for looking at biological motion. In a series of studies, infants were shown pairs of point-light displays with both displays composed of the same number of lights. One display specified biological motion (a moving hen) and the other nonbiological (random) movement. The infants looked significantly longer at the biological than the random motion, suggesting that it was more coherent to them. (A preference for watching biological movement has also been documented in chickens.) Thus, enhanced attention to biological movement is common, both ontogenetically and phylogenetically.

Early Attention to Animals

A primary question addressed in our research is whether infants have a preference for animals. We conducted two experiments to explore this idea. In Experiment 1, we tested whether infants in the first year of life would pay more attention to films of real animals than to films of inanimate objects. Using a standard visual attention protocol, we presented 16 infants of various ages (4–12 months) with 10 pairs of films. Each pair consisted of one film of animals and one of inanimate objects. From films of the infants' eye movements, we recorded how long they looked at the various stimuli. Figure 4.1 shows an infant participating in the research.

All of the highly realistic films depicted one or more animals or objects moving in a natural landscape. For example, the scenes of animals included an elephant walking down a slope, a dolphin swimming through water, and a bird flying. The inanimate object films included automobile traffic on a highway, a sailboat, and a helicopter landing on a building. Because the infants had had little or no exposure to most of the types of animals and objects that appeared in the films, any preference they expressed could not be based on experience. Figure 4.2 shows the average looking times for the animal and object stimuli.

The results were straightforward and quite dramatic: The infants responded substantially more to the animate than to the inanimate stimuli,

Figure 4.1. This 9-month-old is pointing and making excited sounds to the animal that she sees on the screen, ignoring the inanimate object beside it. (Her mother wears a blindfold to ensure that she does not influence her child's behavior.)

both in terms of visual attention and affective behavior. As Figure 4.2 shows, the infants in both age groups looked substantially and significantly longer at the animals than at the inanimate stimuli. Strikingly, not a single infant preferred objects over animals; all but two showed the pattern of looking longer at the animals.

Such a high degree of similarity in the pattern of responses for an entire group of infants is extremely rare, especially for a group comprising such a range of ages. (Most studies with infants involve tightly constrained age groups.) Further evidence of the strength of the difference in responding to animate and inanimate stimuli is the fact that there were no individual differences as a function of either gender or prior experience with animals. The strong preference for animals is also evident in the infants' responses to the 20 individual stimuli. Of the 12 pictures that they looked at longest, 9 were of animals. (Interestingly, the other three—pinwheel, windmill, and lawn ornament—all involved spinning parts.)

Not only did the infants look at the animals more, but they also directed significantly more emotional responses—all positive—toward the animals

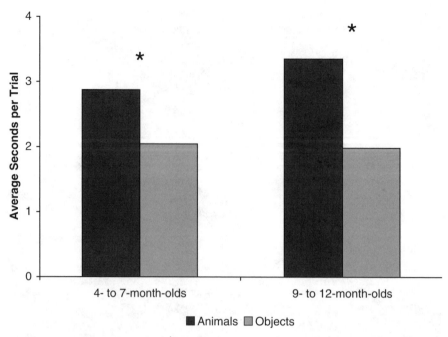

Figure 4.2. Looking times by the two age groups to the animate and inanimate stimuli.

than the objects. They frequently smiled, laughed, and waved at the animals, and one child even blew kisses at some of them. The infants virtually never directed any of these affective behaviors toward the inanimate objects. The results of this study thus document for the first time not only that humans have a preference for animate stimuli from early in life but also that the preference is remarkably robust.

In Experiment 2, we probed the basis for this strong preference for attending to animals. Specifically, we asked whether infants are attracted to animals per se or primarily to animate movement. It seemed reasonable that the basis for the early animal preference we observed could be distinctive differences in how animals and inanimate objects move. If so, the preference for viewing animate entities over inanimate ones should disappear if the stimuli were stationary.

To answer this question, we presented 10 pairs of still color photographs of animals and objects to a new group of infants ages 4 to 12 months. Each photograph depicted a single focal animal or inanimate object set against a white background. (A preliminary study, in which we presented infants with still photos taken from the films used in the earlier research suggested that the stationary animals and objects against the complex natural backgrounds were not readily discernible to them.)

Just as in Experiment 1, the infants in Experiment 2 looked significantly longer at the animals than at the inanimate objects. This difference was particularly strong among the older infants, all but one of whom paid greater attention to the animals.

Thus, the results of these two studies provide strong evidence for the existence of a preference for animate over inanimate stimuli that is evident in the first year of human life. Infants respond more, both in terms of visual attention and emotional engagement, to a range of nonhuman animals than to various inanimate entities. Although this preference is stronger when animate movement is involved, it is also present in response to stationary stimuli.

Attention to Biological Motion

For Experiment 3, we investigated whether infants' animal preference holds when only dynamic information is available to specify animals and objects. Specifically, we used point-light displays—schematic representations of motion made up of moving dots of light[1]—to determine the extent to which entities are recognizable solely by their patterns of movement.

Adults are highly skilled at recognizing the content of point-light displays of humans, accurately identifying type of movement (Walk & Homan, 1984), emotional state (Atkinson, Dittrich, & Gemmell, 2004), gender, age, and even the identity of individuals (Cutting & Kozlowski, 1977; Troje, Westhoff, & Lavriv, 2005). Evidence that these displays are perceived holistically—as coherent biological motion—comes from the fact that inversion disrupts identification. If a point-light display of a person walking that is readily recognizable when shown upright is presented upside-down, adults no longer perceive human movement (Bertenthal, Proffitt, & Cutting, 1984; Bertenthal, Proffitt, & Kramer, 1987).

Infants also perceive coherent movement in point-light displays of human walking. This conclusion is supported by the fact that inversion destroys the illusion of coherent locomotion for infants just as it does for adults. Several species of nonhuman animals, including cats (Blake, 1993), pigeons (Dittrich, Lea, Barrett, & Gurr, 1998), dolphins (Herman, Morrel-Samuels, & Pack, 1990), and even visually inexperienced 1-day-old chicks (Vallortigara, Regolin, & Marconata, 2005) perceive biological motion from point-light displays and are subject to inversion effects just as are humans.

To date, there has been little research exploring humans' reactions to point-light displays depicting nonhuman animals or inanimate objects. Recent

---

[1]Point-light displays of human movement are typically created by attaching lights to the joints of a person and then filming in complete darkness as the person moves. Point-light displays can also be made from digital videos: In each frame of the film, lights are digitally applied to the joints of the target stimulus. When the background in the film is eliminated, the resulting image is a standard point-light display.

evidence suggests that adults, young children, and even infants discriminate between upright point-light films of animals and inanimate objects such as vehicles. However, it is quite difficult for infants or even adults to identify the particular exemplar of a category (for example, dog vs. cow or car vs. truck) being depicted in the point-light display (Arterberry & Bornstein, 2001; Pavlova, Krageloh-Mann, Sokolov, & Birbaumer, 2001).

Some evidence from research using point-light stimuli suggests that infants prefer biological motion per se to other patterns of motion. For example, when presented with upright and inverted human point-light walkers, infants looked longer at the coherent upright human movement (Fox & McDaniel, 1982). As mentioned, even newborns visually prefer point-light displays specifying biological motion (a moving hen) over nonbiological motion (inverted hen or random movement; Simion et al., 2008).

For Experiment 3, we constructed and presented point-light displays of various moving animals and objects. Eliminating all other cues makes it possible to assess the extent to which movement alone affects behavior. The animal point-light displays each consisted of pairs of point-light representations of numerous different animals walking.

The 16 infants participated in two within-subjects conditions. In the first, they saw a pair of upright displays, one of an animal(s) and the other of an inanimate object(s). Assuming that the infants would perceive biological movement in the displays, the prediction was that the infants would look longer at the animals than the objects, as in the earlier studies with realistic films. That is just what they did, suggesting that they perceived animate movement in these abstract displays. In a second condition, the pairs of point-light stimuli were inverted. Because adults and infants alike generally fail to recognize the content of inverted point-light displays (Bertenthal, Proffitt, & Cutting, 1984; Bertenthal, Proffitt, & Kramer, 1987), we expected that the infants would show no preference in this condition. As predicted, the infants looked equally long at the two types of upside-down stimuli.

Attention to "Super" Stimuli

In a further effort to identify what types of information contribute to infants' perception of and preference for animals, we have recently used commercially produced animated cartoons. Animations can give the illusion of life to normally inanimate objects, as exemplified by highly popular movies such as *Beauty and the Beast* and *Cars* (Wargo, 2005). In cartoons, inanimate objects can have features that mimic animates, and they can display biological motion, as well as intentional action and emotion. They also can illustrate any of these characteristics either one at a time or in combination. As a result, any given feature or element can be manipulated independent of the others. By exaggerating particular animate features in isolation, we should be able to get a better idea of which ones are most effective for specifying animals and eliciting the attention of an infant.

In Experiment 4—the first of what will probably become a long series of studies—we showed infants (ages 4–12 months) cartoons of animals, cartoons of inanimate objects, and cartoons in which animate features were applied to inanimate objects. One example of the last category is a car that behaved as if it were a wild animal, using its tires as paws, displaying a ferocious facial expression on its grill, producing screeching calls with its front bumper, and so on. This stimulus was a particular favorite. An interesting result that emerged from this preliminary study was that the infants' highest level of preference was for "super stimuli"—cartoons that imposed greatly exaggerated features and movement patterns onto inanimate objects. (This approach may prove useful in investigating various topics.)

As predicted, there was an overall preference for animals, with infants looking longer at both cartoon animals and animated objects than at inanimate objects. A particularly interesting result was that, overall, the infants looked longer at the animated animals than at the real animals. This result indicates that animate features, such as having a face and moving in an animate manner, are sufficient to elicit a preference in infants, regardless of the specific identity of the entity in question.

GENERAL DISCUSSION

The goal of the experiments described here was to explore the nature of humans' attention to animals. Of specific interest was the extent to which infants' attention is recruited by animals over inanimate stimuli. In two preliminary experiments, this question was examined by presenting infants with pairs of images of animals and objects, and visual attention was assessed. Experiment 1 established that infants strongly prefer moving animals to moving objects. In Experiment 2, in which infants were shown still photographs, older infants showed a strong preference for animals over objects. Overall, the results of the preliminary studies showed that infants prefer animals to objects on the basis of both static and dynamic features. However, the strongest preference was for moving animals.

Two subsequent experiments further explored the nature of infants' attention to animate movement. In Experiment 3, girls but not boys preferred biological motion (depicted in point-light displays) to the motion of inanimate objects. This result suggests that, at least for girls, animate movement, apart from all other cues to identity, is sufficient to elicit an animal preference. In Experiment 4, infants overall preferred cartoons of both animals and animated objects (objects made to move and behave like animals) to cartoons of objects moving as they normally would. This result suggests that features of animals, such as having a face and moving like an animal, are sufficient to elicit preference in infants, regardless of the identity of the object in question.

Overall, the results of the four studies described here suggest that in the first year of life infants possess a preference for animate over inanimate stimuli in numerous forms. This research supports an intrinsic tendency for humans to orient preferentially toward animals. This basic result is consistent with the recently published animate-monitoring hypothesis, that humans have an evolved tendency to preferentially allocate attention to animals (New et al., 2007). In addition, it is consistent with the life-detector hypothesis, the idea that the human visual system readily detects and recognizes patterns of biological motion (Johnson, 2006; Simion et al., 2008). Such tendencies would have likely had adaptive value during mammalian evolution, as a high degree of attention to other animals would have facilitated survival through the rapid detection and identification of predator, prey, and conspecifics.

The results of this research have also established that particular animal features draw infants' attention. First, infants prefer animals to objects on the basis of both dynamic (as demonstrated in Experiments 1, 3, and 4) and static (as demonstrated in Experiment 2) features, even when the entity being depicted with those features is not actually an animal but rather an object made to look like an animal (as in Experiment 4).

Future work is needed to determine to a higher level of precision which dynamic and static elements of animals draw infants' attention. For example, static features of animals include (but are not limited to) facial features, eyes, legs, tails, and a particular body shape (e.g., animal bodies never possess right angles or perfectly straight lines). We know infants discriminate animals from objects on the basis of these features (e.g., Jones, Smith, & Landau, 1991; Rakison & Butterworth, 1998; Rakison & Poulin-Dubois, 2001) and, in the case of faces, actually show a preference (Cassia, Turati, & Simion, 2004; Fantz, 1961). However, more work is needed to determine precisely which of these features attracts infants' attention and to what extent.

In terms of dynamic features of animals, the results of the research described here suggest that the pattern of animal movement (as depicted in point-light displays) is sufficient to elicit an animal preference in infants, at least for girls. However, there are numerous other dynamic elements of living creatures that infants recognize as distinctly animate, such as patterns of movement with smooth trajectories (Arterberry & Bornstein, 2001; Bertenthal, 1993; Fox & McDaniel, 1982), self-initiation (Spelke, Phillips, & Woodward, 1995), and apparent agency and intentionality (Gergely, Nadasdy, Csibra, &

Bíró, 1995; Johnson, 2003; Poulin-Dubois & Shultz, 1990; Rakison & Poulin-Dubois, 2001). Although quite a bit is known of infants' developing understanding of these concepts, future work is needed to examine which of these features of animals actually draw infants' attention. Do dynamic patterns that encompass these features draw attention to a greater extent than other types of movement?

One striking element of the studies described here is that experience with animals seems to have no effect on whether infants express an animal preference. In combination with the fact that the observed patterns of preference were relatively consistent across children, this suggests that the results of these studies reflect an intrinsic, low-level attentional bias that is immune to effects of experience (at least beyond the normative changes related to age). There are reasons to suspect that experience with animals might have had an effect on infants' preference for animals. The most likely reason is that infants with more experience with animals might find animals to be generally more familiar and thus might attend to them to a greater extent than do infants with less experience with animals. Alternatively, infants with a high degree of experience with animals might have found the novelty of the inanimate objects to be highly appealing and thus show the opposite pattern of results, a preference for inanimate objects. However, both of these cases can be ruled out because no effects of experience on patterns of preference were observed.

It is possible that the measure of experience with animals employed in these studies was not precise enough to detect subtle effects of experience. One possible reason is that the questions asked were not specific. A second possibility is that the population tested was too homogenous in terms of individuals' experiences with animals to detect any effects of experience. Testing populations with extreme degrees of animal experience, such as urban versus rural children, might yield a more heterogeneous sample, and more subtle effects of experience may thus be observable.

The question remains whether particular types of animals may draw attention more than others. There is some evidence that particular types of animals elicit specific types of responses. For example, snakes and spiders, two animals that have posed a significant threat throughout evolution, are detected more quickly than other nonthreatening entities by both adult and infant humans (DeLoache & LoBue, 2009; LoBue, 2008; LoBue & DeLoache, 2008; Ohman, Flykt, & Esteves, 2001; Ohman, Lundqvist, & Esteves, 2001) and by non-human primates (Shibasaki & Nobuyuki, 2008). The ability to respond quickly and efficiently to threat is highly adaptive and serves as an important survival mechanism for humans and other animals (Ohman, 1993; Ohman, Lundqvist, & Esteves, 2001). Still unresolved is the extent to which particular animals attract infants' attention over other types of animals. For example, would infants attend differentially to animals that have posed a significant threat throughout evolution versus nonthreatening animals, humans versus non-human animals, prototypical versus nontypical or unusual animals, or specific classes of animals, such as mammals versus birds versus fish versus reptiles.

A related question is whether humans' attention to different types of animals changes with age. According to one theory, for example, a wariness of large mammals is likely to emerge in toddlerhood, at the point in development when children begin to explore their surroundings somewhat independently, often a distance from the safety and protection of parents or other adults (Heerwagen & Orians, 2001). A question for future research is whether children's attention to particular types of animals changes over the course of development as a result of these types of developmental changes.

Finally, the question remains, how does an intrinsic attentional bias toward animals benefit humans? One possibility, according to the animate-monitoring hypothesis, is that humans are quicker and more accurate to allocate attention to animals, thus facilitating survival through the rapid detection and identification of predator, prey, and conspecifics. Evidence for such a tendency comes from the fact that adults are quicker and more accurate in identifying changes to an animal in a scene than in an object (New et al., 2007). Does a similar monitoring bias exist in infants? Future work will examine this question.

A second possibility is that an attentional bias toward animals in infancy scaffolds conceptual development. If attention is drawn so strongly to animals over other elements of the environment, what is the impact on early learning? Might a high degree of attention to animals facilitate learning in this domain, drawing infants' attention early on to the structure and function of animals over other sorts of stimuli. Finally, perhaps the preference for animals observed in these studies among infants represents an early manifestation of biophilia, an interest and affiliation with life. Thus, future research will explore the extent to which an emotional tie to animals develops in children.

Overall, the research described here provides the first comprehensive evidence of an intrinsic attentional bias that leads even infants to preferentially attend to animate stimuli. Future work will continue to explore the nature of this bias and how it changes throughout development.

REFERENCES

Arterberry, M., & Bornstein, M. (2001). Three-month-old infants' categorization of animals and vehicles based on static and dynamic attributes. *Journal of Experimental Child Psychology, 80*, 333–346.

Atkinson, A., Dittrich, W., & Gemmell, A. (2004). Emotion perception from dynamic and static body expressions in point-light and full-light displays. *Perception, 33,* 717–746.

Barton, N., Briggs, D., Eisen, J., Goldstein, D., & Patel, N. (2007). *Evolution.* Cold Spring Harbor, NY: Cold Spring Harbor Laboratory Press.

Bertenthal, B., Proffitt, D., & Cutting, J. (1984). Infant sensitivity to figural coherence in biomechanical motion. *Journal of Experimental Child Psychology, 37,* 213–230.

Bertenthal, B., Proffitt, D., & Kramer, S. (1987). Perception of biomechanical motions by infants: Implementation of various processing constraints. *Journal of Experimental Psychology, 13,* 577–585.

Bertenthal, B. (1993). Infants' perception of biomechanical motions: Intrinsic image and knowledge-based constraints. In C. Granrud (Ed.), *Visual perception and cognition in infancy* (pp. 175–214). Hillsdale, NJ: Erlbaum.

Blake, R. (1993). Cats perceive biological motion. *Psychological Science, 4,* 54–57.

Cassia, V., Turati, C., & Simion, F. (2004). Can a nonspecific bias toward top-heavy patterns explain newborns' face preference? *Psychological Science, 15,* 379–383.

Curtis, G. (2006). *The cave painters: Probing the mysteries of the world's first artists.* New York, NY: Alfred A. Knopf.

Cutting, J., & Kozlowski, L. (1977). Recognizing friends by their walk: Gait perception without familiarity cues. *Bulletin of the Psychonomic Society, 9,* 353–356.

DeLoache, J. S., & LoBue, V. (2009). The narrow fellow in the grass: Human infants associate snakes and fear. *Developmental Science, 12*(1), 201–207.

Dittrich, W., Lea, S., Barrett, J., & Gurr, P. (1998). Categorization of natural movements by pigeons: Visual concept discrimination and biological motion. *Journal of the Experimental Analysis of Behavior, 70,* 281–299.

Fox, R., & McDaniel, C. (1982). The perception of biological motion by human infants. *Science, 218,* 486–487.

Franz, R. L. (1961). The origin of form perception. *Scientific American, 204,* 66–72.

Gergely, G., Nadasdy, Z., Csibra, G., & Bíró, S. (1995). Taking the intentional stance at 12 months of age. *Cognition, 56,* 165–193.

Hart, D., & Sussman, R. (2005). *Man the hunted: Primates, predators, and human evolution.* New York, NY: Westview Press.

Heerwagen, J., & Orians, G. (2001). The ecological world of children. In P. Kahn and S. Kellert (Eds.), *Children and nature: Psychological, sociocultural, and evolutionary investigations* (pp. 29–64). Cambridge, MA: MIT Press.

Herman, L., Morrel-Samuels, P., & Pack, A. (1990). Bottlenosed dolphin and human recognition of veridical and degraded video displays of an artificial gestural language. *Journal of Experimental Psychology, 119,* 215–230.

Johnson, M. (2006). Biological motion: A perceptual life detector? *Current Biology, 16,* R376–R377.

Johnson, S. (2003). Detecting agents. *Philosophical Transactions of the Royal Society of London, Series B, 358*, 549–559.

Jones, K., Smith, L., & Landau, B. (1991). Object properties and knowledge in early lexical learning. *Child Development, 62*, 499–516.

Kahn, P., Friedman, B., Gill, B., Hagman, J., Severson, R., Freier, N., . . . Stolyar, A. (2007). A plasma display window? The shifting baseline problem in a technologically mediated natural world. *Journal of Environmental Psychology, 22*, 192–199.

Kaplan, R., & Kaplan, S. (1989). *The experience of nature: A psychological perspective*. Cambridge, England: Cambridge University Press.

LoBue, V. (2010). And along came a spider: Superior detection of spiders in children and adults. *Journal of Experimental Child Psychology, 107*, 59–66.

LoBue, V., & DeLoache, J. S. (2008). Detecting the snake in the grass: Attention to fear-relevant stimuli by adults and young children. *Psychological Science, 19*, 284–289.

LoBue, V., & DeLoache, J. S. (2010). Superior detection of threat-relevant stimuli in infancy. *Developmental Science, 13*(1), 221–228.

Nelson, K. (1973). Structure and strategy in learning to talk. *Monographs of the Society for Research in Child Development, 38*, 1–135.

New, J., Cosmides, L., & Tooby, J. (2007). Category-specific attention for animals reflects ancestral priorities, not expertise. *Proceedings of the National Academy of Sciences, 104*, 6598–6603.

Ohman, A. (1993). Fear and anxiety as emotional phenomena: Clinical phenomenology, evolutionary perspectives, and information-processing mechanisms. In M. Lewis & J. Haviland (Eds.), *Handbook of emotions* (pp. 511–536). New York, NY: Guilford Press.

Ohman, A., Flykt, A., & Esteves, F. (2001). Emotion drives attention: Detecting the snake in the grass. *Journal of Experimental Psychology: General, 130*, 466–478.

Ohman, A., Lundqvist, D., & Esteves, F. (2001). The face in the crowd revisited: An anger superiority effect with schematic faces. *Journal of Personality and Social Psychology, 80*, 381–396.

Pavlova, M., Krageloh-Mann, I., Sokolov, A., & Birbaumer, N. (2001). Recognition of point-light biological motion displays by young children. *Perception, 30*, 925–933.

Poulin-Dubois, D., & Shultz, T. (1990). The infant's concept of agency: The distinction between social and nonsocial objects. *Journal of Genetic Psychology, 151*, 77–90.

Rakison, D., & Butterworth, G. (1998). Infants' attention to object structure in early categorization. *Developmental Psychology, 34*, 1310–1325.

Rakison, D., & Poulin-Dubois, D. (2001). Developmental origin of the animate–inanimate distinction. *Psychological Bulletin, 127*, 209–228.

Shibasaki, M., & Nobuyuki, K. (2008). Rapid detection of snakes by Japanese monkeys (*Macaca fuscata*): An evolutionarily predisposed visual system. *Journal of Comparative Psychology, 123*, 131–135.

Simion, F., Regolin, L., & Buff, H. (2008). A predisposition for biological motion in the newborn baby. *Proceedings of the National Academy of Sciences, 105*, 809–813.

Spelke, E., Phillips, A., & Woodward, A. (1995). Infants' knowledge of object motion and human action. In D. Sperber, D. Premack, & A. James (Eds.), *Causal cognition: A multidisciplinary debate*. New York, NY: Oxford University Press.

Stiner, M. (1994). *Honor among thieves*. Princeton, NJ: Princeton University Press.

Tardif, T., Fletcher, P., Liang, W., Zhang, Z., Kacriroti, N., & Marchman, V. (2008). Baby's first 10 words. *Developmental Psychology, 44*, 929–938.

Troje, N., Westhoff, C., & Lavriv, M. (2005). Person identification from biological motion: Effects of structural and kinematic cues. *Perception & Psychophysics, 67*, 667–675.

Ulrich, R. (1984). View through a window may influence recovery from surgery. *Science, 224*, 420–421.

Vallortigara, G., Regolin, L., & Marconata, F. (2005). Visually inexperienced chicks exhibit spontaneous preference for biological motion patterns. *PLOS Biology, 3*, 1312–1316.

Walk, R., & Homan, C. (1984). Emotion and dance in dynamic light displays. *Bulletin of the Psychonomic Society, 22*, 437–440.

Wargo, E. (2005). Animated expressions. *APA Observer, 18*.

Weise, E. (September 11, 2007). We really love—and spend on—our pets. *USA Today*.

5

THE OTHER SIDE OF THE BOND: DOMESTIC DOGS' HUMAN-LIKE BEHAVIORS

CLIVE D. L. WYNNE, NICOLE R. DOREY, AND MONIQUE A. R. UDELL

The ecological niche for the majority of dogs is the human domicile. In the United States today, families provide homes to more than 70 million pet dogs (American Pet Products Manufacturers Association [APPMA], 2008; American Veterinary Medicine Association [AVMA], 2007). No reliable estimates of the numbers of stray dogs are available. In the contemporary United States, their numbers appear to be small, and even stray dogs depend on human refuse for their survival (Coppinger & Coppinger, 2001).

Nearly 40% of American homes house a pet dog (APPMA, 2008; AVMA, 2007). Indeed, in modern America, more families include a dog than a child (31%; U.S. Census Bureau, n.d.). A study by the APPMA (2008) found that dogs are no more common in families with children than those without (41% compared with 40% in the general population). However, a Humane Society of the United States (2006) study found that pets are more likely to be found in households with children, with rates as high as 75% of these households. An Australian study found that pets, in general, were less commonly found in households with young children (birth to 4 years), but the likelihood of finding pets in a family increased with the age of the children (Shuler, Debess, Lapidus, & Hedberg, 2008).

The fact that these pets are a voluntary acquisition, as well as copious anecdotal evidence, indicates that dogs provide great pleasure to many people. A recent study indicates that people with a strong relationship with their dog release more oxytocin when their dog looks at them than do people with a weaker relationship with their dog whose dog looks at them less (Nagasawa, Kikusui, Onaka, & Ohta, 2009). Oxytocin is a hormone implicated in social affiliative behaviors that is released during birth and lactation.

Dogs are clearly a great source of pleasure to many children in the developed world. On the other hand, children are also the most likely victims of dog attacks (Gershman & Sacks, 1994). In more than half of dog-caused fatalities in the United States, the victims were children (Sacks, Sinclair, Gilchrist, Golab, & Lockwood, 1996), with 5- to 9-year-old children being the group at greatest risk (National Center for Injury Prevention and Control, 2008). Although fatalities remain rare in the United States, the pattern for the approximately 5 million annual nonfatal dog bites is similar: 42% of all bites were to children younger than 14 years (Centers for Disease Control, 2003).

Thus, from the viewpoint of understanding the pleasure that dogs may bring children, and minimizing the harm that dogs can cause them, detailed study of the interaction of dogs and children is of great importance. Unfortunately, to our knowledge there have been no detailed analyses of dog–child interaction. In this chapter, we compile what is known about the responsiveness of pet dogs to human cues (studies in which the cues have all been offered by adult humans) and what is known about factors that precipitate dog attacks on children. These two types of study are necessarily at different levels of analysis; for obvious ethical reasons, no experimental study has been performed to look at the actions of children that might trigger dog attacks. The chapter concludes with an analysis of the importance of appropriate socialization of pet dogs if the pleasure and pedagogic value they can bring to children is to be maximized while the risks are kept to a minimum. The coda is a plea for detailed experimental research on the nature of child–dog interactions: What cues do children present to dogs, how do dogs react to them?

HUMAN–DOG INTERACTION

Research over the last decade has proven pet owners right: Domestic dogs really do have a remarkable sensitivity to human actions and intentions (see Miklósi, 2008, and Udell & Wynne, 2008, for more complete reviews of this literature). In one of the simplest and most widely used tests of dogs' sensitivity to human cuing actions, an experimenter places herself between two containers. These containers are equidistant from the experimenter, usually

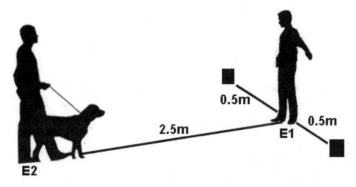

Figure 5.1. Typical setup for a pointing experiment with dogs.

about 1 meter apart. The experimenter points to one of the containers while the dog is attending to her from 2 or 3 meters away (see Figure 5.1). Commonly both containers are baited, but only the food in the pointed-to container can be obtained by the dog. Numerous studies, starting with Miklósi, Polgardi, Topál, and Csanyi (1998), have shown that pet domestic dogs living in human homes are highly proficient at finding food by following human pointing gestures under these circumstances. Typically in studies of this type, the experimenter returns to a resting position with all limbs in a natural position close to the midline before the dog makes its choice. The original study by Miklósi et al. (1998) showed that dogs were able to use human hand and arm pointing, head nodding, bowing, and head turning to locate the container with accessible food. Subsequent studies have extended the range of human gestures dogs can use to locate food to include many forms of pointing with the arm (Hare & Tomasello, 1999; Miklósi et al., 1998; Soproni, Miklósi, Topál, & Csanyi, 2002; Udell, Giglio, & Wynne, 2008), pointing with the leg (Udell, Dorey, & Wynne, 2008), and glancing with the eyes and head (Miklósi et al., 1998; Udell, Giglio, & Wynne, 2008). A similar outcome was found in a study in which a trained dog acted as the "experimenter" to indicate the location of a hidden food item by gazing at it (Hare & Tomasello, 1999).

Although earlier studies suggested that the ability to follow human pointing was present in all dogs, a more recent study has shown that, although most pet dogs living in human homes are able to follow pointing, this ability is not present in dogs living at an animal shelter facility, even after pretesting for willingness to eat from the experimenters' hands and lack of fear responses to the experimenters (Udell, Dorey, & Wynne, 2008).

In addition, one study has shown that dogs can effectively cue their human caregivers to find a food item or toy that the dog, but not the human, had seen hidden. Miklósi, Polgardi, Topál, and Csanyi (1998) showed dogs a hidden item while their owner was out of the room. On the owner's return, the tethered dog was able to communicate the location of the hidden item to the owner by alternation of its gaze between the hidden location and the owner.

Dogs show sensitivity to the attentional state of humans in other ways. For example, dogs are more likely to take food that they have been forbidden to touch if the experimenter cannot see them than if the experimenter's view of the dog remains unobscured. This was found when the experimenter had left the room, had a barrier between her and the dog, or even if her eyes were closed (Brauer, Call, & Tomasello, 2004).

Gácsi, Miklósi, Varga, Topál, and Csanyi (2004) showed that dogs are sensitive to the body orientation and eye visibility of a human being in another way. They gave dogs the choice of two people from whom to beg for treats. One person had a blindfold over her eyes; the other had the blindfold over her forehead so that her eyes were not covered. In another condition, the dogs had to choose between one person looking straight at the dog and another looking away. The dogs were given food no matter from whom they begged on each trial. In both conditions, the dogs showed a significant preference for the person whose vision was unobscured. Cooper et al. (2003) carried out a similar experiment, offering dogs in different conditions choices between people whose vision was obscured by blindfolds, hands over their eyes, a bucket over the head, or a book in front of the face. In each case, a person whose vision was not obscured but who held the same occluder near their head served as the alternative choice. Dogs' performance was above chance in all cases, but the book in front of a person's face was a markedly more salient stimulus for the dogs than the other forms of blindfold.

Kaminski, Call, and Fischer (2004) reported the ability of a dog known as Rico to recognize vocal labels for more than 200 items. Rico was able to select the correct item from a neighboring room when instructed vocally.

This litany of dogs' successes on tasks requiring the comprehension of cues offered by humans often surprises professional comparative psychologists more than it shocks dog owners. For the comparative psychologist, the performance of dogs is remarkable because of the long history of failures to show similar skills in human's closest relatives, the great apes. For example, when chimpanzees were given a choice of two containers, the rewarded container being the one pointed to by a human experimenter, few succeeded in using human cues such as pointing to locate a hidden object unless they were given extensive training (Itakura, Agnetta, Hare, & Tomasello, 1999; Povinelli, Reaux, Bierschwale, Allain, & Simon, 1997; Tomasello, Call, & Gluckman, 1997). The success of dogs compared to the difficulties of chimpanzees on related tasks raises interesting questions about the origin and development of these skills in dogs.

THE DEVELOPMENT OF HUMAN-COMPATIBLE
BEHAVIORS IN DOGS

Over the last decade there has been considerable debate about the origin of human-compatible behavior in the domestic dog. Some researchers have proposed that dogs are born with the skills and cognitive abilities they need to effectively interpret human gestures and interact with humans in beneficial ways throughout their lives (Hare, Brown, Williamson, & Tomasello, 2002; Riedel, Schumann, Kaminski, Call, & Tomasello, 2008). Thus the human–canine bond is sometimes presumed to be inevitable and independent of the rearing history of the dog involved (Hare et al., 2002). However, there is ample evidence to the contrary.

Domestic dogs, like many other species, require experience with conspecifics to form social bonds, and this socialization must occur within a specific window of time for the dog's social behavior to develop normally (Scott & Fuller, 1965). This is also true of the domestic dog's ability to form bonds with members of other species, including humans. Although some breeds of dog are receptive to socialization with humans up to 16 weeks of age (Coppinger & Coppinger, 2001), a study by Freedman, King, and Elliot (1961) demonstrated that, for some breeds, the seventh week of life marks a turning point for optimal socialization with humans. Using cocker spaniels and beagles, the effects of socialization at 2, 3, 5, 7, 9, or after 14 weeks was determined by each dog's attraction to the handler, resistance to leash training, and reactivity to aversive stimuli. The investigators found that dogs socialized each day during only their seventh week of life showed the most stable receptiveness to humans both during their week of socialization and at the end of the 14-week testing period. The full sensitive period of socialization, however, ranged from 2.5 to 13 weeks, and dogs socialized within this window were generally responsive to humans. Dogs that were not socialized by 14 weeks of age became fearful of humans, and even an intense remedial 3-month attempt to socialize one of these dogs with humans improved the dog's behavior only slightly (Freedman et al., 1961). Scott and Fuller (1965) described puppies socialized too late in their development as "like little wild animals and could be tamed only in the way in which wild animals are usually tamed, by keeping them confined so that they could not run away and feeding them only by hand, so that they were continually forced into close human contact" (p. 105).

The United States, like most first-world nations, has institutions for removing unsocialized dogs from human society. If a dog has not been adequately socialized to humans by 14 weeks of age, it is most likely to end up at a dog shelter, classified as abandoned or abused. A visit to the nonadoptable section of a local dog shelter will provide ample encounters with dogs that fit Scott and Fuller's description.

An understanding of domestic dogs' social development can also be used to establish desired relationships. For example, those who raise dogs as livestock guards limit contact with humans and conspecifics during a puppy's sensitive period of social development and instead bond the puppy with the species it will one day protect, such as sheep or goats (Lorenz & Coppinger, 1986). Doing so makes the dog more likely to stay with the species it has been raised to guard, displaying affiliative behaviors toward this species alone, despite the approach of humans or even other dogs.

There is a compounding effect of this initial developmental trajectory. Once a dog has developed a bond with a particular species, it has access to a range of stimuli that it can continue to learn about as long as this contact is maintained. This allows the formation of critical associations between the environment, the behavior of its companions, its own behavior, and various outcomes. For most pet dogs, intense exposure to humans is unavoidable, and because the majority of a pet's reinforcers are provided by humans, there is great benefit to them in learning about human behavior. As mentioned, dogs are sensitive to human actions and readily adjust their behavior in the presence of human stimuli to increase their chances of obtaining desired items, such as food, toys, and attention. In many cases, human action controls dogs' access even to mating opportunities.

Although the domestic dogs' sensitivity to human actions has often been attributed to an evolved human-like social cognition (Hare et al., 2002; Kubinyi & Miklósi, 2007; Miklósi, Topál & Csanyi, 2007), this theory has been brought into doubt by several lines of research. First, Udell, Dorey, and Wynne (2008) demonstrated that intensely socialized wolves are capable of developing sensitivity to human stimuli, whereas some domestic dogs fail to respond to such stimuli on identical tests. Second, experience and age affect performance on human-guided object choice tasks (Dorey, Udell, & Wynne, 2009; Wynne, Udell, & Lord, 2008) and, third, this behavior extinguishes rapidly when reinforcement is withheld (Bentosela, Barrera, Jakovcevic, Elgier, & Mustaca, 2008).

These recent findings prompted a novel account of the origin of dogs' sensitivity to human actions—the two-stage hypothesis (Udell, Dorey, & Wynne, 2010)—which stresses the importance of ontogeny in the development of the human–canine bond. This hypothesis does not deny that domestication and other genetic differences affect developmental stages, motor patterns, and even the ease of socialization found in different species, subspecies, and breeds. Instead, it suggests that all of these features contribute to differences in development and experience that have previously been overlooked by theories that have focused more on the evolution of cognitive faculties.

To increase the probability that a dog will develop sensitivity to human cues to its fullest potential, it is important that two conditions are met: (a) Socialization to humans during a sensitive period of development leading to the acceptance of humans as social companions; and (b) Learning that is not restricted to a particular phase of development to use the location and movement of parts of the human body to find or obtain sought-after objects (through Pavlovian and/or operant conditioning). This interaction between species-specific developmental processes and environmental experience not only provides the basis of a strong bond between humans and dogs but also allows for flexibility in their relationship and in the signals an owner might use to communicate with his dog. Therefore, the interactions between humans and dogs are dynamic as well as interactive, giving both humans and dogs opportunities to develop their unique relationship. However, this knowledge also places the responsibility on every dog owner to provide his dog with the necessary experiences to ensure that it is well adjusted to the human environment throughout its life. This means that a dog that will experience children in its lifetime (as most pets surely will) must be socialized to children at an early age and have regular experiences with them throughout its life. It also means that children who will experience dogs in their lifetimes should be taught how to interact with dogs because each dog is also learning something about children—and adjusting its behavior accordingly—during each interaction. This may include aversive experiences, such as repeatedly getting its tail pulled, which could train the dog to avoid children or to take the offensive next time a child approaches. As with any relationship, effective communication and respect are important factors in promoting positive interactions and avoiding unpleasant or even dangerous outcomes.

DOGS' INTERACTIONS WITH CHILDREN

As noted, few studies have investigated the nature of children's interactions with dogs. The few studies that have been done on child–dog interactions have been correlational and used questionnaires, telephone surveys, dog bite reporting systems such as medical records, and reports collected by veterinarians to attempt to uncover general benefits or disadvantages to dog ownership. For example, Paul and Serpell (1996) compared mothers' impressions of their 8- to 12-year-old children in the year after obtaining a new pet dog to impressions of mothers of matched-age children who did not acquire a dog. The results showed few clear health or psychological impacts of dog ownership. At the end of the first month, the dog-owning children had experienced more visits from their friends and more leisure activities at home with their family, but these changes wore off by the end of the observation year. At the end of the year, the dog-owning children reported more symptoms of ill health than did the children who had not acquired dogs.

Daly and Morton (2006) reported that elementary-school–aged children who owned or preferred both dogs and cats recorded higher scores on a test of empathy than did those who owned or preferred only dogs or cats. Children who were highly attached to their pets were also more empathetic than were those with lower levels of attachment.

Arambasic, Kuterovac-Jagodic, and Vidovic (1999) investigated whether possession of pet dogs or cats acted to buffer elementary-school children's self-esteem during the Balkan wars of the 1990s. Contrary to their hypothesis, no beneficial effects of pet ownership on the self-esteem of war-traumatized children were observed.

Some information about dog–child interactions can be gleaned from studies of children as victims of dog bites. With the number of dogs living in human households increasing, it is not surprising that the number of dog bites inflicted on humans is also on the rise. According to Philips (2008), the number of fatal dog bites almost doubled between 1990 and 2007. Children are the most common victims of these dog bites (Reisner, Shofer, & Nance, 2007; Sacks et al., 2000), with the perpetrator usually being a dog the child is familiar with (Guy et al., 2001b; Wright, 1985, 1990). Presently 2% of the U.S. population is bitten each year. By age 10, the cumulative risk of having been bitten by a dog is about 70% (Sack et al., 2000), with the majority of these bites occurring to the head, face, or neck (Weiss, Friedman, & Coben, 1998).

Surprisingly, there is no clear consensus in the literature whether the sex of a dog and whether it has been sterilized are risk factors for attacks on children. Several papers report more aggression in male dogs than in female dogs (Borchelt, 1983; Gershman & Sacks, 1994; Guy et al., 2001a; Reisner et al., 2007). Nonetheless, one study contradicts these results and found that in small breeds, females were more aggressive toward humans than were males (Guy et al., 2001a), although other authors have suggested this result may be an artifact of the sampling method used (Luescher & Reisner, 2008; Guy et al., 2001b).

There is also little consensus in the literature on breed of dog as a factor in bites of children. Although several studies have found breed differences in temperament (Scott & Fuller, 1965), handling of novel situations (Plutchik, 1971), working performance (Brenoe, Larsgard, Johannessen, & Uldal, 2002), activity and playfulness (Hart & Miller, 1985), and trainability (Serpell & Hsu, 2005), the literature on breed differences in biting remains unclear. Several studies of dog bite rates in the United States report that German shepherd dogs are the most likely to bite humans (Avner & Baker, 1991; Gershman

& Sacks, 1994; Schalamon et al., 2006). However, other investigators have found breeds such as pit bulls (Gandhi, Liebman, Stafford, & Stafford, 1999; Sacks et al., 2000) and English springer spaniels (Guy et al., 2001b; Reisner, Erb, & Houpt, 1994; Reisner, Houpt, & Shofer, 2005) to have the highest rates of such incidents. A recent study by Shuler et al. (2008) reported that dogs categorized by the American Kennel Club as herding breeds (e.g., German shepherd, border collie, old English sheepdog) had the highest rates of biting incidents. Duffy, Hsu, and Serpell (2008) suggested that the inconsistency between studies may result from the context in which the incident occurred. For example, they found that dachshunds were aggressive in most contexts, but rottweilers were more aggressive toward strangers, rather than their owners.

Some investigators have argued that research should focus on environmental risk factors instead of breed differences (AVMA, 2007; O'Sullivan, Jones, O'Sullivan, & Hanlon, 2008). These factors include young and inexperienced owners (Guy et al., 2001b; Miller, Staats, Pertlo, & Rada, 1996), dogs not being socialized during the critical period (O'Sullivan et al., 2008), dogs that have been adopted from shelters (Wells & Hepper, 2000), dogs that are constrained by a leash or chain (Thompson, 1997), and the overall health of the dog (Guy et al., 2001b).

Several studies have attempted to identify behaviors in puppies that might predict the likelihood of biting humans when it gets older. Guy et al. (2001a) reported that dogs that were more excitable when they were puppies were more likely to bite their owners as adults. Furthermore, guarding behaviors over both food and toys that might be considered attractive in a puppy could turn dangerous as the dog gets older (Guy et al., 2001a). Luescher and Reisner (2008) state that in dog bite cases analyzed at two sites, more than half of the dogs labeled as showing dominance-related aggression started displaying these behaviors in their first year of life.

Interestingly, treating a dog like a family member can increase the risk of dog attacks. Families that allowed their dogs onto furniture, to sleep with them in their beds, or handed them scraps of food from the dining room or kitchen table were at a greater risk of being bitten by their dog (Guy et al., 2001b; O'Sullivan et al., 2008). However, more research needs to be done to identify if this is because of the dog's temperament, the owner's approach, or a combination of the two (Guy et al., 2001b).

Another environmental risk factor is the behavior of the children toward the dogs. Children underestimate the dangers that dogs pose and are more careless and inexperienced than adults when it comes to interacting with dogs (Schalamon et al., 2006). Bites may occur because children cannot discriminate between a dog that wants to play and a dog that is feeling threatened (AVMA, 2007). Bites to children occurred more often when they were in the dog's territory (Reisner et al., 2005). Children could be bitten when they engaged in contact classified as aversive for the dog, such as stepping on the dog (Reisner et al., 2007), pulling its ear (Schalamon et al., 2006), and disturbing the dog while it is eating or while protecting its possessions (Schalamon et al., 2006). But bites may also occur when the child engages in nonaversive contact but at the wrong time or place, such as petting, hugging, or kissing the dog while it is sleeping (Reisner et al., 2007).

CONCLUSIONS

Much is at stake in the study of children's interactions with dogs. As mentioned, dogs bring much happiness into the 40% of homes with children that include dogs. On the other hand, children are the most common victims of dog bites (Centers for Disease Control, 2003). Schmitt (1998) likened the emotional trauma that a child of 5 to 11 years experiences as a consequence of dog bite "to an unarmed adult sustaining a bear bite" (p. 1174). Thus, it is most troubling that we have been unable to uncover any studies detailing the nature of dog and child interaction. We have been unable to find any studies specifically focused on the types of behaviors children emit in the presence of dogs or of the behaviors dogs emit in the presence of children. There are several different approaches that could be applied to this problem.

One approach would be to take techniques used in developmental psychology for the study of conspecific interaction to this heterospecific situation. Thus, a child or children might be placed in a room with a dog and their interactions observed through a one-way mirror or by video. The dog would be carefully selected to minimize any risk to the children; indeed, the dog could even be trained to emit particular behaviors to measure the children's reaction to different scenarios. In effect, the dog would become a canine confederate of the experimenter. Such a technique could be used analytically to gain knowledge of the typical behavior of children toward dogs in different circumstances, and it could be used prophylactically to identify, under safe circumstances, dangerous behaviors of specific children, which could then be rectified.

The methods described that have been used to study how dogs respond to human cues could be adapted for use with children. A child could be instructed to occupy the role that is traditionally viewed as that of the experimenter— pointing at one of two food containers, for example. The purpose of these studies would be to see how the dogs' responses differ when a child offers the gesture as compared to the usual scenario, in which an adult offers cues to the dog. Studies of this type would help uncover how dogs perceive children.

A deeper understanding of how dogs behave toward children, and children around dogs, could inform programs to educate children and dog owners to reduce the risk of dogs to children. This knowledge would increase the chances that a child's recollections of his or her time with dogs are among the richest, rather than the most traumatic. It also holds out the promise of reducing the large number of dogs that are rejected from human families each year, many of whom end up destroyed in shelters because their behavior is incompatible with human society (New et al., 2004).

REFERENCES

American Pet Products Manufacturers Association. (2008). Industry statistics and trends. Retrieved April 24, 2008, from http://www.appma.org.

American Veterinary Medicine Association. (2007). *U.S. pet ownership and demographics sourcebook*. Schaumburg, IL: Author.

Arambasic, G. K. L., Kuterovac-Jagodic, G., & Vidovic, V. V. (1999). Pet ownership and children's self-esteem in the context of war. *Anthrozoos, 12*, 218–223.

Avner, J. R., & Baker, M. D. (1991). Dog bites in urban children. *Pediatrics, 88*, 55–57.

Bentosela, M., Barrera, G., Jakovcevic, A., Elgier, A., & Mustaca, A. (2008). Effect of reinforcement, reinforcer omission and extinction on a communicative response in domestic dogs (*Canis familiaris*). *Behavioral Processes, 78*, 464–469.

Borchelt, P. L. (1983). Aggressive behavior of dogs kept as companion animals: Classification and influence of sex, reproductive status and breed. *Applied Animal Ethology, 10*, 45–61.

Brauer, J., Call, J., & Tomasello, M. (2004). Visual perspective taking in dogs. *Journal of Comparative Psychology, 119*(2), 145–154.

Brenoe, U. T., Larsgard, A. G., Johannessen, K. R., & Uldal, S. H. (2002). Estimates of genetic parameters for hunting performance traits in three breeds of gun hunting dogs in Norway. *Applied Animal Behaviour Science, 77*, 209–215.

Centers for Disease Control. (2003). Nonfatal dog bite-related injuries treated in hospital emergency departments—United States, 2001. *Morbidity and Mortality Weekly Report, No. 52*, 605–610. Retrieved December 20, 2008, from http://www.cdc.gov/mmwr/preview/mmwrhtml/mm5226a1.htm

Cooper, J. J., Ashton, C., Bishop, S., West, R., Mills, D. S., & Young, R. J. (2003). Clever hounds: Social cognition in the domestic dog (*Canis familiaris*). *Applied Animal Behavior Science, 81*, 229–244.

Coppinger, R., & Coppinger, L. (2001). *Dogs: A startling new understanding of canine origin, behavior and evolution*. Chicago, IL: Chicago University Press.

Daly, B., & Morton, L. L. (2006). An investigation of human–animal interactions and empathy as related to pet preference, ownership, attachment, and attitudes in children. *Anthrozoos, 19*, 113–127.

Dorey, N. R., Udell, M. A. R., & Wynne, C. D. L. (2009). When do domestic dogs, *Canis familiaris*, start to understand human points? The role of ontogeny in the development of interspecies communication. *Animal Behaviour, 79*, 37–41.

Duffy, D. L., Hsu, Y., & Serpell, J. A. (2008). Breed differences in canine aggression. *Applied Animal Behaviour Science, 114*, 441–460.

Freedman, D. G., King, J. A., & Elliot, O. (1961). Critical period in the social development of dogs. *Science, 133*, 1016–1017.

Gandhi, R. R., Liebman, M. A., Stafford, B. L., & Stafford, P. W. (1999). Dog bite injuries in children: A preliminary survey. *American Surgeon, 65*, 863–864.

Gásci, M., Miklosi, A., Varga, O., Topál, J., & Csanyi, V. (2004). Are readers of our face readers of our mind? *Journal of Animal Cognition, 7*, 144–153.

Gershman, K. A., & Sacks, J. J. (1994). Which dogs bite? A case-control study of risk factors. *Pediatrics, 93*, 913–924.

Guy, N. C., Luescher, U. A., Dohoo, S. E., Spangler, E., Miller, J. B., Dohoo, I. R., & Bate, L. A. (2001a). Demographic and aggressive characteristics of dogs in a general veterinary caseload. *Applied Animal Behaviour Science, 74*, 15–28.

Guy, N. C., Luescher, U. A., Dohoo, S. E., Spangler, E., Miller, J. B., Dohoo, I. R., & Bate, L. A. (2001b). Risk factors for dog bites to owners in a general veterinary caseload. *Applied Animal Behaviour Science, 74*, 29–42.

Hare, B., & Tomasello, M. (1999). Domestic dogs (*Canis familiaris*) use human and conspecific social cues to locate hidden food. *Journal of Comparative Psychology, 113*, 1–5.

Hare, B., Brown, M., Williamson, C., & Tomasello, M. (2002). The domestication of the social cognition in dogs. *Science, 298*, 1634.

Hart, B. L., & Miller, M. F. (1985). Behavioral profiles of dog breeds. *Journal of the American Veterinary Medical Association, 186*, 1175–1180.

Humane Society of the United States. (2006). U. S. pet ownership statistics. Available from http://www.hsus.org/pets/issues_affecting_our_pets/pet_overpopulation_and_ownership_statistics/us_pet_ownership_statistics.html

Itakura, S., Agnetta, B., Hare, B., & Tomasello, M. (1999). Chimpanzees use human and conspecific social cues to locate hidden food. *Developmental Science, 2*, 448–456.

Kaminski, J., Call, J., & Fischer, J. (2004). Word learning in a domestic dog: Evidence for 'fast mapping.' *Science, 304*, 1682–1683.

Kubinyi, E. V. Z., & Miklósi, A. (2007). Comparative social cognition: From wolf and dog to humans. *Comparative Cognition & Behavior Reviews, 2*, 26–46.

Lorenz, J. R., & Coppinger, L. (1986). Raising and training a livestock-guarding dog. *Oregon State University Extension Service: Extension Circular, 1238*, 1–8.

Luescher, A. U., & Reisner, I. R. (2008). Canine aggression toward familiar people: A new look at an old problem. *Veterinary Clinics Small Animal Practice, 38*, 1107–1130.

Miklosi, A. (2008). *Dog behavior, evolution and cognition*. New York, NY: Oxford University Press.

Miklósi, Á., Polgárdi, R., Topál, J., & Csányi, V. (1998). Use of experimenter-given cues in dogs. *Animal Cognition, 1*, 113–121.

Miklosi, A., Topal, J., & Csanyi, V. (2007). Big thoughts in small brains? Dogs as a model for understanding human social cognition. *Neuroreport, 18*, 467–471.

Miller, D., Staats, S. R., Pertlo, C., & Rada, K. (1996). Factors associated with the decision to surrender a pet to an animal shelter. *Journal of American Veterinary Medicine Association, 209*, 738–742.

Nagasawa, M., Kikusui, T., Onaka, T., & Ohta, M. (2009). Dog's gaze at its owner increases owner's urinary oxytocin during social interaction. *Hormones and Behavior, 55*, 434–441.

National Center for Injury Prevention and Control. (2008). WISQARS Leading Causes of Death Reports, 1999–2005: 10 Leading Causes of Death, United States. Retrieved May 2, 2008, from http://webappa.cdc.gov/cgi-bin/broker.exe. 5/2/08.

New, J. C., Kelch, W. J., Hutchison, J. M., Salman, M. D., King, M., Scarlett, J. M., & Kass, P. H. (2004). Birth and death rate estimates of cats and dogs in U.S. households and related factors. *Journal of Applied Animal Welfare Science, 7(4)*, 229–241.

O'Sullivan, E. N., Jones, B. R., O'Sullivan, K., & Hanlon, A. J. (2008). The management and behavioural history of 100 dogs reported for biting a person. *Applied Animal Behaviour Science, 114*, 149–158.

Paul, E. S., & Serpell, J. A. (1996). Obtaining a new pet dog: Effects on middle childhood children and their families. *Applied Animal Behaviour Science, 47*, 17–29.

Plutchik, R. (1971). Individual and breed differences in approach and withdrawal in dogs. *Behaviour, 40*, 301–311.

Povinelli, D. J., Reaux, J. E., Bierschwale, D. T., Allain, A. D., & Simon, B. B. (1997). Exploitation of pointing as a referential gesture in young children, but not adolescent chimpanzees. *Cognitive Development, 12*, 327–365.

Reisner, I. R., Erb, H., & Houpt, K. (1994). Risk factors for behavior-related euthanasia among dominant-aggressive dogs 110 cases (1989–1992). *Journal of American Veterinary Medicine Association, 205*, 855–863.

Reisner, I. R., Houpt, K. A., & Shofer, F. S. (2005). National survey of owner-directed aggression in English springer spaniels. *Journal of the American Veterinary Medicine Association, 227*, 1594–1603.

Reisner, I. R., Shofer, F. S., & Nance, M. L. (2007). Behavioral assessment of child-directed canine aggression. *Injury Prevention, 13*, 348–351.

Riedel, J., Schumann, K., Kaminski, J., Call, J., & Tomasello, M. (2008). The early ontogeny of human–dog communication. *Animal Behaviour, 75*, 1003–1014.

Sacks, J. J., Lockwood, R., Hornreich, J., & Sattin, R. W. (1996). Fatal dog attacks, 1989-1994. *Pediatrics, 97*, 891–895.

Sacks, J. J., Sinclair, L., Gilchrist, J., Golab, G. C., & Lockwood, R. (2000). Breeds of dogs involved in fatal human attacks in the United States between 1979 and 1998. *Journal of the American Veterinary Medical Association, 217,* 836–840.

Schalamon, J., Ainoedhofer, H., Singer, G., Petnehazy, T., Mayr, J., Kiss, K., & Hollwarth, M. E. (2006). Analysis of dog bites in children who are younger than 17 years. *Pediatrics, 117,* 374–379.

Schmitt, R. L., White, D. J., & Wallace, M. T. (1998). Injuries from dog bites. JAMA, *279,* 1174.

Scott, J. P., & Fuller, J. L. (1965). *Genetics and the social behavior of the dog.* Chicago, IL: University of Chicago Press.

Serpell, J. A., & Hsu, Y. (2005). Effects of breed, sex, and neuter status on trainability in dogs. *Anthrozoos, 18,* 196–207.

Shuler, C. M., Debess, E. E., Lapidus, J. A., & Hedberg, K. (2008). Canine and human factors related to dog bite injuries. *Journal of the American Veterinary Medical Association, 232,* 542–546.

Soproni, K., Miklósi, A., Topál, J., & Csanyi, V. (2002). Comprehension of human pointing gesture in dogs. *Journal of Comparative Psychology, 116,* 27–34.

Thompson, P. G. (1997). The public health impact of dog attacks in a major Australian city. *Medical Journal of Australia, 167,* 129–132.

Tomasello M., Call, J., & Gluckman, A. (1997). Comprehension of novel communicative signs by apes and human children. *Child Development,* 68(6), 1067–1080.

Udell, M. A. R., & Wynne, C. D. L. (2008). A review of domestic dogs' (*Canis familiaris*) human-like behaviors: Or why behavior analysts should stop worrying and love their dogs. *Journal of the Experimental Analysis of Behavior, 89,* 247–261.

Udell, M. A. R., Dorey, N. R., & Wynne, C. D. L. (2008). Wolves outperform dogs in following human social cues. *Animal Behaviour, 76,* 1767–1773.

Udell, M. A. R., Dorey, N. R., & Wynne, C. D. L. (2010). What did domestication do to dogs? A new account of dogs' sensitivity to human actions. Manuscript submitted for publication. *Biological Reviews of the Cambridge Philosophical Society, 85,* 327–345.

Udell, M. A. R., Giglio, R. F., & Wynne, C. D. L. (2008). Domestic dogs (*Canis familiaris*) use human gestures but not nonhuman tokens to find hidden food. *Journal of Comparative Psychology, 122,* 84–93.

U.S. Census Bureau. (n.d.). Table: S1101. Households and families. Dataset: 2006 American Community Survey. Available at http://factfinder.census.gov/servlet/STTable?_bm=y&-geo_id=01000US&-qr_name=ACS_2006_EST_G00_S1101&-ds_name=ACS_2006_EST_G00_&-_lang=en&-redoLog=false&-format=&-CONTEXT=st

Wells, D. L., & Hepper, P. G. (2000). Prevalence of behaviour problems reported by owners of dogs purchased from an animal rescue centre. *Applied Animal Behavior Science, 69,* 55–65.

Weiss, H. B., Friedman, D. I., & Coben, J. H. (1998). Incidence of dog bite injuries treated in emergency departments. *Journal of the American Medical Association, 279*, 51–53.

Wright, J. C. (1985). Severe attacks by dogs: Characteristics of the dogs, the victims, and the attack settings. *Public Health Reports, 100*, 55–61.

Wright, J. C. (1990). Reported dog bites: Are owned and stray dogs different? *Anthrozoos, 4*, 111–119.

Wynne, C. D. L., Udell, M. A. R., & Lord, K. A. (2008). Ontogeny's impacts on human–dog communication. *Animal Behaviour, 76*, e1–e4.

6

ANIMAL ABUSE AND DEVELOPMENTAL PSYCHOPATHOLOGY

FRANK R. ASCIONE AND MIKA MARUYAMA

> To the young child, there is no gap between his soul and that of animals.
> (Hall, 1904, p. 220)

While the authors of other chapters in this book explore the various dimensions of positive interactions between humans and animals and their potential benefits for human physical and psychological health, our task is to describe recent research findings related to cases where animals are abused by humans and their implications for mental health and developmental psychopathology. We discuss the challenges of defining and assessing animal abuse, as well as the relationship between animal abuse and conduct disorder.

Numerous reviews of the animal abuse literature are now available (e.g., Ascione, 2008; McPhedran, 2009; Petersen & Farrington, 2007) and reflect the increasing research attention to this phenomenon, especially within the past decade (see Figure 6.1[1]). We will not duplicate these research summaries but instead will highlight studies relevant to child mental health. It is our belief that progress in both the development of theory and the refinement of empirical research on animal abuse will be enhanced by developments in our ability to assess this important, yet often covert, form of antisocial behavior, a behavior commonly ignored in the research literature on violence. We trust

---

[1]We thank Shelby McDonald for preparing this figure.

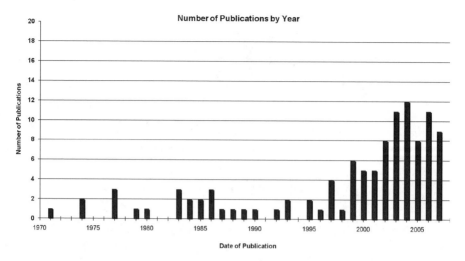

Figure 6.1. Frequency of animal-abuse related publications, 1971–2007. Literature Search [6.3.2008] using PsycINFO and Psychology and Behavioral Sciences Collection. Search terms: "cruel to animals" or "cruelty to animals" or "animal abuse."

that we will convince the reader that attention to animal abuse is relevant not only for the field of developmental psychopathology but also for sociology, criminology, social work, and child and animal welfare.

PRIOR APPROACHES TO DEFINITION AND ASSESSMENT

Currently, there is no universally agreed-upon definition of animal abuse or cruelty to animals. In the United States, state anticruelty statutes vary dramatically in language, content, and the species that are included, and they were developed from a law enforcement perspective. In Australia, Gullone and Clarke (2008) note that prevention-of-cruelty legislative acts also vary by state and territory. For example, three states define "animals" to include fish and crustaceans; the other three states and two territories do not. General conceptions of human cruelty are the subject of continuing dialogue (Nell, 2006), and the scope of our definitions of animal cruelty (individual, group, institutional, and societal) is the subject of debate (Munro, 2005). Our working definition of animal abuse, developed to serve empirical research, is "non-accidental, socially unacceptable behavior that causes pain, suffering, or distress to and/or the death of an animal" (Ascione & Shapiro, 2009). This definition permits the inclusion of both acts of commission and omission. The parallel to definitions of child maltreatment (which includes physical, sexual, and emotional/ psychological abuse, as well as various forms of neglect) is deliberate, but in some ways, defining animal abuse is a more challenging task. Veterinarians are now better able to document nonaccidental physical injuries to animals (Sinclair, Merck, & Lockwood, 2006), and they acknowledge animals' capacity for emotional suffering (McMillan, 2005). But our own definition of animal abuse does not specify the species of animal in question, a variable recently shown to be related to empathy (Westbury & Neumann, 2008). Humans vary in the extent of their circle of compassion (intrusive insects are killed, family pets are doted on), and the same human act may be injurious or lethal for one species of animal but inconsequential for another species. We have not resolved this dilemma in our own work (Pagani, Robustelli, & Ascione, 2008), but we assume it will continue to be a challenge to defining animal abuse in empirical studies.

One of the first formal listings of childhood antisocial behaviors that include reference to animal abuse was developed by Cyril Burt in 1925. Under symptoms of "anger," he noted, "cruelty to children or animals (with bodily injury)" and "cruelty to children or animals (without bodily injury)" (Burt, 1925, p. 14). Although we have not been able to document use of Burt's diagnostic system by other scientists, it was not until publication of the *Diagnostic and Statistical Manual of Mental Disorders* (3rd ed., revised; *DSM-III-R*; American Psychiatric Association, 1987) that "cruelty to animals" was added to the symptom list for conduct disorder. The symptom has thus far been retained in *DSM-IV* (American Psychiatric Association, 1994) and *DSM-IV-TR* (American Psychiatric Association, 2000).

In a report on the field trials for the development of *DSM-III-R*, Spitzer, Davies, and Barkley (1990) noted that, for the cruelty-to-animals symptom, a comparison of children diagnosed with conduct disorder and children without this diagnosis yielded an odds ratio of 5.07. The symptom has high specificity (.94) but low sensitivity (.23), values that are similar to those for the symptom of physical cruelty to people. A more recent study by Gelhorn, Sakai, Price, and Crowley (2007), using a retrospective assessment of adults, found an odds ratio of 4.6 for cruelty to animals when comparing adults who would have received a diagnosis of conduct disorder or antisocial personality disorder and adults who would not have received either of these diagnoses. Gelhorn et al. also reported high specificities (.82 for males; .68 for females) and low sensitivities (.22 for males; .05 for females) in their analyses. The item used to assess animal abuse was phrased as follows, "In your entire life, did you ever . . . hurt or be cruel to an animal or pet on purpose?"

A variety of assessment instruments now include one or more items related to animal abuse. A question about physical cruelty to animals is found in the Child Behavior Checklist (CBCL) parent report form (Achenbach, 1991) for children 4 to 16 years of age, the Achenbach-Connors Quay Behavior Checklist (ACQ; Achenbach, Howell, Quay, & Conners, 1991), the Interview for Antisocial Behavior (IAB; Kazdin & Esveldt-Dawson, 1986), and a recently developed computer-based assessment, the Dominic Interactive (Valla et al., 2002) for children 6 to 11 years of age. The Dominic Interactive uses a child self-report format, an advantage discussed later in this chapter. However, like the other assessments, it includes only one item that taps the animal-abuse symptom ("Have you ever hurt an animal on purpose?"). The limitations of single-item assessments are captured by Kruesi in this observation of a 12-year-old girl diagnosed with conduct disorder: "In response to the Diagnostic Interview for Children and Adolescents (DICA; Herjanic & Campbell, 1982) question, 'Have you ever injured or killed a small animal such as a cat or a squirrel just for fun?' the patient answered no. However, she then described having found a baby bird and throwing it in the air repeatedly to watch it attempt to fly, until it died. Parents noted that the child had mistreated her pet hamsters by attempting to cram them into confined spaces (e.g., the interior of toys)" (1989, p. 115).

The instruments described focus on the presence or absence of animal abuse, with the CBCL and ACQ querying respondents about whether the symptom has been present "sometimes" or "often" during a designated time period, for example, the past 6 months (as distinct from lifetime prevalence). The Interview for Antisocial Behavior, a parent-report assessment developed by Kazdin and Esveldt-Dawson (1986), includes a question about "being cruel to animals." If responded to affirmatively, parents are further queried on the severity of the behavior and how recently the problem has existed (6 months or less, more than 6 months, always). Another commonly used psychiatric assessment instrument for children 9 to 17 years of age, the Diagnostic Interview Scale for Children (DISC-IV; Shaffer & Fisher, 1996) goes further by assessing not only lifetime prevalence but also frequency, recency, and age of onset. The main question is phrased as follows: "Have you *ever* been physically cruel to an animal and hurt it on purpose?" If the response is affirmative, follow-up questions ask about the age of onset of such cruelty and the presence of the behavior in the past year and in the past 6 months. If 1-year prevalence was acknowledged, the interviewer asks whether the behavior occurred more than once, more than 5 times, or more than 10 times. The DISC-IV is available in both a parent-report form and a youth self-report form.

The availability of self-report assessments is a decided advantage, because there is empirical evidence that parents may underreport this symptom in their children (Offord, Boyle, & Racine, 1991), and other informants, such as teachers, may not have opportunities to observe this behavior in their students. Children may abuse animals covertly, and the evidence of such abuse (unlike, for example, evidence of fire setting) may not come to the attention of others.

In closing this section, we note that scant attention has been given to assessing children's sexual acting out with animals. Friedrich's (1997) Child

Sexual Behavior Inventory is a notable exception and includes one item phrased, "touches animals' sex parts." Parents and guardians of sexually abused children are more likely to endorse this item than are caregivers for nonabused children (Ascione, Friedrich, Heath, & Hayashi, 2003). We are not aware of any self-report assessments that address bestiality in young people; such measures are more commonly used with adult clinical and forensic samples (e.g., Simons, Wurtele, & Durham, 2008).

RECENT DEVELOPMENTS IN THE ASSESSMENT OF ANIMAL ABUSE

Because of the limitations of single-item assessments of animal abuse, one of us developed the Children and Animals Assessment Instrument (CAAI; Ascione, Thompson, & Black, 1997), a structured interview that can be administered to parents or children older than 4 years. The child version of the CAAI asks about animal abuse with the following question, "Can you remember a time when you were mean to a (pet, stray, wild, or farm) animal or hurt a (pet, stray, wild, or farm) animal?" A similar assessment, the Childhood Trust Survey on Animal Related Experiences, has been developed by Boat, Loar, and Phillips (2008). Both are lengthy assessments and have not yet been used widely. Other variations on structured interviews that include questions about animal abuse have been developed, such as the Physical and Emotional Tormenting Against Animals Scale (PET; Baldry, 2003); the Survey on Children's Relationships with Animals (Pagani et al., 2008); and the Children's Treatment of Animals Questionnaire (Thompson & Gullone, 2003). Several of these assessments tap abusive, as well as positive, behaviors toward animals.

As noted, the CAAI was developed to fill a void in the assessment of animal abuse in childhood and adolescence. It had the advantage of assessing abuse of various types of animals (pets, strays, wild, and farm animals), as well as assessing the frequency and severity of abuse, the child's affective (empathic or nonempathic) response to animal abuse, whether the abuse was perpetrated alone or with others, and whether it was perpetrated covertly or with no effort at concealment. It was also designed in two formats: a parent/guardian report form and a child self-report form. Although inter-rater agreement on scoring responses to the CAAI was acceptable, no other psychometric properties (e.g., internal consistency, test–retest reliability) were calculated.

Guymer, Mellor, Luk, and Pearse (2001) used the CAAI as the basis for developing their Children's Attitudes and Behavior Toward Animals (CABTA) assessment. The CABTA allows for a distinction to be made between what might be called "typical, normative cruelty" toward animals and more severe, malicious abuse. It also included fewer items than the CAAI, making it easier and less time consuming to administer and score. However, the CABTA was only designed as a parent report and would not capture incidents of abuse that were covertly committed.

In a study in Japan, we collected data from 853 students (in grades 2–5) from 10 elementary schools to investigate their attitudes toward animals (Maruyama, Ascione, & Nakagawa, 2005). Among the many surveys collected, one was used specifically to examine students' animal abuse experiences (i.e., intentional harm to animals), both as a perpetrator and a witness. Because of the sensitivity of the questions, only fourth and fifth graders were asked about their experiences of animal abuse for the past 6 months (n = 448). Students were asked about the following: (a) self as an abuser of socially valued animals (e.g., dog, cat); (b) self as an abuser of less socially valued animals (e.g., fish, insect); (c) self as a witness of a friend/family member's abusive behaviors of socially valued animals (e.g., dog, cat); and (d) self as a witness of a friend/family member's abusive behaviors of less socially valued animals (e.g., fish, insect).

For socially valued animals, 19.6 % of students reported their own intentional abusive experiences, and 44% reported witnessing such events. For less socially valued animals, 41.2 % of students reported intentional abusive experiences and 45.6% reported witnessing such abuse. Students who reported abusive experiences toward socially valued animals (M = 95.55, SD = 8.96) scored significantly lower (less humanely) on a measure assessing students' attitudes toward animals (Intermediate Assessment Scale; Ascione, 1988) than did students who reported no such experiences (M = 102.02, SD = 8.29), t (430) = 2.42, $p < .05$. Male students reported significantly more animal abuse episodes than did female students (χ^2 (1, n = 85) = 17.81, $p < .01$).

In our view, the most encouraging development in the assessment of animal abuse by children and adolescents is the construction and evaluation of the Children and Animals Inventory (CAI; Dadds et al., 2008; Dadds, Whiting, Bunn, Fraser, & Charlson, 2004) for use with 6- to 13-year-old children. The CAI addresses the same aspects of animal abuse that were identified in the development of the CAAI but distills these aspects into 13 dimensions, each of which receives a numerical score (0–4 for the first dimension, 0–2 for one other dimension, and 0–3 for the remaining ones) based on the parent or child's response. Total scores can range from 0 to 39. Animal abuse is described as either "hurting an animal on purpose" or treating animals "cruelly." The dimensions are as follows:

- Lifetime presence or absence of animal abuse and a frequency estimate if animal abuse is reported (two items)
- The category or categories of animal abused (wild, stray, farm, or pet)
- The number of different animals that were victims

- The presumed sentience level of the animal (from invertebrate to warm-blooded vertebrate)
- The period of time during which animal abuse occurred (1 month to over 6 months)
- The most recent occurrence of animal abuse (over 1 year ago to within the past 6 months)
- Whether the animal abuse occurred in the presence of peers or when the child was alone (a measure of covert behavior)
- Whether the animal abuse involved other human participants
- Whether the child attempted to conceal the behavior
- Whether the child expressed remorse or empathy, or was callous and uncaring about the animal victim (two items)
- Severity of abuse inflicted determined by scoring degree of injury to the animal based on the child's free response to an item asking the child to describe the manner of abuse and its physical effects on the animal

The CAI was first evaluated with a convenience sample of 36 Australian parent–child pairs; parents and children (6–13 years of age with an equal number of boys and girls) independently completed the CAI (Dadds et al., 2004). Internal consistency for the CAI was excellent (.88 for the parent version and .96 for the child self-report), as was 1-week test–retest reliability (parent r = .80, child r = .75). The relationship between parent reports and child self-reports yielded a correlation coefficient of .51. As predicted by earlier research (Offord et al., 1991), children's reports of animal abuse were higher than their parents' reports, and boys scored higher on the CAI than did girls. A second study in this same report involved a larger sample of children (N = 330) in the same age range and yielded similar results. One final study in this series was restricted to boys and their mothers. Total scores on the CAI child self-report (0, 1–12, or 13–22) were used to create three groups of 10 boys. Each child was observed interacting with a small caged mammal in a classroom context (measures were taken to ensure that the animal was not harmed). Children's interactions with the animal were scored along dimensions of cruel or nurturing behaviors (inter-rater agreement ranged from .77–.85). As expected, cruel and nurturing behaviors were inversely related (r = -.92). More important, scores on the CAI were correlated with actual behaviors toward the classroom pet. CAI parent scores correlated +.38 with cruelty and -.41 with nurturing; CAI child scores correlated +.55 with cruelty and -.52 with nurturing.

Tani (2007), in the first empirical study on this topic conducted in Japan, administered the Children and Animals Inventory (Dadds et al., 2004) to 125 junior high school students (aged 13–15 years, M = 13.8) and 61 offenders from a juvenile correctional facility (aged 15–19 years, M = 17.8) to investigate differences in histories of animal cruelty between these two groups. Approximately half of the juvenile offender group had been incarcerated in the correctional facility more than twice and had criminal histories. Tani categorized criminal activities into two categories: violent crimes (murder, bodily injury, violent attack, rape, robbery with force, threat of violence, and interruption of police investigation) and nonviolent crimes (other criminal activities, such as robbery, illegal drug use, violating traffic regulations).

Tani (2007) found that 41.6% of junior high school students and 65.5% of juvenile offenders reported having had experiences of animal cruelty. For the juvenile offenders, 54.5% who had committed nonviolent crimes reported animal cruelty experiences, and 78.6% who had committed violent crimes reported animal cruelty experiences. Juveniles who committed violent crimes reported significantly more experiences of animal cruelty than did other juveniles ($\chi^2 = 12.924$, $p < .005$). This finding indicates that juveniles who committed violent crimes were twice as likely to have had experiences of animal cruelty compared with junior high school students. Although differences between types of animals the two groups reported abusing were not significant, junior high school students frequently reported abusing frogs (53.1%), whereas juvenile offenders reported abusing birds (30.0%). Additionally, juvenile offenders were twice as likely to abuse socially valued animals, such as dogs, cat, or birds, than were junior high school students ($\chi^2 = 33.88$. $p < .005$). Both groups reported that they had engaged in animal cruelty in elementary schools (60.5% of junior high school students, 57.7% of juvenile offenders), and both reported having engaged in animal cruelty more than five times (42.4% of junior high school students and 40.3% of juvenile offenders).

There is much to recommend the use of the CAI in research on animal abuse with children and young adolescents. The instrument has excellent internal consistency, high test–retest reliability, and demonstrates convergent validity. Further support for use of the CAI comes from a recent study by Dadds, Whiting, and Hawes (2006). A community sample of 131 six- to 13-year-old boys and girls were assessed with the CAI as well as Frick and Hare's (2001) Antisocial Process Screening Device, which includes a subscale measuring callous and unemotional traits. The authors report that CAI scores for both boys and girls were significantly and positively related to callous/unemotional trait scores. Replication of this study with a clinical sample (for example, children diagnosed with conduct disorder [CD]) would be informative. Questions such a study could address include: Are CAI scores related to the severity of CD? Do CAI scores differ for children with early versus later onset CD? With what other CD symptoms are CAI scores most strongly correlated?

Before concluding this section on assessment issues, we will briefly discuss measures that ask about children's *exposure to* animal abuse perpetrated by others. Studies of children's exposure to intimate partner violence (e.g., Fantuzzo & Fusco, 2007) and to community or neighborhood violence (e.g.,

Brandt, Ward, Dawes, & Flisher, 2005) are common, but assessing the impact on young people of exposure to animal abuse is in its infancy. Retrospective studies of adults suggest that such exposure may be related to perpetrating animal abuse, but the direction of this relation is, as yet, undetermined. For example, Henry (2004b) found that exposure to animal abuse was reported by 64.9% of men and 39.1% of women. Those exposed to animal abuse were more likely to admit to having abused animals (25.6%) than were those not so exposed (9.6%). The perpetration rate for animal abuse was higher (32%) if exposure to animal abuse first occurred before age 13 years than if it occurred later (11.5%). In an intriguing sex difference, Henry reports that scores on a measure of humane attitudes toward animals were lower (i.e., less humane) for men exposed to animal abuse (than for men not exposed) but higher for women exposed to animal abuse (than for women not exposed).

Two similar studies enlisted the participation of incarcerated men. Merz-Perez and Heide (2004) found that violent and nonviolent criminals (N = 50 in each group) reported comparable rates of exposure to animal abuse, but nonviolent criminals expressed greater remorse about such exposure. Hensley and Tallichet (2005) studied 261 incarcerated men and reported a correlation coefficient of .30 between witnessing and perpetrating animal abuse. The younger the age at which animal abuse was witnessed, the younger the age at which animal abuse was first perpetrated (r = .49).

Assessments of exposure to animal abuse are embedded in several of the animal abuse instruments mentioned in this chapter. Exposure to animal abuse is included in the CAAI (Ascione et al., 1997). The Children's Observation and Experiences with Pets (COEP, Ascione et al., 2007) was designed to query children at domestic violence shelters about their experiences with animal abuse, including exposure to abuse perpetrated by others. However, both of these studies involved relatively small samples, and we are not aware of any other studies that have used these instruments to assess the prevalence of such exposure.

Baldry's (2003) PET, which includes questions about exposure to animal abuse, was used in a survey of more than 1,300 school children between the ages of 9 and 17 years who resided in Rome, Italy. Reports of exposure to animal abuse were as follows: abuse perpetrated by peers, 63.7%; by nonparental adults, 60.9%; by mothers, 5.1%; by fathers, 9%. Echoing the results of the previously cited studies with adults, exposure to animal abuse correlated with perpetration of animal abuse. A follow-up study (Baldry, 2005) with 532 Roman children between 9 and 12 years of age yielded similar findings. Exposure to animal abuse perpetrated by others was reported by 70.1% of boys and 60.3% of girls. Children exposed to animal abuse (or to parental intimate partner violence) were about three times more likely than nonexposed children to admit to engaging in animal abuse.

Pagani, Robustelli, and Ascione (2007) reported the responses of 800 Italian young people (9- to 18-year-old individuals). Exposure to "socially unacceptable" animal abuse was reported by 65% of respondents. Regarding their emotional response to such exposure, girls were significantly more likely to report feeling "very sorry" (65%) than were boys (36%). However, in this study, perpetration of animal abuse was not related to exposure to animal abuse. Despite these provocative findings, we know little about the developmental sequencing of exposure to and perpetration of animal abuse.

Thompson and Gullone (2006) assessed perpetrating and witnessing animal abuse in a sample of 281 Australian 12- to 18-year-old individuals. Respondents were asked if they had witnessed animal abuse and, if so, how often and who had been the perpetrator (strangers versus relatives or friends). Of these adolescents, 77.5% reported witnessing animal abuse; perpetrating animal abuse was higher for these adolescents than for adolescents who had not witnessed animal abuse.

An encouraging development related to this issue is the recent release of the Children's Exposure to Domestic Violence Scale (CEDV; Edleson, Johnson, & Shin, 2007). Although the CEDV was specifically designed to be used with 10- to 16-year-old children whose mothers were victims of intimate partner violence, it does contain one item related to animal abuse. Respondents are asked, "How often has your mom's partner hurt, or tried to hurt, a pet in your home on purpose?" The scale authors report that, in a study of 65 young people, 9 (13.8%) said that this had sometimes occurred (note that this percentage may be an underestimate because young people were not screened for the presence of a pet or pets in their homes). Of these children, two saw the outcome of the abuse, one heard about it afterward, one heard it as it was occurring, and five saw the abuse and were near when it occurred. Were this scale to become widely used in domestic violence research, we would have an additional source of data about young people's exposure to animal abuse (EAA), albeit in a clinical context. Used in conjunction with assessments of intimate partner violence (IPV) victims, numerous research questions become evident. Is the severity of IPV related to EAA? Is the form of IPV (physical, sexual, and/or emotional) related to EAA? Is the mental health of children who are exposed to both IPV and animal abuse more severely compromised than that of children exposed only to IPV? Is EAA in the context of IPV related to risk for or existing child maltreatment? (See Ascione, 2009, and Ascione & Shapiro, 2009, for a discussion of these issues.)

Not only is defining and assessing animal abuse a continuing challenge, but also assessing the motivations for perpetrating such abuse warrants more careful analysis (Ascione, 2005: Tallichet, Hensley, & Singer, 2005). As noted by Pinizzotto (2008, p. x), "Recording an incident of animal abuse without clear definitions and criteria and without an understanding of the context in which the incident occurred and the physical and emotional effects it had on the individual might well be meaningless."

RESEARCH FINDINGS ON ANIMAL ABUSE WITH CHILDREN AND ADOLESCENTS

Reviews of research on animal abuse and its relation to child and adolescent development are now available (Ascione, 2005; 2008). In this final section of the chapter, we highlight numerous recent research studies that illustrate the potential value of incorporating animal abuse variables when studying the mental health characteristics and psychological development of children and adolescents. These studies include both normative samples as well as samples where developmental psychopathology may be indicated. We close with several recommendations for future research.

Animal Abuse and Empathy

Dadds et al. (2008) used CAI scores to assign 6- to 12-year-old boys to three groups: low CAI (N = 10), medium CAI (N = 10), and high CAI (N = 8). These 28 boys also received scores on a measure of empathy and participated in a behavioral assessment in which cruel behavior toward a caged mouse was observed. Cruel behavior scores correlated more highly with total empathy scores (-.31) and the subscale on affective empathy (-.35) than with the cognitive subscale (-.12; see Henry, 2006, for a similar study with adults).

Animal Abuse and Bullying

Using self-reports, Gullone and Robertson (2008) studied 241 twelve- to 16-year-old children, assessing both witnessing and perpetrating animal abuse (using Baldry's PET scale), as well as perpetrating bullying. Multiple regression analysis revealed that witnessing animal abuse was a significant predictor of engaging in both animal abuse and in bullying.

Animal Abuse and Exposure to Intimate Partner Violence

Currie (2006) studied 47 mothers who self-identified as victims of domestic violence and had received counseling and 45 mothers who were not victims of domestic violence. All mothers were selected on the basis of having children in the 5- to 17-year-old age range. Based on maternal reports on the CBCL, Currie reported that children of abused mothers were nearly three times more likely to have been cruel to animals than were children of nonabused mothers (17% vs. 7%, odds ratio = 2.95). It should be noted that the reported percentages may be underestimates because neither the children's access to animals nor their pet ownership was assessed. In addition, exposure to animal abuse perpetrated by others was not measured (Ascione et al., 2007; see Ascione, 2007, for a review).

Animal Abuse and Sibling Violence

In Scotland, Khan and Cooke (2008) interviewed 91 male and 20 female offenders who were between 10 and 19 years old. The authors developed and used a measure of severe intersibling violence (SISV) that assessed the form and severity of such violence (dichotomized as violence with or without a weapon). Background and historical variables were also assessed with the SISV (Khan, 2005). Questions related to animal abuse were as follows: "If you are, or when you were aged 17 years old or younger, did you hurt animals? (if YES) Do you know why you did this? How did you feel when doing it? How old were you when you first did this? How often did you do this?" With regard to sibling violence, inflicting minor injuries was reported by 31.5% of the sample and inflicting serious injuries by 36%. Multiple regression analysis revealed a strong relation between animal abuse (derived from interview questions) and sibling violence that involved a weapon. For sibling violence perpetrated without a weapon, animal abuse again emerged as a significant, albeit weaker, predictor.

Animal Abuse and Child Maltreatment

One hundred boys, ages 8 to 17 years, in residential treatment for conduct disorder were enlisted for a study by Duncan, Thomas, and Miller (2005). The boys were recruited in such a manner that half the boys had a history of animal cruelty and the other half did not. This grouping was based on symptoms noted during assessments for conduct disorder. Boys whose symptoms included animal cruelty were significantly more likely to have been physically abused, sexually abused, or exposed to intimate partner violence (as assessed from chart reviews) than were boys without animal cruelty.

Animal Abuse and the Experiences of Therapists

Schaefer, Hays, and Steiner (2007) received replies from 174 practicing therapists (34% response rate) whose backgrounds included psychotherapy or clinical counseling or child clinical psychology. They were asked to report on their experiences with clients, within the past 5 years, in which animal abuse issues emerged. Overall, 28% had encountered animal abuse issues. Of these, one in five (21%) described cases in which a child or adolescent was the perpetrator of animal abuse. Most of these clinicians admitted that questions about animal abuse were not a routine part of their initial client assessments.

AN AGENDA FOR FUTURE RESEARCH

We close by offering suggestions for future empirical research, suggestions we hope will advance our understanding of the etiology, developmental trajectories, and predictive value of animal abuse. This understanding could inform efforts to prevent and intervene in cases of animal abuse, a form of antisocial behavior that continues to be relevant for our understanding of mental health in childhood and adolescence.

It is unlikely that there will ever be agreement on a single definition of "cruelty to animals". We suggest that the term "animal abuse" be adopted instead and that operational definitions of this term include, at a minimum, the types of abuse that humans can inflict on animals, the type of harm that animals may experience, and specification of the species of animals included as potential victims. We believe that the CAI comes closest to meeting this requirement and that it should be more widely used. Several other animal abuse assessments are now available (e.g., the CAAI, CABTA, and PET); their existence is an indicator of increased attention to the challenging task of assessing this behavior. However, these assessments have different formats and content. To more effectively compare results across studies, agreement on (or, at least, specification of) the following dimensions of animal abuse is encouraged (this is not meant to be an exhaustive list):

- Is lifetime prevalence being measured, or does the assessment cover a particular time period (e.g., past 6 months? 12 months? 2 years?)?
- Is there a method for assessing the age of onset of animal abuse?
- Is animal abuse defined as a threat of harm or as actual harm to an animal?
- Does the assessment include measuring the frequency of the behavior? Does it include a scale to estimate the severity of animal abuse?
- Is there a process for obtaining information on the possible motivations for and likely reinforcers associated with the behavior?

The inclusion of "cruelty to animals" among the symptoms of conduct disorder was surely a diagnostic advance. Although the meaning of other symptoms in the conduct disorder list may be self-evident (e.g., setting fires, vandalism, stealing with confrontation of a victim), "cruelty" remains open to subjectivity and the personal interpretation of the diagnostician and the person being diagnosed. We recommend that if "cruelty to animals" is retained in future revisions of the *DSM*, it be defined more objectively and that examples of behaviors that would be considered "cruel" be listed as a guide.

Although the assessment of animal abuse will continue to be embedded in various child behavior problem checklists (such as the CBCL and Dominic Interactive) and given the concerns we've raised about single-item assessments of animal abuse, we encourage researchers who have gathered data with these checklists to disaggregate scores for this item and make those data available to other researchers for secondary analyses.

A few studies have now examined animal abuse in the context of developing subtypes of conduct disorder. These subtypes include those based on symptom severity, early versus late onset, and the presence of callous/unemotional traits. As is clear from specificities and sensitivities, young people diagnosed with conduct disorder do not all display animal abuse, and young people who display animal abuse do not all receive conduct disorder diagnoses. It will be useful to examine whether animal abuse co-occurs with other particular symptoms of conduct disorder (e.g., lying to "con" others, fire setting, bullying) and whether the pattern of a child's symptoms adds to the prognostic value of the diagnosis.

Dadds (2008) has offered numerous essential considerations for future research, including the following: "Given that cruelty is a relatively low-occurrence behavior, we need longitudinal studies of children already showing cruel behaviors . . . (in which) the predictive power of early cruelty is compared with that afforded by more general aspects of the child's adjustment" (p. 124). Longitudinal designs would allow comparison of young people who engage in animal abuse at one developmental period and then desist from further abuse with those who persist in abuse across two or more developmental periods (Tapia, 1971). Prospective designs would also permit analysis of how animal abuse may be related to the development of other antisocial behaviors.

It is time for greater collaboration among researchers studying the development of antisocial behavior. Those of us who focus on animal abuse should consider joint projects with scientists who examine genetic and psychobiological aspects of violence and aggression (Dodge & Sherrill, 2007; Henry, 2004a; Raine et al., 2006; Stoff & Susman, 2005), bullying (Smith, Pepler, & Rigby, 2004), fire setting (Becker, Stuewig, Herrera, & McCloskey, 2004; Dadds & Fraser, 2006; Kolko, 2002), prodromal aspects of psychopathy (Kotler & McMahon, 2005; Lahey & Waldman, 2007), and approaches to violence prevention (Farrington & Coid, 2003; Lutzker, 2005).

Fernando Tapia (1971), the author of what we believe was the first empirical analysis of animal abuse and developmental psychopathology, has noted, "I still feel that the psychopathology of these interesting children needs further unraveling" (personal communication, June 22, 1990). Now, nearly 20 years later, Tapia's observation still rings true.

REFERENCES

Achenbach, T. M. (1991). *Manual for the Child Behavior Checklist/4-18 and 1991 Profile*. Burlington: University of Vermont Department of Psychiatry.

Achenbach, T. M., Howell, C. T., Quay, H. C., & Conners, C. K. (1991). National survey of problems and competencies among four- to sixteen-year-olds. *Monographs of the Society for Research in Child Development*, 56(3), 1–131.

American Psychiatric Association. (1987). *Diagnostic and statistical manual of mental disorders* (3rd ed., rev.). Washington, DC: Author.

American Psychiatric Association. (1994). *Diagnostic and statistical manual of mental disorders* (4th ed.). Washington, DC: Author.

American Psychiatric Association. (2000). *Diagnostic and statistical manual of mental disorders* (4th ed., text rev.). Washington, DC: Author.

Ascione, F. R. (1988). *The Intermediate Attitude Scale*. Logan: Utah State University.

Ascione, F. R. (2005). *Children and animals: Exploring the roots of kindness and cruelty*. West Lafayette, IN: Purdue University Press.

Ascione, F. R. (2007). Emerging research on animal abuse as a risk factor for intimate partner violence. In K. Kendall-Tackett & S. Giacomoni (Eds.), *Intimate partner violence* (pp. 3.1–3.17). Kingston, NJ: Civic Research Institute.

Ascione, F. R. (Ed.). (2008). *International handbook of animal abuse and cruelty: Theory, research, and application*. West Lafayette, IN: Purdue University Press.

Ascione, F. R. (2009). Examining children's exposure to violence in the context of animal abuse: A review of recent research. In A. Linzey (Ed.), *The link between animal abuse and human violence* (pp. 106–126). East Sussex, England: Sussex Academic Press.

Ascione, F. R., Friedrich, W. N., Heath, J., & Hayashi, K. (2003). Cruelty to animals in normative, sexually abused, and outpatient psychiatric samples of 6- to 12-year-old children: Relations to maltreatment and exposure to domestic violence. *Anthrozoös, 16*, 194–212.

Ascione, F. R., & Shapiro, K. J. (2009). People and animals, kindness and cruelty: Research directions and policy implications. *Journal of Social Issues, 65*, 569–587.

Ascione, F. R., Thompson, T. M., & Black, T. (1997). Childhood cruelty to animals: Assessing cruelty dimensions and motivations. *Anthrozoös, 10*, 170–177.

Ascione, F. R., Weber, C. V., Thompson, T. M., Heath, J., Maruyama, M., & Hayashi, K. (2007). Battered pets and domestic violence: Animal abuse reported by women experiencing intimate violence and by non-abused women. *Violence Against Women, 13*, 354–373.

Baldry, A. C. (2003). Animal abuse and exposure to interparental violence in Italian youth. *Journal of Interpersonal Violence, 18*, 258–281.

Baldry, A. C. (2005). Animal abuse among preadolescents directly and indirectly victimized at school and at home. *Criminal Behaviour and Mental Health, 15*, 97–110.

Becker, K. D., Stuewig, J., Herrera, V. M., & McCloskey, L. A. (2004). A study of firesetting and animal cruelty in children: Family influences and adolescent outcomes. *Journal of the American Academy of Child and Adolescent Psychiatry, 43,* 905–912.

Boat, B. W., Loar, L., & Phillips, A. (2008). Collaborating to assess, intervene, and prosecute animal abuse: A continuum of protection for children and animals. In F. R. Ascione (Ed.), *The international handbook of animal abuse and cruelty: Theory, research, and application* (pp. 393–422). West Lafayette, IN: Purdue University Press.

Brandt, R., Ward, C. L., Dawes, A., & Flisher, A. J. (2005). Epidemiological measurement of children's and adolescents' exposure to community violence: Working with the current state of the science. *Clinical Child and Family Psychology Review, 8,* 327–342.

Burt, C. (1925). *The young delinquent.* New York, NY: D. Appleton and Co.

Currie, C. L. (2006). Animal cruelty by children exposed to domestic violence. *Child Abuse and Neglect, 30,* 425–435.

Dadds, M. R. (2008). Conduct problems and cruelty to animals in children: What is the link? In F. R. Ascione (Ed.), *The international handbook of animal abuse and cruelty: Theory, research, and application* (pp. 111–131). West Lafayette, IN: Purdue University Press.

Dadds, M. R., & Fraser, J. A. (2006). Fire interest, fire setting and psychopathology in Australian children: A normative study. *Australian and New Zealand Journal of Psychiatry, 40,* 581–586.

Dadds, M. R., Hunter, K., Hawes, D. J., Frost, A. D. J., Vassallo, S., Bunn, P., Merz, S., & El Masry, Y. (2008). A measure of cognitive and affective empathy in children using parent ratings. *Child Psychiatry and Human Development, 39,* 111–122.

Dadds, M. R., Whiting, C., Bunn, P., Fraser, J., & Charlson, J. (2004). Measurement of cruelty in children: The Cruelty to Animals Inventory. *Journal of Abnormal Child Psychology, 32,* 321–334.

Dadds, M. R., Whiting, C., & Hawes, D. J. (2006). Associations among cruelty to animals, family conflict, and psychopathic traits in childhood. *Journal of Interpersonal Violence, 21,* 411–429.

Dodge, K. A., & Sherrill, M. R. (2007). The interaction of nature and nurture in antisocial behavior. In D. J. Flannery, A. T. Vazsonyi, & I. D. Waldman (Eds.), *The Cambridge handbook of violent behavior and aggression* (pp. 215–242). New York, NY: Cambridge University Press.

Duncan, A., Thomas, J. C., & Miller, C. (2005). Significance of family risk factors in development of childhood animal cruelty in adolescent boys with conduct problems. *Journal of Family Violence, 20,* 235–239.

Edleson, J. L., Johnson, K. K., & Shin, N. (2007). *Children's Exposure to Domestic Violence Scale.* St. Paul: Minnesota Center against Domestic Violence.

Fantuzzo, J., & Fusco, R. (2007). Children's direct sensory exposure to substantiated domestic violence crimes. *Violence and Victims, 22,* 158–171.

Farrington, D. P., & Coid, J. W. (Eds.). (2003). *Early prevention of adult antisocial behaviour*. Cambridge, England: Cambridge University Press.

Frick, P. J., & Hare, R. (2001). *Antisocial process screening device*. North Tonawanda, NY: Multi-Health Systems.

Friedrich, W. N. (1997). *Child sexual behavior inventory: Professional manual*. Odessa, FL: Psychological Assessment Resources.

Gelhorn, H. L., Sakai, J. T., Price, R. K., & Crowley, T. J. (2007). DSM-IV conduct disorder criteria as predictors of antisocial personality disorder. *Comprehensive Psychiatry, 48*, 529–538.

Gullone, E., & Clarke, J. P. (2008). Animal abuse, cruelty, and welfare: An Australian perspective. In F. R. Ascione (Ed.), *The international handbook of animal abuse and cruelty: Theory, research, and application* (pp. 305–334). West Lafayette, IN: Purdue University Press.

Gullone, E., & Robertson, N. (2008). The relationship between bullying and animal cruelty behaviours in Australian adolescents. *Journal of Applied Developmental Psychology, 29*, 371–379.

Guymer, E. C., Mellor, D., Luk, E. S. L., & Pearse, V. (2001). The development of a screening questionnaire for childhood cruelty to animals. *Journal of Child Psychology and Psychiatry, 42*, 1057–1063.

Hall, G. S. (1904). *The psychology of adolescence* (Vol. 2). New York, NY: D. Appleton and Co.

Henry, B. C. (2004a). The relationship between animal cruelty, delinquency, and attitudes toward the treatment of animals. *Society and Animals, 12*, 185–207.

Henry, B. C. (2004b). Exposure to animal abuse and group context: Two factors affecting participation in animal abuse. *Anthrozoös, 17*, 290–305.

Henry, B. C. (2006). Empathy, home environment, and attitudes toward animals in relation to animal abuse. *Anthrozoös, 19*, 17–34.

Hensley, C., & Tallichet, S. E. (2005). Animal cruelty motivations: Assessing demographic and situational influences. *Journal of Interpersonal Violence, 20*, 1429–1443.

Herjanic, B., & Campbell, W. (1982). Differentiating psychiatrically disturbed children on the basis of a structured interview. *Journal of Child Abnormal Psychology, 10*, 173–189.

Kazdin, A. E., & Esveldt-Dawson, K. (1986). The interview for antisocial behavior: Psychometric characteristics and concurrent validity with child psychiatric inpatients. *Journal of Psychopathology and Behavioral Assessment, 8*, 289–303.

Khan, R. (2005). *Severe inter-sibling violence (SISV) perpetration in young offenders and anti social youths: Implications for valid risk assessments*. Unpublished doctoral dissertation, Glasgow Caledonian University, Scotland.

Khan, R., & Cooke, D. J. (2008). Risk factors for severe inter-sibling violence: A preliminary study of a youth forensic sample. *Journal of Interpersonal Violence, 23*, 1513–1530.

Kolko, D. (Ed.). (2002). *Handbook on firesetting in children and youth*. New York, NY: Academic Press.

Kotler, J. S., & McMahon, R. J. (2005). Child psychopathy: Theories, measurement, and relations with development and persistence of conduct problems. *Clinical Child and Family Psychology Review, 8,* 291–325.

Kruesi, M. J. P. (1989). Cruelty to animals and CSF 5HIAA. *Psychiatry Research, 28,* 115–116.

Lahey, B. B., & Waldman, I. D. (2007). Personality dispositions and the development of violence and conduct problems. In D. J. Flannery, A. T. Vazsonyi, & I. D. Waldman (Eds.), *The Cambridge handbook of violent behavior and aggression* (pp. 260–287). New York, NY: Cambridge University Press.

Lutzker, J. R. (Ed.). (2005). *Preventing violence: Research and evidence-based intervention strategies.* Washington, DC: American Psychological Association.

Maruyama, M., Ascione, F. R., & Nakagawa, M. (2005, August). *The effects of animals in the classroom on children's empathy in Japanese elementary schools.* Paper presented at the 55th Annual Meeting of the Society for the Study of Social Problems, Philadelphia, PA.

McMillan, F. D. (2005). Emotional maltreatment in animals. In F. D. McMillan (Ed.), *Mental health and well-being in animals* (pp. 167–179). Ames, IA: Blackwell Publishing.

McPhedran, S. (2009). Animal abuse, family violence, and child wellbeing. *Journal of Family Violence, 24,* 41–52.

Merz-Perez, L., & Heide, K. M. (2004). *Animal cruelty: Pathway to violence against people.* Walnut Creek, CA: AltaMira Press.

Munro, J. (2005). *Confronting cruelty: Moral orthodoxy and the challenge of the animal rights movement.* Leiden, Netherlands: Brill.

Nell, V. (2006). Cruelty's rewards: The gratifications of perpetrators and spectators. *Behavioral and Brain Sciences, 29,* 211–224.

Offord, D. R., Boyle, M. H., & Racine, Y. A. (1991). The epidemiology of antisocial behavior in childhood and adolescence. In D. J. Pepler & K. H. Rubin (Eds.), *The development and treatment of childhood aggression* (pp. 31–54). Hillsdale, NJ: Lawrence Erlbaum Associates.

Pagani, C., Robustelli, F., & Ascione, F. R. (2007). Italian youths' attitudes toward and concern for animals. *Anthrozoös, 20,* 279–293.

Pagani, C., Robustelli, F., & Ascione, F. R. (2008). Animal abuse experiences described by Italian school-aged children. In F. R. Ascione (Ed.), *The international handbook of animal abuse and cruelty: Theory, research, and application* (pp. 247–268). West Lafayette, IN: Purdue University Press.

Petersen, M L., & Farrington, D. P. (2007). Cruelty to animals and violence to people. *Victims and Offenders, 2,* 21–43.

Pinizzotto, A. J. (2008). Foreword. In F. R. Ascione (Ed.), *The international handbook of animal abuse and cruelty: Theory, research, and application* (pp. ix–x). West Lafayette, IN: Purdue University Press.

Raine, A., Dodge, K., Loeber, R., Gatzke-Kopp, L., Lynam, D., Reynolds, C., Stouthamer-Loeber, M., & Liu, J. (2006). The Reactive-Proactive Aggression Questionnaire: Differential correlates of reactive and proactive aggression in adolescent boys. *Aggressive Behavior, 32*, 159–171.

Schaefer, K. D., Hays, K. A., & Steiner, R. L. (2007). Animal abuse issues in therapy: Survey of therapists' attitudes. *Professional Psychology: Research and Practice, 38*, 530–537.

Shaffer, D., & Fisher, P. W. (1996). *The diagnostic interview for children.* New York, NY: Columbia University.

Simons, D. A., Wurtele, S. K., & Durham, R. L. (2008). Developmental experiences of child sexual abusers and rapists. *Child Abuse and Neglect, 32*, 549–560.

Sinclair, L., Merck, M., & Lockwood, R. (Eds.). (2006). *Forensic investigation of animal cruelty: A guide for veterinary and law enforcement professionals.* Washington, DC: Humane Society Press.

Smith, R. K., Pepler, D., & Rigby, K. (Eds.). (2004). *Bullying in schools: How successful can interventions be?* Cambridge, England: Cambridge University Press.

Spitzer, R. L., Davies, M., & Barkley, R. A. (1990). The DSM-III-R field trial of disruptive behavior disorders. *Journal of the American Academy of Child and Adolescent Psychiatry, 29*, 690–697.

Stoff, D. M., & Susman, E. J. (Eds.). (2005). *Developmental psychobiology of aggression.* Cambridge, England: Cambridge University Press.

Tallichet, S. E., Hensley, C., & Singer, S. D. (2005). Unraveling the methods of childhood and adolescent cruelty to nonhuman animals. *Society and Animals, 13*, 91–107.

Tani, T. (2007). Seishounen ni okeru doubutsu gyakutai no jittai: Hikoushounen to taijinbouryoku tono kanrenwo chushin to shite. [Investigation of animal cruelty among youths: Focusing on relationships between juvenile offenders and interpersonal violence]. *Seishinigaku, 4*, 727–733.

Tapia, F. (1971). Children who are cruel to animals. *Child Psychiatry and Human Development, 2*, 70–77.

Thompson, K. L., & Gullone, E. (2003). The Children's Treatment of Animals Questionnaire [CTAQ]: A psychometric investigation. *Society and Animals, 11*, 1–15.

Thompson, K. L., & Gullone, E. (2006). An investigation into the association between the witnessing of animal abuse and adolescents' behavior toward animals. *Society and Animals, 14*, 221–243.

Valla, J. P., Kovess, V., Chan Chee, C., Berthiaume, C., Vantalon, V., Piquet, C., . . . Alles-Jardel, M. (2002). A French study of the Dominic Interactive. *Social Psychiatry and Psychiatric Epidemiology, 37*, 441–448.

Westbury, H. R., & Neumann, D. L. (2008). Empathy-related responses to moving film stimuli depicting human and non-human animal targets in negative circumstances. *Biological Psychiatry, 78*, 66–74.

III

HUMAN–ANIMAL
INTERACTION
AND HUMAN HEALTH

7

CHILDHOOD OBESITY AND HUMAN–ANIMAL INTERACTION

JO SALMON AND ANNA TIMPERIO

This chapter presents available evidence about human–animal inter-action and obesity and health among children. Childhood obesity and related health issues are currently recognized as significant public health concerns in many Western countries. Identifying influences on these dis-eases is critical for developing prevention strategies. Associations between animals and obesity and other health outcomes among children is an under-explored area of study that is currently gaining popularity. This chapter focuses mainly on the influence of dog ownership and dog walking on chil-dren's health and health behaviors. Some data based on adult populations is used where studies in child populations are lacking. Future research direc-tions are also suggested.

The authors wish to acknowledge individual support from the National Heart Foundation of Australia, Sanofi-Aventis, and the Victorian Health Promotion Foundation. The Children's Leisure Activities Study Survey was funded by the Foundation for Children, Australia, and analysis of data examining associations between dog ownership, physical activity and weight status in that study was funded by PetCare Advisory Service Inc.

139

RATES OF CHILD OBESITY AND OTHER
LIFESTYLE-RELATED DISEASE RISK FACTORS

Childhood and adolescent overweight and obesity and type 2 diabetes have increased at an alarming rate in the last 15 to 20 years. In particular, children from developed countries such as the United States, the United Kingdom and Europe, parts of Asia, and Australia have seen increases in overweight and obesity from 5% to 15% in the mid-1970s to 25% to 30% in 2000 (Lobstein, Baur, & Uauy, 2004). Type 2 diabetes and impaired glucose tolerance have also dramatically increased in prevalence among children and adolescents in the United States in recent years (American Diabetes Association [ADA], 2000). A study of more than 4,000 U.S. adolescents found that 11% of teenagers who reported not having diabetes had impaired fasting glucose levels ($\geq$100 mg/dl; Duncan, 2006).

Overweight and obese children are at high risk of becoming overweight adults and suffer increased morbidity during adulthood, even after weight loss (Deckelbaum & Williams, 2001; Dietz, 1998). Adiposity (weight, body mass index, and sum of skinfolds) persists from 13 years of age to young adulthood (21 years; Boreham et al., 2004). It is estimated that almost 30% of overweight children have impaired glucose tolerance, a precursor to type 2 diabetes (Sinha, Fisch, Teague, Tamborlane, & Banyas, 2002). Furthermore, young people who are overweight are more likely to have cardiovascular disease (CVD) risk factors, such as high cholesterol levels and elevated blood pressure (ADA, 2000). The Bogalusa Heart Study of 5- to 17-year-old children in the United States found that approximately 60% of overweight children in the study had at least one CVD risk factor, and one-quarter had two or more CVD risk factors (Freedman, Dietz, Srinivasan, & Berenson, 1999).

The Amsterdam Growth and Health study found that children who displayed CVD risk factors such as high cholesterol and adiposity at 13 to 16 years were highly likely to retain these risk factors at 21 to 27 years (Twisk, Kemper, Van Mechelen, & Post, 1997). There is also evidence that over a 25-year period there has been a substantial increase in conduct and emotional problems among adolescents (Collishaw, Maughan, Goodman, & Pickles, 2004). Therefore, primary prevention during early childhood years is critical not only for young people's physical and mental health in the short term but also for reducing the likelihood of poor health in adulthood.

INFLUENCES ON HEALTH AND HEALTH BEHAVIORS

Physical activity is an important health behavior that contributes to healthy growth. In particular, physical inactivity is an important risk factor in the development of overweight and obesity through its impact on creating a positive energy imbalance, and it is linked to all of the health issues previously outlined, including risk factors for CVD, type 2 diabetes, and psychosocial outcomes (e.g., self-esteem; Biddle, Gorely, & Stensel, 2004). Considering the long-term health impact of these conditions, physical activity during childhood is an important preventive health behavior. Several countries recommend that children and adolescents accumulate at least 60 minutes of moderate- to vigorous-intensity physical activity per day (Salmon & Timperio, 2007). However, compliance with these recommendations in the United Kingdom is estimated at 70% of boys and 60% of girls (London Department of Health, 2004), and a recent population survey in Australia suggests that only 38% of boys and 25% of girls met the recommendations on each of the days they were assessed (Australian Government Department of Health and Ageing, 2008).

With higher proportions of children and adolescents showing poor physical and mental health profiles, it is important to identify potentially modifiable factors that may be incorporated into population-based interventions and programs. Socioecological models of health posit that there are multiple levels of influence that explain engagement in health behaviors and ultimately health outcomes (Bronfenbrenner, 1979). These influences include at the individual level, for example, biological, demographic, and psychological influences; at the social/cultural level, friends, family members, teachers, employers, cultural mores/practices, and neighbors; at the physical environment level, the built environment, natural environment, and behavioral settings; and at the policy environment level, laws/legislation, and formal and informal policies.

The most important influences on child and adolescent health behavior originate in the home. Parents are the gatekeepers of children's health behaviors, and other members of the household (those living with the child or adolescent) are also an important source of influence. Apart from family members in the home, pets may also positively benefit young people's emotional and physical health. In particular, levels of attachment to dogs are higher than attachment to other pets, with dogs often being considered members of the family (Albert & Bulcroft, 1988). A study of 120 children from kindergarten through to fifth grade found that older children had stronger levels of attachment to their pets than did younger children (Melson, Peet, & Sparks, 1991). In single-parent families the attachment to dogs is higher than in two-parent families, and in single-child families, the attachment is higher than in families with more than one child (Albert & Bulcroft; Bodsworth, & Coleman, 2001).

Owning a pet may increase children's perceived social support in the family and can also increase children's opportunities to learn responsibility (i.e., they can learn from adults how to take care of, play with, and share their emotions with pets). Furthermore, through play and games, and general care of pets (e.g., taking the dog for a walk), these physical and emotional interactions may also benefit children's mental and physical health. The following section reviews evidence of associations between pet ownership and children's physical activity.

PET OWNERSHIP AND PHYSICAL ACTIVITY

Much of the evidence of associations between pet ownership and physical activity is from studies of adults' physical activity and dog ownership (Cutt, Giles-Corti, Knuiman, & Burke, 2007). Several studies have shown that dog ownership is associated with higher levels of physical activity among adults, primarily through dog walking (Bauman, Russell, Furber, & Dobson, 2001; Brown & Rhodes, 2006; Ham & Epping, 2006; Schofield, Mummery, & Steele, 2005).

A recent Canadian study (Brown & Rhodes, 2006) found adult dog owners walked almost twice as much (300 minutes/week) as those who didn't own dogs (168 minutes/week). A California study found that dog owners spent 19 minutes/week more time walking than did those who didn't own pets, whereas owning a cat had no impact on walking (Yabroff, Troiano, & Berrigan, 2008). In Australia, one study found that, even after adjusting for sociodemographic, neighborhood, social, and intrapersonal factors, dog owners were 57% more likely than those who didn't own dogs to meet physical activity recommendations for adult health (150 minutes/week) and 59% more likely to walk for at least 150 minutes/week (Cutt, Giles-Corti, Knuiman, Timperio, & Bull, 2008). Furthermore, during a 12-month period, adults who acquired a dog increased their walking by 36 minutes/week more than did those who continued to not own a dog (Cutt, Knuiman, & Giles-Corti, 2008). Two studies found little difference in the prevalence of meeting physical activity guidelines (Schofield et al., 2005) and in the objectively assessed (accelerometry) duration of moderate- to vigorous-intensity physical activity (MVPA) between dog owners and those who did not own dogs (Coleman et al., 2008); however, both studies found that dog owners who walked their dog were more likely to meet physical activity recommendations than were those who did not walk a dog.

Evidence of links between dog ownership and physical activity in children is limited. An Australian study (the Children's Leisure Activities Study Survey [CLASS]) conducted in 2001 surveyed approximately 1,200 children (aged 5–6 and 10–12 years) and their parents. CLASS data revealed that 53% of families owned a dog and that within these families 50% of 5- to 6-year-old children and 66% of 10- to 12-year-old children walked a dog at least once per

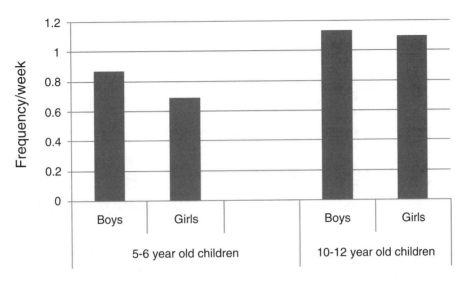

Figure 7.1. Frequency children walk a dog per week: from the Children's Leisure Activities Study (CLASS), 2001. Data from Salmon et al. (2010).

week (proxy-report survey by parents; Salmon, Timperio, Chu, & Veitch, in press). However, 51% of younger children and 38% of older children whose family owned a dog never walked a dog. Figure 7.1 shows that boys walked a dog more often (as reported by parents) than did girls, irrespective of age group.

The proportion of families reporting walking a dog as a family (defined as at least one parent/caregiver with the child) once per week or more also varied slightly by children's age and sex, with a higher proportion of parents with younger boys reporting doing this (Figure 7.2). The CLASS project found that, on average, young girls who owned a dog spent 29 minutes/day more in objectively assessed physical activity (using accelerometry) compared to those without a dog (Salmon et al., 2010). This comprises approximately 50% of daily physical activity recommendations for children in several countries (e.g., United States, United Kingdom, Australia). Among dog owners, for each single increase in frequency of walking the dog as a family, young girls spent 28 minutes per day and older girls spent 8 minutes per day more in objectively assessed physical activity. CLASS also found that dog ownership was significantly associated with children's frequency of total walking per week (approximately 1.3 more walking sessions per week among dog owners compared with nonowners), particularly among older girls. It is important to note that the physical activity benefits of dog ownership among children may not be limited to those accrued through dog walking. Playing with the dog informally (e.g., running around with the

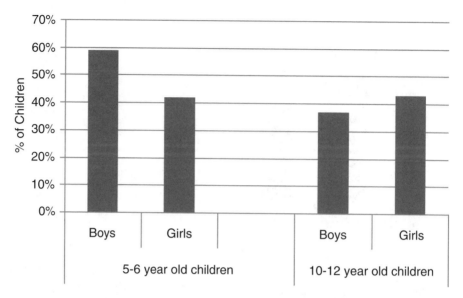

Figure 7.2. Proportion of children who walk a dog as a family once per week or more: from the Children's Leisure Activities Study (CLASS), 2001. Data from Salmon et al. (2010).

dog or throwing a ball or stick for the dog to fetch) may also be a means of accruing physical activity in this age group. However, there have not been any studies to date that have quantified the contribution of playing with dogs to physical activity.

These findings suggest that the promotion of dog ownership and dog walking in children and families may be a potentially effective strategy for promoting participation in physical activity for children. It is a concern that high proportions of dog owners do not appear to walk their dog regularly. Further research is required to examine why this is the case, particularly among children. Among adults, previous research suggests that dog owners who did not perceive that their dog provided motivation or social support to walk more, or who felt no "obligation" to walk the dog, were less likely to do so (Cutt, Giles-Corti, & Knuiman, 2008) and that lack of availability and access to public open spaces for dogs may also be a barrier (Cutt, Giles-Corti, Wood, Knuiman, & Burke, 2008).

One study among children and adolescents found that signage (e.g., dogs allowed only on leashes, dogs allowed off leashes, no dogs allowed) regarding dogs in the closest public open space was associated with almost 7 more minutes of MVPA/day in the after-school period (objectively assessed by accelerometry) among adolescent girls (Timperio, Giles-Corti, et al., 2008). Other studies have found that dog walking is more common in neighborhoods deemed to have enhanced walkability, that is, the neighborhood has grid-like street patterns, mixed land use (residential and commercial), and high-density housing (Coleman et al., 2008), and among women who perceive their neighborhood to have average levels of safety (Suminski, Poston, Petosa, Stevens, & Katzenmoyer, 2005). Given that traffic safety and stranger danger are key concerns that limit children's use of their neighborhood for play and physical activity (Carver, Timperio, & Crawford, 2008), walking with a dog may alleviate children's and/or their parents' concerns about safety by providing a sense of "protection" from personal harm. However, it should be noted that the presence of dogs may not always be positive; one study found that adolescents' concern about roaming dogs in the neighborhood was related to less walking/cycling for recreation among girls and for transport among boys (Carver et al., 2005).

One of the few studies to examine factors associated with young people walking their dog was the Nepean birth cohort study that examined just under 350 adolescents (mean age, 13 years) from Sydney, Australia (Carver et al., 2005). The study found that among adolescent girls, being concerned about roaming dogs in the neighborhood was inversely associated with frequency of walking a dog on weekends, whereas perceiving roads in the neighborhood as safe and the neighborhood as having good places for young people to be physically active was positively associated. More studies, particularly longitudinal studies, are required to elucidate the barriers to and facilitators of dog walking among children. An understanding of such factors is essential for informing the development of effective interventions promoting this behavior among children.

POTENTIAL ROLE OF DOG WALKING AND WEIGHT STATUS

Few epidemiologic studies have examined associations between pet ownership and young people's health. Among adults, dog or other pet ownership can provide psychological and physical health benefits (Serpell, 1991). Having a dog as a companion can enhance social interaction and social support (Allen, Blascovich, & Mendes, 2002; McNicholas & Collis, 2000; Robins, Sanders, & Cahill, 1991). An intervention study conducted by Allen et al. demonstrated that the presence of dogs reduces stress, resting heart rates, and blood pressure. A previous study of adult pet owners, mainly of dogs and cats, reported that owning a pet significantly reduced the systolic blood pressure and plasma triglycerides of the owners compared with nonowners of pets (Anderson, Reid, & Jennings, 1992). Several studies have examined the beneficial effects of human–animal interaction (HAI), but many focus on adults in clinical studies and are therefore beyond the scope of this chapter, which focuses on associations between interaction with pets and children's health at the population level.

A small number of studies have reported on associations between dog ownership, dog walking, and overweight and obesity. A U.S. study of more than 2,000 adults examined variations in weight status among households with and without dogs (Coleman et al., 2008). As shown in Figure 7.3, the prevalence of overweight was highest among dog owners who walked their dog more than 0 minutes per week (43%) compared to dog owners who were non-walkers and those who did not own a dog (both groups 34%). Interestingly, however, this trend was reversed for obesity. Overall, fewer dog owners who walked their dog (17%) were obese, compared with 28% of dog owners who were nonwalkers and 22% of nonowners of dogs (Coleman et al., 2008). Being a cross-sectional study, it may be that dog owners who are overweight walk their dog for weight-control purposes, although why this is not also the case for those who are obese is unclear. To elucidate such relationships, longitudinal or experimental research into the association between dog walking and weight status is needed.

The CLASS project (described earlier) also examined cross-sectional associations between dog ownership, dog walking, and overweight and obesity in children and their parents (Timperio, Salmon, et al., 2008). After adjusting analyses for potential confounders (sex, physical activity, mothers' and

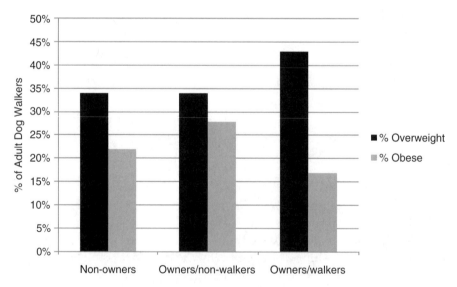

Figure 7.3. Weight status of adult dog walkers (derived from data reported in Coleman et al., 2008). Data from Salmon et al. (2010).

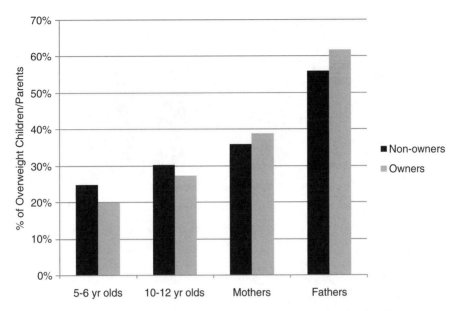

Figure 7.4. Proportion of children and their parents who were overweight/obese according to dog ownership: from the Children's Leisure Activities Study (CLASS), 2001. Data from Salmon et al. (2010).

fathers' weight status, maternal education, neighborhood socioeconomic status and clustering by school), younger children whose family owned a dog were 50% less likely to be overweight or obese than were those who did not own a dog (Figure 7.4).

Consistent with the study by Coleman and colleagues (2008), the CLASS study also found that mothers whose families walked the dog together were 30% more likely to be overweight or obese, suggesting that associations between dog walking and weight status among adults are not always in the anticipated direction (Timperio, Salmon, et al., 2008). However, there were no significant associations between the frequency with which the child walked a dog, frequency of dog walking as a family, and child's weight status (Figure 7.5).

CONCLUSIONS/FUTURE RESEARCH NEEDS

With the rates of overweight and obesity and other health conditions among children in many developed nations increasing, it has never been so urgent to identify potential opportunities to prevent further increases. Owning a pet, most particularly a dog, is cross-sectionally associated with physical

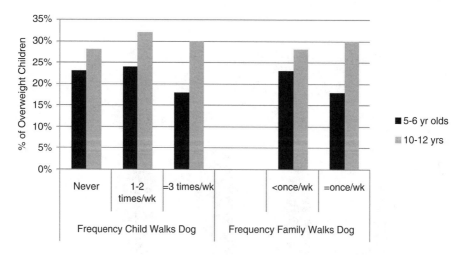

Figure 7.5. Proportion of children who were overweight/obese according to child dog walking and dog walking as a family: from the Children's Leisure Activities Study (CLASS), 2001. Data from Salmon et al. (2010).

activity (and walking) among adults and children. Cross-sectional associations with overweight and obesity have also been found but not always in the anticipated direction. Few studies have examined these associations at the population level, and the quality of evidence is weak. Longitudinal studies would at least provide some insights into temporal associations between pet ownership and human health. However, the most powerful level of evidence, the randomized controlled trial, is yet to be reported among adults or children. Additional studies with children and adolescents are needed. Longitudinal and experimental study designs should be prioritized for all population groups.

The cross-sectional studies of associations between dog ownership and physical activity have found that substantial proportions of dog owners never walk their dog. Identifying barriers and motivations for dog walking are required for informing the development of opportunities to promote child health through increased physical activity with pets. Some studies have examined this issue among adults (Coleman et al., 2008; Cutt, Giles-Corti, & Knuiman, 2008; Cutt, Giles-Corti, Wood, Knuiman, & Burke, 2008), finding that perceiving that the dog provides motivation and social support, access to dog-friendly open spaces, and a physical environment that supports walking (walkability) may influence dog walking. However, very few studies have explored the facilitators and barriers to dog walking among children and adolescents.

Understanding why dog ownership may promote higher levels of physical activity is important for the development of interventions. One incentive

148   SALMON AND TIMPERIO

may be owners' concerns about their dog's health. As it has with humans, the incidence of obesity in the pet population has increased, with 22% to 40% of the dog population overweight or obese (German, 2006). A study in Australia found that 41% of dogs could be classified as overweight or obese (McGreevy et al., 2005). As noted, being responsible for the health and well-being of a pet could be a motivating factor for walking or playing with the animal. Brown and Rhodes (2006) found that dog owners who felt an "obligation" to walk their dog were more likely to do so than were owners who felt no such obligation. Owners of a small dog or owners who reported not feeling attached to their dog also were less likely to take their dog for walks (Schofield et al., 2005). These are all potential factors important to consider in the development of interventions to promote dog walking and health. For children, it is also important to understand the nature of their interactions with their dog. For example, what is the nature of their play and what contribution does this make to overall physical activity and subsequent health outcomes?

Future studies should examine a range of individual, social, and environmental factors that may restrict or support dog walking among children. Factors that may be specific to children and youth include levels of parental and child confidence in the child's ability to handle the dog or to handle the dog in specific situations (e.g., while crossing roads, when off-lead), the type/breed and temperament of the dog and the level of dog obedience. Other factors that are specific barriers to children's mobility and physical activity within neighborhoods, for instance traffic volumes, the need to cross roads, and lack of crossing infrastructure (Davison & Lawson, 2006), may also come into play. However, parental concerns about some of these safety issues may be alleviated if the child is accompanied by the family dog.

Finally, although this chapter has focused primarily on dog ownership and dog walking, this is not the only source of HAI that may benefit children's health. Few studies have examined the importance of interaction with animals, other than dogs, on children's health in primary prevention or nonclinical populations. There is a long way to go in the field of HAI; the preliminary evidence of associations with children's health is currently limited by study design (cross-sectional), by being opportunistic, and focusing only on weight status. Future research should incorporate purpose-designed longitudinal or randomized controlled trial studies that examine interactions with a range of animals and various health outcomes among children.

REFERENCES

Albert, A., & Bulcroft, K. (1988). Pets, families, and the life course. *Journal of Marriage and the Family, 50,* 543–552.

Allen, K., Blascovich, J., & Mendes, W. B. (2002). Cardiovascular reactivity and the presence of pets, friends, and spouses: The truth about cats and dogs. *Psychosomatic Medicine, 64,* 727–739.

American Diabetes Association. (2000). Type 2 diabetes in children and adolescents. *Diabetes Care, 23,* 381–389.

Anderson, W. P., Reid, C. M., & Jennings, G. L. (1992). Pet ownership and risk factors for cardiovascular disease. *Medical Journal of Australia, 157,* 298–301.

Australian Government Department of Health and Ageing, Department of Agriculture Fisheries and Forestry, Australian Food and Grocery Council. (2008). *Australian National Children's Nutrition and Physical Activity Survey (2007).* Canberra, Australian Capital Territory: Author.

Bauman, A., Russell, S. J., Furber, S. E., & Dobson, A. J. (2001). The epidemiology of dog walking: An unmet need for human and canine health. *The Medical Journal of Australia, 175,* 631–634.

Biddle, S. J., Gorely, T., & Stensel, D. J. (2004). Health-enhancing physical activity and sedentary behavior in children and adolescents. *Journal of Sports Science, 22,* 679–701.

Bodsworth, W., & Coleman, G. J. (2001). Child-companion animal attachment bonds in single and two-parent families. *Anthrozoos, 14,* 216–223.

Boreham, C., Robson, P. J., Gallagher, A. M., Cran, G. W., Savage, J. M., & Murray, L. J. (2004). Tracking of physical activity, fitness, body composition and diet from adolescence to young adulthood: The Young Hearts Project, Northern Ireland. *International Journal of Behavioral Nutrition & Physical Activity, 1,* 14.

Bronfenbrenner, U. (1979). *The ecology of human development.* Cambridge, MA: Harvard University Press.

Brown, S. G., & Rhodes, R. E. (2006). Relationships among dog ownership and leisure-time walking in Western Canadian adults. *American Journal of Preventive Medicine, 30,* 131–136.

Carver, A., Salmon, J., Campbell, K., Baur, L., Garnett, S., & Crawford, D. (2005). How do perceptions of local neighborhood relate to adolescents' walking and cycling? *American Journal of Health Promotion, 20,* 139–147.

Carver, A., Timperio, A., & Crawford, D. (2008). Playing it safe: The influence of neighborhood safety on children's physical activity—A review. *Health & Place, 14,* 217–227.

Coleman, K. J., Rosenberg, D. E., Conway, T. L., Sallis, J. F., Saelens, B. E., Frank, L. D., & Cain, K. (2008). Physical activity, weight status, and neighborhood characteristics of dog walkers. *Preventive Medicine, 37,* 309–312.

Collishaw, S., Maughan, B., Goodman, R., & Pickles, A. (2004). Time trends in adolescent mental health. *Journal of Child Psychology and Psychiatry, 45,* 1350–1362.

Cutt, H., Giles-Corti, B., & Knuiman, M. (2008). Encouraging physical activity through dog walking: Why don't some owners walk with their dog? *Preventive Medicine, 46,* 120–126.

Cutt, H., Giles-Corti, B., Knuiman, M., & Burke, V. (2007). Dog ownership, health and physical activity: A critical review of the literature. *Health & Place, 13,* 261–272.

Cutt, H., Giles-Corti, B., Knuiman, M., Timperio, A., & Bull, F. (2008). Understanding dog owners' increased levels of physical activity: Results from RESIDE. *American Journal of Public Health, 98,* 66–69.

Cutt, H. E., Giles-Corti, B., Wood, L. J., Knuiman, M. W., & Burke, V. (2008). Barriers and motivators for owners walking their dog: Results from qualitative research. *Health Promotion Journal of Australia, 19,* 118–124.

Cutt, H. E., Knuiman, M. W., & Giles-Corti, B. (2008). Does getting a dog increase recreational walking? *International Journal of Behavioral Nutrition & Physical Activity, 5,* 17.

Davison, K. K., & Lawson, C. T. (2006). Do attributes of the physical environment influence children's physical activity? A review of the literature. *International Journal of Behavioral Nutrition and Physical Activity, 3,* 19.

Deckelbaum, R. J., & Williams, C. L. (2001). Childhood obesity: The health issue. *Obesity Research, 9,* 239S–243S.

Dietz, W. H. (1998). Childhood weight affects adult morbidity and mortality. *Journal of Nutrition, 128,* 411–414.

Duncan, G. E. (2006). Prevalence of diabetes and impaired fasting glucose levels among US adolescents: National health and nutrition examination survey, 1999–2002. *Archives of Pediatric & Adolescent Medicine, 160,* 523–528.

Freedman, D. S., Dietz, W. H., Srinivasan, S. R., & Berenson, G. S. (1999). The relation of overweight to cardiovascular risk factors among children and adolescents: The Bogalusa Heart Study. *Pediatrics, 103,* 1175–1182.

German, A. J. (2006). The growing problem of obesity in dogs and cats. *Journal of Nutrition, 136,* 1940S–1946S.

Ham, S. A., & Epping, J. (2006). Dog walking and physical activity in the United States. *Preventing Chronic Disease, 3,* A47.

Lobstein, T., Baur, L., & Uauy, R. (2004). Obesity in children and young people: A crisis in public health. *Obesity Reviews, 5,* 4–85.

London Department of Health. (2004). *At least five a week: Evidence on the impact of physical activity and its relationship to health.* London, England: Author.

Melson, G. F., Peet, S., & Sparks, C. (1991). Children's attachment to their pets: Links to socio-emotional development. *Children's Environments Quarterly, 8,* 55–65.

McGreevy, P. D., Thomson, P. C., Pride, C., Fawcett, A., Grassi, T., & Jones, B. (2005). Prevalence of obesity in dogs examined by Australian veterinary practices and the risk factors involved. *The Veterinary Record, 156,* 695–702.

McNicholas, J., & Collis, G. M. (2000). Dogs as catalysts for social interactions: Robustness of the effect. *British Journal of Psychology, 91,* 61–70.

Robins, D. M., Sanders, C. R., & Cahill, S. E. (1991). Dogs and their people. *Journal of Contemporary Ethnography, 20,* 3–25.

Salmon, J., & Timperio, A. (2007). Prevalence, trends and environmental influences on child and youth physical activity. *Medicine and Sport Science, 50,* 183–199. In G. Tomkinson & T. Olds (Eds.), *Fitness of children.* Medicine and Science Book Series: Worldwide variation and secular trends in children's fitness. Basel, Switzerland: Karger Publishers.

Salmon, J., Timperio, A., Chu, B., & Veitch, J. (2010). Dog ownership, dog walking and children's and parents' physical activity. *Research Quarterly for Exercise & Sport, 81*(3), 264–271.

Schofield, G., Mummery, K., & Steele, R. (2005). Dog ownership and human health-related physical activity: An epidemiological study. *Health Promotion Journal of Australia, 16,* 15–19.

Serpell, J. (1991). Beneficial effects of pet ownership on some aspects of human health and behaviour. *Journal for the Royal Society of Medicine, 84,* 717–720.

Sinha, R., Fisch, G., Teague, B., Tamborlane, W., & Banyas, B. (2002). Prevalence of impaired glucose tolerance among children and adolescents with marked obesity. *New England Journal of Medicine, 346,* 802–810.

Suminski, R. R., Poston, W. S., Petosa, R. L., Stevens, E., & Katzenmoyer, L. M. (2005). Features of the neighborhood environment and walking by U.S. adults. *American Journal of Preventive Medicine, 28,* 149–155.

Timperio, A., Giles-Corti, B., Crawford, D., Andrianopoulos, N., Ball, K., Salmon, J., & Hume, C. (2008). Features of public open spaces and physical activity among children: Findings from the CLAN Study. *Preventive Medicine, 47,* 514–518.

Timperio, A., Salmon, J., Chu, B., & Andrianopoulos, N. (2008). Is dog ownership or dog walking associated with weight status in children and their parents? *Health Promotion Journal of Australia, 19,* 60–63.

Twisk, J., Kemper, H., Van Mechelen, W., & Post, G. (1997). Tracking of risk factors for coronary heart disease over a 14 year period: A comparison between lifestyle and biologic risk factors with data from the Amsterdam Growth and Health Study. *American Journal of Epidemiology, 145,* 888–898.

Yabroff, K. R., Troiano, R. P., & Berrigan, D. (2008). Walking the dog: Is pet ownership associated with physical activity in California? *Journal of Physical Activity and Health, 5,* 216–228.

8

HEALTH CORRELATES OF PET OWNERSHIP FROM NATIONAL SURVEYS

BRUCE HEADEY AND MARKUS GRABKA

This chapter reviews evidence from nationally representative surveys, including longitudinal panel surveys, about links between dog and cat ownership and adult health, focusing on three specific issues: (a) determining whether the frequently reported link between pet ownership and better health is causal or merely correlational—could it be that the apparent link results from pet owners being healthier in the first place, rather than benefiting from the presence of a pet; (b) obtaining improved estimates of the *magnitudes* of relationships between pet ownership and better health outcomes; and (c) estimating national health cost savings resulting from pet ownership.

Evidence about the first of these issues comes mainly from the German Socio-Economic Panel Survey (Wagner, Frick, & Schupp, 2007) in which questions about pet ownership and health have been asked at 5-year intervals. These data enable analysis of whether health improves subsequent to acquisition of a pet and declines if pet ownership ends. Evidence about the second issue comes mainly from China, where pet ownership was more or less banned until 1992; after that date, there was a rapid spread of pet ownership among families with, of course, having no previous pet history. Therefore, the conditions of a "natural experiment" existed, making it more feasible to estimate the magnitude of health benefits than is the case in the West, where families have long histories of ownership and nonownership of pets. The final issue is treated only preliminarily. Initial but crude estimates of national health cost savings owing to pet ownership are made for Australia and Germany, two countries in which large-sample national representative surveys have been conducted.

PREVIOUS RESEARCH

The first wave of research on pets and human health consisted of *small-scale interventions*, in which specific groups of (mainly) older and institutionalized people were given a pet in the hope or expectation of benefits to their health and/or psychological well-being. Many positive results were reported, but from a methodological standpoint, there was a concern that many participants may have known or suspected that the aim was to improve their well-being, and this could have affected their responses in evaluation surveys (Garrity & Stallones, 1998; Robb & Stegman, 1983).

An apparent breakthrough was made by Friedmann, Katcher, Lynch, and Thomas (1980), who found that patients who owned dogs were far less likely to die in the year following a heart attack than were patients with no pet. The methods used in this study were criticized by Wright and Moore (1982), but the findings have since been replicated on a larger scale and seem fairly well established (Friedmann & Thomas, 1995).

A landmark British study by Serpell (1991) showed that people who had not recently owned a dog or cat and then acquired one or were given one by the researchers showed improvements during the next 10 months in their health, psychological well-being, self-esteem, and exercise levels, compared with a control group who did not get a pet. Results were clearly statistically significant, but the study has not yet been replicated and is open to the previously mentioned criticism that some participants may well have guessed that they were given a pet to improve their health. This last objection cannot be leveled at Siegel's (1990) study of 938 U.S. Medicaid enrollees, some of whom owned pets and some of whom did not. During the follow-up period, pet owners were less distressed by adverse life events and made fewer doctor visits. Similarly, Raina, Bonnett, and Waltner-Toews (1998) found that elderly people who had pets declined less in physical and mental health in a 1-year period than did a matched group without pets. Those who were closely attached to their pets recorded better outcomes than did those less closely attached. However, in this study, the people who had pets were somewhat healthier than were nonowners of pets when the research began, and this casts some doubt on results.

There have been several investigations of physiological response to the presence of pets. The most promising of these, conducted in Japan, showed that elderly people's stress levels, measured by changes in autonomic nervous activity, were substantially lower when walking a dog than when walking alone (Motooka, Koike, Yokoyama, & Kennedy, 2006). In fact, simply being in a room with a friendly dog also reduced stress. More generally, research on the effects of "pet therapy" has indicated that interaction with pets reduces depressive symptoms and lowers blood pressure (Allen & Blascovich, 1991; Allen, Blascovich, & Mendes, 2002). Indeed, having a pet dog in the room lowers blood pressure more effectively than ace inhibitor therapy (Allen & Shykoff, 2001). However, this result was not replicated in a study in which "stranger" dogs were introduced to participants in an experimental setting (Kingwell, Lomdahl, & Anderson, 2001).

In this context, it is relevant that there is some evidence that "companion animals" are a form of both "bonding" and "bridging" social capital; that is, they bond closely with their owners and provide links or bridges to other potential friends (Wood, Giles-Corti, & Bulsara, 2005). Social capital, in turn, is linked to better health (Putnam, 2000). But if an animal is a "stranger" and an experimental setting provides a "strange" environment, then benefits are presumably less likely. However, that does not mean they can never occur. The Japanese study mentioned (Motooka et al., 2006) involved introducing stranger dogs to elderly participants.

It should be noted that several studies have found no relationship between pet ownership and general health or concluded that the sequence might be that people who already enjoy good health are more likely to get pets (Beck & Katcher, 1984; Jorm et al., 1997; Ory & Goldberg, 1983; Parslow & Jorm, 2003; Robb & Stegman, 1983). However, these studies were limited to small samples or to local area populations rather than applying to nationwide samples.

METHODS: CONTRIBUTION OF NATIONAL REPRESENTATIVE SURVEYS, ESPECIALLY LONGITUDINAL SURVEYS

Evidence based on national representative surveys is crucial for public policy purposes. Population estimates are much more convincing to policymakers than are estimates from special samples or samples of convenience. Longitudinal data are particularly needed to enable researchers to come closer to establishing causal direction than is possible with cross-sectional surveys. As noted, a crucial issue is whether people who acquire pets show subsequent improvements in health or whether the pets–health link is seen because future owners were healthier in the first place.

In designing surveys, it is desirable that questions be sequenced in such a way that respondents cannot guess that the aim is to assess links between pets and health. The survey should be introduced in general terms (e.g., "it is about lifestyle issues") and questions about health should be placed before questions about pets to avoid the possibility that the warm, "fuzzy" subject of pets might induce a favorable mood and lead respondents to make unduly benign reports of their current health. Finally, it is important to find out in the course of the survey who in the family is the main caregiver of the pet and/or how closely attached to the family pet particular respondents are. Some negative findings about the pets–health link appear to result from not identifying who in the family is closely attached and who is not. In general, one would expect that only those who are closely attached would gain health benefits.

ISSUE 1: CAUSAL DIRECTION—DO PEOPLE WHO ACQUIRE PETS SHOW SUBSEQUENT IMPROVEMENTS IN HEALTH?

Our first research issue was addressed with evidence from the huge German Socio-Economic Panel (Wagner et al., 2007). This panel began in 1984 with a sample of approximately 12,000 individuals in approximately 5,000 households. Everyone in the household aged 16 years and older is interviewed annually. The representativeness of the national sample is maintained by following "split-offs" from the original sample households (e.g., young people who leave the parental home to get married) and also by including refresher samples of immigrants and other groups. Most of the questions in the survey are about economic and labor force issues. However, a few questions about health are asked every year. These include the number of doctor visits (general practice visits and all other medical doctors) in the past 3 months and the number of nights in the hospital in the past year.

In 1996, for the first time, and again in 2001, questions were added about pet ownership. Respondents were simply asked whether the family owned a dog, cat, horse, fish, bird, or other pet. It is important to note that questions about pets were buried in a section of the survey on economic issues and came long after the health questions. Respondents could not have guessed that the researchers had any interest in the pets–health link; indeed, the main researchers did not.

The sample used here comprises the 9,723 respondents who answered exactly the same health and pet questions in 1996 and 2001. In this 5-year period, more than 1,000 respondents had acquired a pet, and more than 1,200 had ceased to have a pet. So plenty of change occurred, which is vital for the current analysis. The two largest groups, however, were those who had a pet at both dates, and those who lacked a pet at both dates.

The results of main interest relate to numbers of doctor visits made by dog and cat owners compared with non-owners. The healthiest group was those who had a pet at both dates, and the next healthiest group was those who had acquired a pet by 2001, having not had one in 1996 (Headey & Grabka, 2007).

Both these groups were healthier by a statistically significant margin ($p < .01$) than those who lacked a pet at both dates or those who ceased to have one.

These results held in regression analyses in which the effects of other variables that are related to health were netted out (or controlled).[1] The control variables included gender, age, marital/partnership status, education, income, occupation, and self-reported health status at the time of the 1996 interview. The evidence to this point suggested, although it certainly did not prove, that gaining a pet caused a subsequent gain in health, as indicated by fewer doctor visits. To try to firm up the causal inference, we then analyzed based on "propensity score matching." Matched groups of pet owners and non-owners were identified within the sample; groups were matched on all variables significantly related to ownership. In other words, the two groups were matched on all variables that mattered, except that one group had chosen to own a pet and the other had not. Based solely on these two subsamples (and omitting the rest), dog and cat owners made 24% fewer doctor visits than did nonowners (Headey & Grabka, 2007).

As is almost always the case, one still cannot be completely sure that pet ownership *causes* improved health. It might be that some variable or variables omitted from analysis account for the link (omitted variable bias). Another possibility, perhaps implausible, is that people acquire pets immediately after their health has improved or is about to improve.

ISSUE 2: THE MAGNITUDE OF HEALTH EFFECTS—A "NATURAL EXPERIMENT" IN CHINA

Unknown to most of us, a "natural experiment" has been going on in China for the last 15 years (Headey, Fu Na, & Zheng, 2008). A natural experiment occurs when events in the real world conspire to approximate the situation that would apply in a laboratory if one had the chance to conduct an experiment there. In China, pets were banned as a bourgeois indulgence until 1992 and then were more or less suddenly permitted. There was a sharp break, a specific moment in time when conditions changed and an "experiment" began. People who had no history of pet ownership began to own animals as pets. As noted, it is in these conditions that researchers can get a better fix on the magnitude of health benefits (if any) than is possible in the West, where families have on–off histories of ownership.

Preliminary work indicated that since 1992 approximately 10% of households in large cities have acquired a dog, with younger women forming the largest group of owners and being "main carers" closely attached to their pets

---

[1]Poisson (negative binomial) regression analysis was used, rather than ordinary least squares, because number of doctor visits is a count variable (0, 1, 2 . . .) rather than being normally distributed.

(Fu Na & Zheng, 2003). Accordingly, a telephone sample of just more than 3,000 women aged 25 to 40 years, half dog owners and half nonowners, was drawn equally from the three major cities of Beijing, Shanghai, and Guangzhou. The sample was obtained by random digit dialing, using the standard procedures of CVI, a subsidiary of China Television, which regularly conducts surveys. Participation was of course voluntary, with ethical clearance being given by Beijing Normal University.

To avoid any possible bias that might have arisen from disclosing that the interviews were about the subject of pets, respondents were initially told that the survey was about lifestyle issues. The opening question then asked which of the following the respondent's household owned: a computer, a house plant, a dog, and a home theater. Then respondents were asked a series of questions about exercise and health. All these were completed before the respondents who owned a dog were asked specific questions about their pet, who cared for it, how attached they were to it, and such.

Six main health-related questions provided the dependent (outcome) variables in this research. The first dealt with frequency of exercising continuously for 20 minutes or more, asked on a 6-point scale, where point 1 was labeled "every day" and point 6 was "less than once a month."[2] For analysis purposes, a variable labeled "exercise frequency per week" was constructed by interpolating a frequency for each scale point.[3] Then came a question about the exact number of times respondents had been seen by a doctor in the last 3 months. The survey then asked about the number of days respondents had been off sick from work in the last year, and also about how many nights they had slept badly in the last month.[4] The two remaining health questions asked for a self-rating of health on a 1-to-5 scale running from "very good" to "very poor," then a self-rating of physical fitness on the same scale. The self-rated health question has been asked in surveys all over the world and is found to correlate well with medical assessments (Schwarze, Andersen, & Anger, 2000).

Strength of attachment to one's dog was measured by the pet attachment scale of Raina et al. (1998). This simply requires owners to say how closely attached they are to their pet on a 0-to-10 response scale ("not at all attached" = 0, "strongly attached" = 10).

The results of regression analyses indicated that "new" dog owners in China are considerably healthier on all measures than are nonowners.[5] Dog

---

[2] It should be noted that this exercise question did not refer to walking the dog and was asked before pet-specific questions were raised.

[3] For example, point 3 on the scale was "exercises 1–2 times each week." A midpoint of 1.5 was interpolated.

[4] Frequencies were interpolated at scale midpoints for these two questions.

[5] As in the German analyses, ordinary least-squares analysis was not appropriate because of the distribution of the dependent variables. Poisson regressions were used for count-dependent variables, and ordinal scale (ordered probit) regressions were used when the dependent variables were the 1-to-5 health and fitness scales.

owners exercised 36% more often per week than did nonowners; they had 46% fewer nights of bad sleep; and reported just less than half the number of doctor visits and less than half the number of days off sick from work. They also scored significantly higher ($p < 0.001$) on the self-rated health and fitness scales. All regression results held, net of the effects of age, marital/partnership status, education, occupation, income, employment status, and city of residence. Effects were particularly strong for those who reported very close attachment to their pets.

The Chinese evidence could be interpreted as suggesting that the health benefits of pet dogs run as follows: Dog owners exercise more, so they sleep better, so they feel fitter and healthier. It is not just a subjective matter, a matter of self-report. They actually go to the doctor much less and are off sick less from work. This account, it must be said, is not based on any kind of "path analysis." It is just offered as a set of plausible linkages among the health variables.

In general, the health benefits of dog ownership found in China are more than twice as large as those found in the West, or at least in German and Australian surveys (Headey et al., 2008; Headey & Grabka, 2007; Headey, Grabka, Kelley, Reddy, & Tseng, 2002). For reasons given, they are more likely to be accurate estimates of the magnitude of benefits than are Western results.

ISSUE 3: PRELIMINARY ESTIMATES OF NATIONAL HEALTH COST SAVINGS DUE TO PETS

If it is the case that pets benefit their owners' health, then an important area for research should be the national economic benefits of pet ownership. If pet owners go to the doctor less, which seems to be true in several countries, and if they take fewer days off sick from work, as is the case in China, then health cost savings must result. There may also be gains in production. For Australia and Germany, we have made some preliminary crude estimates of health cost savings (Headey, 1999; Headey et al., 2002). The calculations are possible only because nationally representative sample data are available for these two countries, together with accurate figures on national health expenditure. For China we do not have national data—our sample was restricted to women aged 25 to 40 years in three cities—so estimates cannot yet be made.

Our calculations of cost savings rest on the assumption that if, in an alternative world, pet dogs and cats were abolished, then pet owners would start going to the doctor and using the health system more. They would use it as frequently as matched non-owners of the same gender, age, marital status, income, and such already do. We also made the drastic assumption that frequency of doctor visits serves as a proxy measure for use of the entire health system and thus for all health costs incurred.[6] Having made these assumptions, it was then straightforward to use our regression results to extrapolate the extra costs that would accrue if pets were abolished.

In Australia (2001), where more than 50% of households own a dog or cat or both, the projected extra health costs resulting from abolition of pets would be $4.5 to $5 billion, which is approximately 7% of national health expenditure and 0.5% of gross domestic product (GDP). In Germany (2001), where pet ownership rates are around 35%, extra health costs would amount to about 7 billion Euros.

Clearly, these calculations are crude and need adjusting and refining in several ways. One factor that probably causes them to err on the high side is that about half of all health expenditures that people incur in their lifetimes are incurred during the last 2 years before death. It is likely that pet owners cost just as much as nonowners during this final period. So it may be that all expenditures incurred at this stage should be excluded from calculations. By contrast, a factor that may cause estimates to err on the low side is that we have not so far considered the extra production pet owners may be responsible for, given that they appear to be fitter and healthier and take fewer days off sick from work.

DISCUSSION

It now seems well established that pet dogs and, less certainly, cats, confer some health benefits on their owners. Owners see general practitioners and other physicians less often and so presumably make less use of the whole health system. The evidence on whether their health outcomes are actually better is less clear cut, but the Chinese "natural experiment" results are a strong pointer.

In future research, it is important to investigate more closely the physiological mechanisms through which pets benefit health. Understanding these mechanisms would enhance confidence that health benefits are genuine and also make it more feasible to design health promotion interventions. The experimental study by Motooka et al. (2006) of physiologically measured (not self-reported) stress reduction in elderly Japanese citizens who walked King Charles spaniels is a promising piece of research that shows the way forward.

Our own interests are primarily in the public policy implications of the pet–health linkage. The German Socio-Economic Panel Survey continues to collect valuable longitudinal data on this linkage, so it should prove possible in the next few years to make more detailed and disaggregated estimates of health benefits accruing to different subsets of the population.

---

[6]Only current health expenditures, and not one-off capital costs, was included.

REFERENCES

Allen, K. M., & Blascovich, J. (1991). Presence of human friends and pet dogs as moderators of autonomic responses to stress in women. *Journal of Personality and Social Psychology, 79,* 582–589.

Allen, K. M., Blascovich, J., & Mendes, W. B. (2002). Cardiovascular reactivity and the presence of pets, friends and spouses: The truth about cats and dogs. *Psychological Medicine, 64,* 727–739.

Allen, K. M., & Shykoff, B. E. (2001). Pet ownership, but not Ace Inhibitor Therapy, blunts human blood pressure responses to mental stress. *Hypertension, 38,* 815–820.

Beck, A. M., & Katcher, A. H. (1984). A new look at pet-facilitated psychotherapy. *Journal of the American Veterinary Association, 184,* 414–421.

Friedmann, E., Katcher, A. H., Lynch, J. J., & Thomas, S. A. (1980). Animal companions and one year survival of patients after discharge from a coronary care unit. *Public Health Reports, 95,* 307–312.

Friedmann, E., & Thomas, S. A. (1995). Pet ownership, social support and one year survival after acute myocardial infarction in the Cardiac Arrhythmic Suppression Trial, CAST. *American Journal of Cardiology, 76,* 1213–1217.

Fu, Na, & Zheng, R. (2003). Influences of pet ownership on the empty nester family. *Chinese Mental Health Journal, 17,* 31–39.

Garrity, T. F., & Stallones, L. (1998). Effects of pet contact on human well-being: Review of recent research. In C. C. Wilson & D. C. Turner (Eds.), *Companion animals in human health* (pp. 32). London, England: Sage.

Headey, B. W. (1999). Health benefits and health cost savings due to pets: Preliminary estimates from an Australian national survey. *Social Indicators Research, 47,* 233–243.

Headey, B. W., Grabka, M., Kelley, J., Reddy, P., & Tseng, Y. P. (2002). Pet ownership is good for your health and saves public expenditure too: Australian and German longitudinal evidence. *Australian Social Monitor, 5,* 93–99.

Headey, B. W., & Grabka, M. (2007). Pets and human health in Germany and Australia: National Longitudinal Results. *Social Indicators Research, 80,* 297–311.

Headey, B. W., Fu Na, & Zheng, R. (2008). Pet dogs benefit owners' health: A 'natural experiment' in China. *Social Indicators Research, 87,* 481–493.

Jorm, A. F., Jacomb, P. A., Christensen, H., Henderson, S., Korten, A. E., & Rodgers, B. (1997). Impact of pet ownership on elderly Australians' use of medical services: An analysis using Medicare data. *Medical Journal of Australia, 166,* 376–377.

Kingwell, B. A., Lomdahl, A., & Anderson, W. P. (2001). Presence of a pet dog and human cardiovascular responses to mild mental stress. *Clinical Autonomic Response, 11,* 313–317.

Motooka, M., Koike, H., Yokoyama, T., & Kennedy, N. L. (2006). Effect of dog-walking on autonomic nervous activity in senior citizens. *Medical Journal of Australia, 184,* 60–63.

Ory, M. G., & Goldberg, E. L. (1983). Pet possession and life satisfaction in elderly women. In A. H. Katcher & E. S. Beck (Eds.), *New perspectives on our lives with companion animals* (pp. 303–317). Philadelphia, PA: University of Pennsylvania Press.

Parslow, R. A., & Jorm, A. F. (2003). The impact of pet ownership on health and human service use: Results from a community sample of Australians aged 40 to 44 years. *Anthrozoos, 16*, 43–56.

Putnam, R. D. (2000). *Bowling alone: The collapse and revival of American community.* New York, NY: Simon & Schuster.

Raina, P., Bonnett, B., & Waltner-Toews, D. (1998). *Relationship between pet ownership and health care use among seniors*, 8th Conference of the International Association of Human–Animal Interaction Organisations, Prague, September 10–11.

Robb, S., & Stegman, C. (1983). Companion animals and elderly people: A challenge for evaluations of social support. *Gerontologist, 23*, 277–282.

Schwarze, J., Andersen, H., & Anger, S. (2000). *Self-rated health and changes in self-rated health as predictors of mortality— first evidence from the German Panel Data*, DIW Discussion Paper No. 203, Berlin, DIW.

Serpell, J. A. (1991). Beneficial aspects of pet ownership on some aspects of human health and behaviour. *Journal of the Royal Society of Medicine, 84*, 717–720.

Siegel, J. M. (1990). Stressful life events and the use of physician services among the elderly: The moderating effects of pet ownership. *Journal of Personality and Social Psychology, 58*, 1081–1086.

Wagner, G. G., Frick, J. R., & Schupp, J. (2007). Enhancing the power of household panel studies—The case of the German Socio-Economic Panel (SOEP). *Schmoeller's Jahrbuch, 127*, 139–152.

Wood, L., Giles-Corti, B., & Bulsara, M. (2005). 'The pet connection': Pets as a conduit for social capital? *Social Science & Medicine, 61(6)*, 1159–1173.

Wright, J. C., & Moore, D. (1982). Comments on animal companions and one-year survival of patients after discharge. *Public Health Reports, 97*, 380–381.

9

PHYSIOLOGICAL CORRELATES OF HEALTH BENEFITS FROM PETS

ERIKA FRIEDMANN, SANDRA B. BARKER, AND KAREN M. ALLEN

Popular beliefs accompanied by numerous anecdotal reports indicate that pets are good for people's health. The research to support health benefits for people interacting with pets began 3 decades ago with a study of patients admitted to a coronary care unit, indicating better outcomes among pet owners than non-owners (Friedmann, Katcher, Lynch, & Thomas, 1980). A growing body of research since that time supports the benefits of pets and animal companions for people's health. However, the research has not systematically addressed different populations and the types of interactions with animals that will benefit people, under what conditions, or what individual human or animal characteristics are associated with these benefits. Researchers are just now beginning to develop the scientific research that will enable us to understand the scope, mechanisms, and circumstances of people's health benefits from pets. The biopsychosocial model has provided a structure for understanding the individual and interactive biological, psychological, and social contributors to health and, conversely, to the development and progression of chronic diseases.

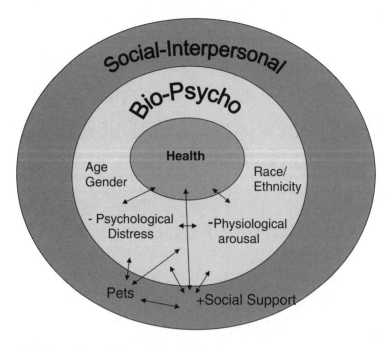

Figure 9.1. Biopsychosocial model for health.

HUMAN–ANIMAL INTERACTION FROM A BIOPSYCHOSOCIAL PERSPECTIVE

The biopsychosocial model (see Figure 9.1) provides a framework for understanding human–animal interaction within the context of health. Health is conceptualized as ranging from minimum to maximum in a continuous dynamic process that requires ongoing adaptation to challenges. The biopsychosocial model emphasizes the interactive nature of the biological, psychological, and social realms (Lindau, Laumann, Levinson, & Waite, 2003). Disruptions or enhancements in any realm affect the others, and together they comprise health status.

Psychosocial distress (see Figure 9.2), including loneliness, anxiety, and depression, is associated with hyperactivity of the hypothalamic–pituitary–adrenocortical (HPA; Brown, Varghese, & McEwen, 2004; Cameron, Abelson, & Young, 2004; Joynt, Whellan, & O'Connor, 2004; Young, Abelson, & Cameron, 2004) and the sympathetic–adrenomedullary (SAM) systems (Gold, Gabry, Yasuda, & Chrousos, 2002; Maas et al., 1994; Watkins, Blumenthal, & Carney, 2002). Activation of the HPA system causes corticosteroid release into the blood, whereas SAM hyperactivity causes increased catecholamine release, reduced heart rate variability (HRV), increased sym-

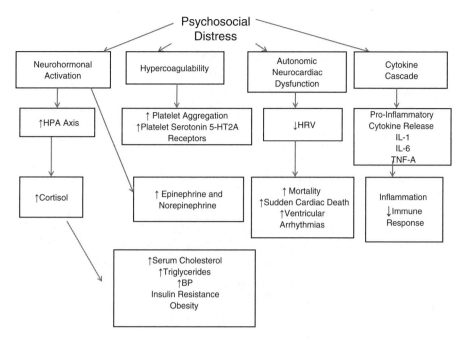

Figure 9.2. Schematic diagram of relationship of psychosocial distress and physiological mechanisms for stress-related health outcomes.

pathetic tone, decreased myocardial perfusion and ventricular instability, and disruption of immune system function, as understood within the psychoneuroimmunology paradigm (see Figure 9.2). This paradigm provides a framework for understanding how psychosocial, behavioral, and physiological (neuroendocrine) interactions influence the immune system (McCain, Gray, Walter, & Robins, 2005c). In activating the HPA and SAM systems, chronic stress induces suppression of the immune system, enhancing vulnerability to infection and cancer and increasing the likelihood of chronic disease morbidity and mortality (McCain, Gray, Walter, & Robins, 2005b; Thomas et al., 2008).

In the biopsychosocial model, pets or companion animals are conceptualized within the psychosocial realm as a form of social support that can affect all other realms and, ultimately, health. Companion animals may directly influence physiological arousal (Allen, Shykoff, & Izzo, 2001; Barker, Knisely, McCain, & Best, 2005), reduce depression (Souter & Miller, 2007) or anxiety (Barker & Dawson, 1998), or increase social support (Allen, Blascovich, & Mendes, 2002), each of which, in turn, decreases physiological arousal. Being in the presence of or observing friendly animals and interacting with friendly animals are conceptualized as means of reducing the chronic stress physiology caused by loneliness, anxiety, and depression, as well as decreasing the physiological stress responses caused by acute stressors.

Research on the physiological correlates of the health benefits of companion animals has addressed both the effects of being in the presence of or observing companion animals and the effects of interacting with companion animals on physiological indicators of chronic stress and acute stress responses. Evidence from these studies is presented in this chapter. Survey, epidemiological, and experimental research all contribute to our understanding of the potential for physiological effects of companion animals on people. Studies specifically examining physiological correlates of health benefits generally use experimental or quasi-experimental designs. This research largely has been carried out on the cardiovascular system and components of the stress response. Physiological indicators that have been studied with respect to the effects of human–animal interactions (HAI) include blood pressure (BP), cortisol, epinephrine, norepinephrine, heart rate (HR), HRV, immunoglobulin A (IgA), and lymphocyte proliferation. A limited number of studies have addressed benefits in children. These are discussed in each application. Recent studies of other populations that could be applicable to children's health are discussed when studies of children are not available.

A relatively brief overview of studies below is organized into four major categories: those indicating the effects of an animal's presence on indicators of chronic and acute stress and the effects of direct interaction on these indicators.

EFFECTS OF BEING IN THE PRESENCE OF OR OBSERVING COMPANION ANIMALS ON INDICATORS OF CHRONIC STRESS

We are not aware of any studies in children looking at the effects of being in the presence of companion animals or observing companion animals on physiological indicators of chronic stress. The best evidence for the effects of being in the presence of companion animals on these indicators comes from population surveys that compare the health or health risk factors between people who do and those who do not own pets. This evidence is presented in Headey and Grabka, Chapter 8. Two small observational studies provide weak evidence for a decrease in physiological arousal as indicated by lower BP when a familiar animal is present than in periods of relaxation without the animal present. A case study of a snake owner (Eddy, 1995) and a study of a chimpanzee caregiver and eight student assistants (Eddy, 1996) revealed lower BP while participants were looking at the animals than when they were relaxing without the animals present. Unfortunately, the order of the conditions was not varied, so BP could just be decreasing as time progressed. The presence

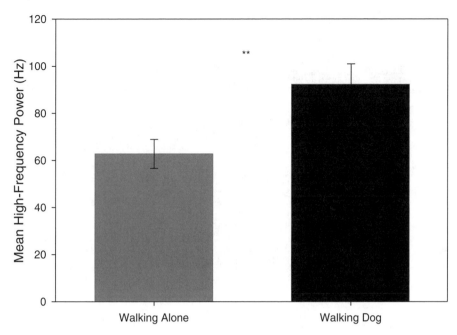

Figure 9.3. Average heart rate variability of 13 older adults while walking for 30 minutes with a friendly dog and while walking for 30 minutes while walking alone. The ** indicates p < .01 for the difference in means while walking with and without a dog. From "Effect of Dog-Walking on Autonomic Nervous Activity in Senior Citizens," by M. Motooka, H. Koike, T. Yokoyama, and N. L. Kennedy, 2006, *Medical Journal of Australia, 184*(2), 60–63. Copyright 2006, by Australasian Medical Publishing Company. Reprinted with permission.

of an aquarium in a patient waiting room had no effect on heart rate or systolic or diastolic BP of psychiatric patients while they waited for electroconvulsive therapy (Barker, Rasmussen, & Best, 2003); participants in this within-subject, crossover study were not asked to attend to or interact in any way with the aquarium.

A small study of older adults lends preliminary but convincing evidence that the presence of animal companions decreases physiological arousal in a less-structured setting (Motoooka, Koike, Yokoyama, & Kennedy, 2006). Older adult participants (n = 13) wore a portable electrocardiograph monitor to measure HRV while they walked for 30 minutes alone and for 30 minutes with an unfamiliar dog. The order of walking activities was varied randomly. Heart rate variability is an indicator of autonomic nervous system arousal. Higher HRV is associated with decreased sympathetic nervous system arousal, increased parasympathetic nervous system arousal, and lower cardiac mortality. HRV was significantly higher while participants walked with the dog than while they walked alone (see Figure 9.3).

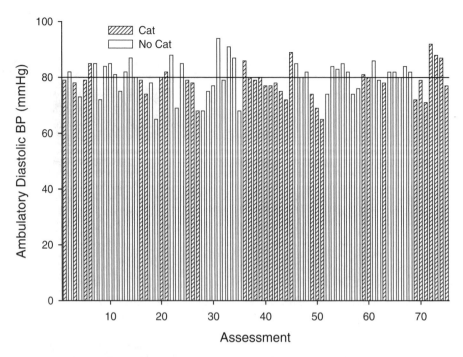

Figure 9.4. Diastolic blood pressures (BPs) obtained via ambulatory BP monitoring every 20 minutes on one older adult woman while she was in her home. Monitoring occurred on 3 days. Each bar indicates one BP assessment. Crosshatched bars indicate that her cat was present and solid bars indicate that her cat was not present at the time the BP was measured. The reference line of 80 mmHg represents the cutpoint for pre-hypertension.

In an ongoing study, Friedmann and colleagues currently are extending the research that evaluates the anti-arousal effects of the presence of an animal companion to examine what happens during people's normal daily lives under completely natural circumstances. To address whether there are physiological benefits from the presence of pets during normal daily activities, they are having 30 older adults wear an ambulatory BP monitor for 24 hours (during awake hours only) on 3 separate days. Blood pressure is measured every 20 minutes, and participants complete a diary indicating where they are, who is with them, and what they are doing each time BP is measured. All participants are taking antihypertensive medication and have their BP under control or have BP in the pre- to mild hypertensive range (systolic BP between 120 and 150 or diastolic BP between 80 and 110 mmHg). Figure 9.4 is a graph of each of the BP measurements taken when the first participant was at home. Significantly more BP measures are below the threshold for the prehypertension level (80 mmHg) when she was at home with her cat present (64.7%) than without her cat present (36.5%). There are no studies of children examining the effect of being in the presence of or observing a pet or animal companion on physiological indicators of chronic stress, but the evidence from older populations suggests that the presence of a pet may reduce physiological indicators of chronic stress in children.

EFFECTS OF BEING IN THE PRESENCE OF OR OBSERVING COMPANION ANIMALS ON INDICATORS OF ACUTE STRESS

Many occurrences during people's daily lives lead to immediate or acute stress responses. These responses cause immediate changes in physiological indicators of stress. The presence of a companion animal has been proposed as a buffer or moderator of these stress responses. Several studies provide evidence that substantiates this effect in both children and adults. As in the previous discussion, study design is crucial to demonstrating these effects due to the extreme variability in physiological indicators both between and within individuals. In the studies of the stress-moderating effects of companion animals for children, the moderation was demonstrated in those studies that had the same children participate in both situations, with and without the animal present, but not in those in which each child participated in only one situation.

The first study, establishing a stress-moderating effect of the presence of a companion animal on physiological indicators of a stress response (Friedmann, Katcher, Thomas, Lynch, & Messent, 1983), used reading aloud as a stressor and was conducted in a home setting. BPs of 9- to 16-year-old children (n = 36) were recorded while they rested and read aloud twice, once with a friendly dog in the room with the child and the researcher and once without the dog present. The order of the dog's presence was assigned randomly. Overall, having the dog present first was associated with lower BPs throughout the study. Blood pressure increased significantly when the children read aloud. There was a significant interaction between the order and the presence of the dog. BP levels were similar with the dog present in both groups, but they were significantly higher without the dog present when that was the first situation than when the dog was not present when that was the second situation (see Figure 9.5; Friedmann et al., 1983).

Several studies used the stressor of children undergoing a health procedure to examine whether the presence of a companion animal would moderate the children's physiological stress responses. In the study by Nagengast, Baun, Megel, and Leibowitz (1997) with a crossover design, 3- to 6-year-old children (n = 23) underwent two 10-minute standardized physical examinations, one with a friendly dog present, the other without the dog. The order of the dog's

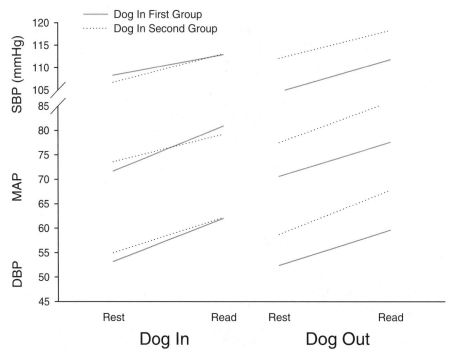

Figure 9.5. Average systolic (SBP), diastolic (DBP), and mean arterial (MAP) blood pressures of children (n = 36) while they rested silently and read aloud both with only the researcher present (dog out) and with the unfamiliar friendly dog and the researcher present (dog in). Participants were randomly assigned to have the dog present during the first (dog in first group: solid line) or second (dog in second group: dotted line) half of the protocol. From "Social Interaction and Blood Pressure: Influence of Animal Companions," by E. Friedmann et al., 1983, *Journal of Nervous and Mental Disease, 171*(8), 461–465, Copyright 1983, by Wolters Kluwer Health. Reprinted with permission.

presence was assigned randomly. The children's systolic BP and HR decreased more during the medical examination with the dog present than with the dog absent. A similar study without a crossover design (Hansen, Messenger, Baun, & Megel, 1999) found no effect of the presence of a friendly dog on physiological responses of 2- to 6-year-old children (n = 34) who were assigned to either a dog or a no-dog condition during their physical examination. Although there was no physiological effect of the presence of the dog, children whose physical examination occurred with the dog present exhibited less behavioral distress. Another study (Havener et al., 2001) without a crossover design examined the effect of the presence of a dog on physiological stress indicators of 7- to 11-year-old children (n = 40) during a dental procedure. In this study, peripheral skin temperature was used as an indicator of stress (lower skin temperature indicates greater physiological stress), and children were assigned to have a dog

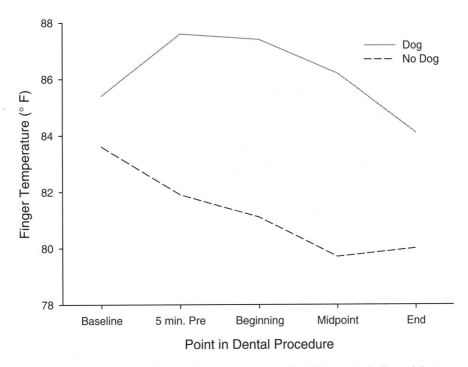

Figure 9.6. Average peripheral skin temperature of 17 children who indicated that they were distressed about having a dental procedure. The solid line represents the average for the children who underwent the procedure with the dog lying beside them, and the dashed line represents the children who underwent the procedure without the dog lying beside them. Peripheral skin temperature was measured on the finger 5 times before, during, and after the dental procedures. From "The Effects of a Companion Animal on Distress in Children Undergoing Dental Procedures," by L. Havener et al., 2001, *Issues in Comprehensive Pediatric Nursing, 24*(2), 137–152, Copyright 2001, by Taylor & Francis. Reprinted with permission.

lying beside them during a dental procedure or not. On average, children's peripheral skin temperature during a dental procedure was not affected by a dog lying beside them. However, a subgroup of 17 of the children indicated that they were stressed by coming to the dentist. In this group of stressed children, the dog's presence moderated the stress response. The changes in physiological stress from baseline to midpoint were significantly different in the two groups. As illustrated in Figure 9.6, there was less decrease in peripheral skin temperature occurring in the children who had the dog present during the dental procedure.

BP and HR responses to numerous everyday mild stressors did not differ between dog owners with their dogs present and nonowners (Kingwell, Lomdahl, & Anderson, 2001; Rajack, 1997). However, the cardiovascular stress response to a standard laboratory stress task was reduced for women who owned dogs (n = 45) with their dog present compared with the presence of another person. Using methodology that mirrored social support research about the role of human friends, HR, systolic BP, and diastolic BP responses to both mental and physical stressors were significantly lower with a woman's own dog present than when a close friend the participant chose to provide support was present. The women were devoted to their dogs and described them as supportive and, unlike human friends, totally nonjudgmental (Allen, Blascovich, Tomaka, & Kelsey, 1991).

Most of the studies conducted to examine the stress-moderating effects of companion animals were conducted with dogs as the companion animals. In a study by Allen and colleagues (2002), cardiovascular reactivity to stress was examined among 240 married couples, half of whom owned either a cat or a dog. Pet owners had significantly lower resting HR and BP; exhibited significantly lower HR, systolic BP, and diastolic BP during mental stress; and returned to baseline levels more quickly than did those who did not own pets. All participants had the highest reactivity to mental stress while in the presence of their spouses, and for pet owners, the lowest stress responses were in the company of their pets. When both spouse and pet were present, reactivity was dramatically reduced, suggesting that a pet may ameliorate the negative effect of a spouse or a judgmental person. There were no differences in the effects of cats and dogs. Wells (2005) conducted a unique study of physiological arousal during a stressful activity after viewing videos of various animals and control videos, demonstrating the potential of many different species to provide physiological stress-response moderating effects. The HR and BP of 100 young adults were lower during a moderately stressful activity after viewing videos of birds, primates, and fish than after viewing a TV show or a blank television screen.

The only randomized clinical trial of the effect of companion animals on chronic and acute stress responses evaluated the effectiveness of pets as an antihypertensive intervention (Allen et al., 2001). BP and HR levels at rest and in response to standardized mental stressors were obtained, in their homes, from hypertensive adults (n = 48) who were employed in a high-stress occupation before beginning angiotensin-converting enzyme (ACE) inhibitor medication. Half were randomly assigned to adopt a cat or dog of their choice at the time they started ACE inhibitor therapy; the others were not assigned to adopt a pet. BP and HR levels at rest and in responses to standardized mental stressors were obtained in their homes 6 months after the beginning of therapy. Resting BPs were lower after 6 months of ACE therapy for patients who were and were not assigned to adopt pets, although they did not differ between the groups. As illustrated in Figure 9.7, BP responses to mental stress of those with hypertension who adopted a pet were lower with the pet present 6 months after starting ACE inhibitors than were the responses of those who

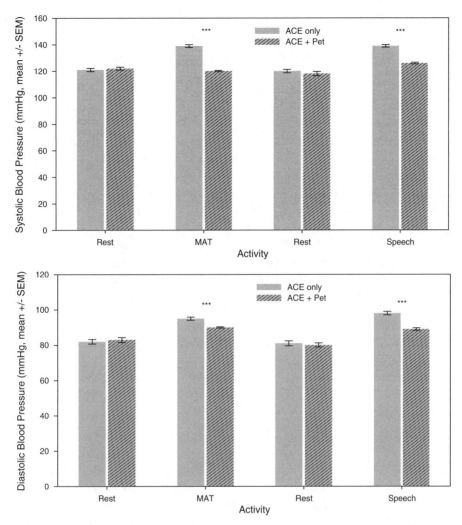

Figure 9.7. Systolic and diastolic blood pressures (BPs) while resting and during 2 stressful tasks (Mental arithmetic: MAT and Speaking: Speech) 6 months after the initiation of the ACE inhibitor therapy for 48 adults with hypertension; half of whom were randomly assigned to obtain pet dogs or cats in addition to ACE inhibitors. *** p < .001. From "The Human-Companion Animal Bond: How Humans Benefit," by E. Friedmann and H. Son, 2009, *Veterinary Clinics of North America: Small Animal Practice, 39*(2), 293–326. Copyright 2009, by Elsevier. Reprinted with permission.

started ACE inhibitors at the same time but did not adopt a pet. Allen and colleagues' findings suggest that having the pet in the home was effective at lowering the physiological stress response, beyond the effect of the anti-hypertensive medication.

Allen (2007) is extending her research to examine the stress response moderating effect of pets for patients with arthritis, another disease with strong stress-related components. Women with arthritis who lived alone were randomly assigned to adopt a dog or to be placed on a waiting list for a dog. The presence of a dog was associated with significantly lower BP and HR response to a standard speech task in participants' homes. The women with rheumatoid arthritis (n = 50), which involves immune-related inflammation, had higher reactivity to everyday and speech tasks and experienced greater benefit from the presence of the pet than those with osteoarthritis (n = 50).

Taken in their totality, these studies suggest a buffering effect on physiological stress response associated with pet presence. Although most studies have been conducted with adult populations, the few studies with children show promise of a similar benefit.

EFFECTS OF INTERACTION WITH COMPANION ANIMALS ON INDICATORS OF CHRONIC STRESS

Several studies before 1990 found BP levels for individuals interacting with pets were similar to their BP levels while they were resting and lower than their BP levels while they were talking or reading (Friedmann, Thomas, & Eddy, 2000). None of these studies included children. Recent studies have not looked at the effect of interaction with pets on chronic stress indicators in children. Four of the older women who participated in the study of Motooka, Koike, Yokoyama, and Kennedy (2006) of adults walking with and without a dog also agreed to have the dog spend additional time with them at their homes while wearing the portable electrocardiograph monitors. During the 6 hours of home monitoring, each spent two 30-minute periods specifically interacting with the dog. Physiological arousal was lower when the dog was in the participant's home, as indicated by higher HRV when interacting with the dog than when the dog was not present. As with the larger group, HRV (see Figure 9.8) in these four participants was also higher while the individuals walked a dog than while they walked alone (Motooka et al., 2006).

Another recent study (Cole, Gawlinski, Steers, & Kotlerman, 2007) involving patients with heart failure also provides evidence of the benefit of brief human–companion animal interaction on physiological stress and cardio-

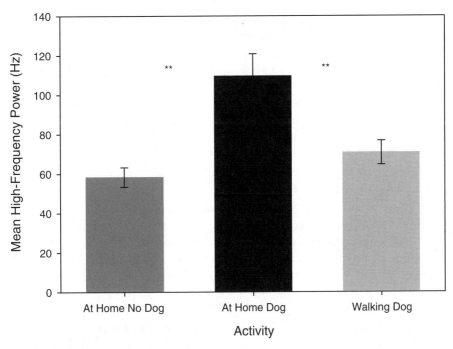

Figure 9.8. Average heart rate variability (+/– sem) of 4 older adults while at home without the dog for 30 minutes, while at home interacting with the friendly dog for 30 minutes, and while walking for 30 minutes with the friendly dog. ** p < .01 for the difference in means from the mean at home with the dog. From "Effect of Dog-Walking on Autonomic Nervous Activity in Senior Citizens," by M. Motooka, H. Koike, T. Yokoyama, and N. L. Kennedy, 2006, *Medical Journal of Australia, 184*(2), 60–63. Copyright 2006, by Australasian Medical Publishing Company. Reprinted with permission.

pulmonary health indicators. Seventy-six patients with heart failure were randomly assigned to a 12-minute animal-assisted interaction (AAI) with a volunteer and a therapy dog, a 12-minute interaction with a volunteer only, or usual care. The AAI group had significantly greater reductions in epinephrine and norepinephrine levels during and after the intervention compared with the volunteer group and significantly greater reductions in systolic pulmonary artery pressure and pulmonary capillary wedge pressure during and after AAI compared with the usual care group.

Barker and colleagues (Barker, Knisely, McCain, Schubert, & Pandurangi, 2010) are extending their research on psychological and physiological stress-response patterns associated with AAI in chronically ill populations to patients with end-stage renal disease undergoing dialysis. Comparing AAI with a similar interaction with a volunteer without a pet, preliminary results in four subjects suggest higher HRV associated with AAI compared with the visit by only the dog owner.

EFFECTS OF INTERACTING WITH COMPANION ANIMALS ON INDICATORS OF STRESS

The data in the previous section support the effectiveness of having a companion animal present for reducing both chronic and acute physiological stress responses. The effectiveness of interacting with a companion animal during a stressful task to moderate the stress responses is much more difficult to support. Interacting with an animal often may interfere with a task one is trying to accomplish. Therefore, the presence of the animal may increase, rather than decrease, stress levels. Furthermore, research to evaluate this effect is difficult.

There are no studies of the effects of interaction with companion animals on physiological stress indicators of children. In one study examining the effect of having a dog on the lap during a stressful task, the intervention did not reduce stress-indicator response (Straatman, Hanson, Endenburg, & Mol, 1997). In this study, 36 adults 18 to 30 years old, were randomly assigned to have a friendly but unfamiliar dog sit on their laps during preparation and delivery of a videotaped, locally televised speech. The BP and HR of those with the dog on their lap and the control group members did not differ during the preparation and the speech periods, even after controlling for the effects of daily stress.

One study provides evidence that having an animal present is more effective at stress reduction than interacting with the animal. DeMello (1999) studied the recovery of BP and HR of 50 adult (26 to 50 years old) individuals with normal blood pressure after the termination of mild cognitive stressors. Each person participated in three conditions: no pet present, pet present with visual but not tactile interaction, and pet present with tactile interaction. The sequence of the conditions was varied and the type of pet used, a dog or a goat, also varied. Reductions were greater with the pet present than not present, and reductions with visual contact were greater than with tactile contact.

Variation in how individuals interact with animals is difficult to control and quantify. Those more actively interacting (e.g., talking, playing) with a pet would be expected to show greater BP and HR levels than individuals more passively interacting (e.g., sitting quietly touching or gently stroking) with a pet. Individuals more excited to be with the animal would also be expected to show increased vital signs than those less interested in the animal. Equally important is the effect an animal's response has on the study participant. These factors make it difficult to accurately and completely assess the actual contribution of interacting with an animal to physiological indicators of chronic or acute stress.

As HAI researchers begin to measure neuroendocrine and immune stress indicators, it is imperative to know the optimum times to measure these indicators after a HAI. To that end, Barker et al. (2005) measured salivary and serum cortisol, epinephrine, norepinephrine, salivary IgA, and lymphocyte proliferation in a small group of health care professionals before a 5-minute AAI, 20-minute AAI, or 20 minutes of quiet rest; these parameters were measured again at 5, 15, 30, 45, and 60 minutes post-condition for each condition. Reductions in salivary and serum cortisol reached significance 45 and 60 minutes after each condition. With no significant between-group differences, a 5-minute AAI may provide the equivalent relaxation as 20 minutes of quiet rest. Changes in salivary cortisol reflected underlying changes in serum cortisol, thus providing support for the collection of salivary cortisol in future studies. Significant reductions from baseline following the two AAI conditions were not found for the other physiological variables measured.

Barker and colleagues are currently extending their research on the effect of companion animal interaction on indicators of psychoneuroimmune function to investigate patterns of response in owners interacting with their own dogs and owners interacting with an unfamiliar therapy dog (as occurs in AAI) after a mental stress task (Barker et al., 2010). On measures of neurophysiologic brain activity and autonomic and endocrine indicators of stress in a small group of 10 healthy adults ranging in age from 26 to 66 years, response patterns support a relaxation effect associated with interacting with one's own dog that is mirrored in interactions with an unfamiliar therapy dog (Barker et al., 2009).

CONCLUSIONS AND FUTURE RESEARCH DIRECTIONS

Based on research on adults, there is consensus that the presence of pets or animal companions is associated with reductions in chronic levels of physiological stress indicators and reductions in stress response to mild to moderate stressors; no research has addressed the effect of pet presence on ameliorating the effects of major stressors. The few studies of children tend to support the generalization of these findings to children.

Results of research examining the physiological health effects of companion animals on children so far are intriguing. Reported findings indicate that companion animals are beneficial to the physiological health of children in some circumstances. Because of extreme physiological variation between children, within-subject designs may be more efficient for obtaining the power needed to quantify benefits for individuals.

There are no data on the health effects of children's own pets; all data have been obtained from studies using friendly but unfamiliar animals. Additional research is necessary to evaluate the effect of pets on children's health. This may be accomplished by incorporating information about pet ownership in large population-based epidemiological studies of children's health as well as through research on the physiological effects of pets on an individual's physiological responses.

The experimental and quasi-experimental research to date has largely evaluated people's responses to friendly but unfamiliar animals. When pet owners have been studied with their own dogs or cats, positive results related to physiological indicators of health have been reported. Both approaches are important to consider, especially since pet ownership currently is not allowed in many living situations.

Although most of the studies considering the physiological effect of companion animals on people have examined them on a one-time basis, recent research has focused on the importance of repeated data collection over several months or years. In addition, the use of ambulatory monitoring equipment has allowed assessment of ongoing interaction of pet animals and their owners in natural home settings. This approach is especially useful in increasing our understanding of the possible role of pets in the reduction of physiological responses to chronic stress resulting from uncontrollable life circumstances, such as caregiving for family members.

Equally important are studies investigating the effect of AAI in health care settings. As AAI programs become more accepted in hospitals, clinics, and nursing homes, researchers must identify appropriate evidence-based interventions, health outcomes, and the proposed mechanisms through which AAI affects those outcomes. As with pet ownership studies, it is important to identify models to guide AAI research. The biopsychosocial (Lindau et al., 2003) and psychoneuroimmunological (McCain, Gray, Walter, & Robins, 2005a) models are particularly useful for guiding research on interventions designed to affect chronic stress or response to acute stressors. The biopsychosocial model concentrates on how biological, psychological, and social realms interact with each other and contribute to health. The psychoneuroimmunological model concentrates on the interaction of psychobehavioral–neuroendocrine–immune systems and the mediating role of elevated cortisol in the suppression of the immune system.

These mechanisms underlie numerous interactions within the biopsychosocial model. AAI is considered a biobehavioral intervention in this model, affecting the immune system indirectly through the neuroendocrine system. Thus, AAI affects the biological realm, which in turn, affects the psychological and social realms of the biopsychosocial model. AAI has been shown to improve mood (Barker & Dawson, 1998; Souter & Miller, 2007; Turner, Rieger, & Lorenz, 2003), reduce loneliness (Banks & Banks, 2002, 2005), and lower perceived stress in varied populations (Barker et al., 2009; Wilson, 1991), thereby reducing psychological distress. Psychological distress increases cortisol, which in turn, suppresses immune function, demonstrating the effect of the psychological realm on the biological realm and ultimately on health.

Although AAI has been associated with reduced cortisol in a few studies (Barker et al., 2010; Barker et al., 2005; Odendaal & Meintjes, 2003), attempts to document the effects of AAI on indicators of immune function have not yielded significant findings. Including neuroendocrine and immune system indicators in AAI research presents a challenge for investigators because of the resources required for collecting, processing, and analyzing these measures.

Some of the same questions raised regarding pet presence and interaction with owners in daily living apply to research on AAI. There are no published studies investigating physiological health benefits of AAI that describe a structured intervention capable of replication. Little is known about the animal in the intervention or how the animal's reaction to the study participant affects the participant's physiological response. With few exceptions, we do not know the contribution of the therapy animal owner/handler (who is present during the intervention) to reported effects. The interaction of the human component of AAI may represent the major source of social support provided by AAI.

AAI studies need to address possible dose effects. For example, what is the ideal length of an AAI session for maximum benefit, and do repeated AAI sessions produce a cumulative effect on stress indicators? The answers have important implications for AAI programs and how they coordinate patient visits. Also important, yet largely unknown, is how patients' attitudes toward pets or other patient characteristics (e.g., underlying anxiety) may affect the outcomes associated with AAI. As with other behavioral or supportive interventions, AAI may be effective at reducing stress for people who are experiencing psychological distress but not have any effect on those who are not distressed. Evidence from the study by Havener et al. (2001) of children during a dental procedure supports this possibility.

The existing data suggest that companion animals provide health benefits in specific situations. It is unclear, however, whether the effects that are demonstrated in such situations generalize to daily lives. In addition, little is known about how choosing, caring for, and bonding with an animal are related to physiological responses. Because researchers from many diverse disciplines study the effects of companion animals, there is currently no agreement on research variables and methodology design. Also, although several explanatory models of the effects of pets on human health have been developed, these models have not been routinely tested in published reports. Increased attention among researchers to employing at least some common research questions and physiological variables in their designs would further our understanding of the role of pets in human health.

The popular media have tended to overgeneralize the research findings about the potential health benefits of having a pet. Having a pet may help a person with hypertension or other diseases that are exacerbated by stress handle reactions to stressful situations and thus reduce the physiological responses that occur during stress. Long-term reductions in stress responses may reduce the effect on health outcomes of a variety of stress-related diseases. However, considerable research is needed to conclusively establish the effectiveness of pets or animal companions to make specific contributions to health. The field really does not have evidence that "pets lower blood pressure"; however, it has been demonstrated that they can be a healthy adjunct to lifestyle changes and drug therapy.

REFERENCES

Allen, K. M. (2007). Pet dogs attenuate cardiovascular stress responses and pain among women with rheumatoid arthritis. *Psychophysiology, 44,* S89.

Allen, K., Blascovich, J., & Mendes, W. (2002). Cardiovascular reactivity and the presence of pets, friends and spouses: The truth about cats and dogs. *Psychosomatic Medicine, 64,* 727–739.

Allen, K. M., Blascovich, J., Tomaka, J., & Kelsey, R. M. (1991). Presence of human friends and pet dogs as moderators of autonomic responses to stress in women. *Journal of Personality and Social Psychology, 61,* 582–589.

Allen, K., Shykoff, B. E., & Izzo, J. L. (2001). Pet ownership, but not ACE inhibitor therapy, blunts home blood pressure responses to mental stress. *Hypertension, 38,* 815–820.

Banks, M. R., & Banks, W. A. (2002). The effects of animal-assisted therapy on loneliness in an elderly population in long-term care facilities. *Journals of Gerontology, Series A, Biological Sciences and Medical Sciences, 57*(7), M428–M432.

Banks, M. R., & Banks, W. A. (2005). The effects of group and individual animal-assisted therapy on loneliness in residents of long-term care facilities. *Anthrozoos, 18*(4), 396–408.

Barker, S. B., & Dawson, K. S. (1998). The effects of animal-assisted therapy on anxiety ratings of hospitalized psychiatric patients. *Psychiatric Services, 49*(6), 797–801.

Barker, S. B., Knisely, J. S., McCain, N. L., & Best, A. M. (2005). Measuring stress and immune response in healthcare professionals following interaction with a therapy dog: A pilot study. *Psychological Reports, 96,* 713–729.

Barker, S. B., Knisely, J. S., McCain, N. L., Schubert, C. M., & Pandurangi, A. K. (2010). Exploratory study of stress-buffering response patterns from interaction with a therapy dog. *Anthrozoös, 23*(1), 79–91.

Barker, S. B., Pandurangi, A. K., Knisely, J. S., McCain, N. L., Schubert, C. M., & Buragkazi, E. (2009). *Autonomic, endocrine and neurophysiologic correlates of human–animal interaction.* Annual meeting of the American Psychiatric Association: Program book, syllabus, and new research abstracts, Arlington, VA.

Barker, S. B., Rasmussen, K. G., & Best, A. M. (2003). Effect of aquariums on electroconvulsive therapy patients. *Anthrozöos, 16,* 229–240.

Brown, E. S., Varghese, F. P., & McEwen, B. S. (2004). Association of depression with medical illness: Does cortisol play a role? *Biological Psychiatry, 55*, 1–9.

Cameron, O. G., Abelson, J. L., & Young, E. A. (2004). Anxious and depressive disorders and their comorbidity: Effect on central nervous system noradrenergic function. *Biological Psychiatry, 56*, 875–883.

Cole, K. M., Gawlinski, A., Steers, N., & Kotlerman, J. (2007). Animal-assisted therapy in patients hospitalized with heart failure. *American Journal of Critical Care, 16*, 575–585.

DeMello, L. R. (1999). The effect of the presence of a companion-animal on physiological changes following the termination of cognitive stressors. *Psychology and Health, 14*, 859–868.

Eddy, T. J. (1995). Human cardiac responses to familiar young chimpanzees. *Anthrozöos, 4*, 235–243.

Eddy, T. J. (1996). RM and Beaux: Reductions in cardiac activity in response to a pet snake. *Journal of Nervous and Mental Disease, 184*, 573–575.

Friedmann, E., Katcher, A. H., Lynch, J. J., & Thomas, S. A. (1980). Animal companions and one-year survival of patients after discharge from a coronary care unit. *Public Health Reports, 95*, 307–312.

Friedmann, E., Katcher, A. H., Thomas, S. A., Lynch, J. J., & Messent, P. R. (1983). Social interaction and blood pressure: Influence of animal companions. *The Journal of Nervous and Mental Disease, 171*, 461–465.

Friedmann, E., Thomas, S. A., & Eddy, T. J. (2000). Companion animals and human health: Physical and cardiovascular influences. In A. L. Podberscek, E. Paul, & J. A. Serpell (Eds.), *Companion animals and us: Exploring the relationships between people and pets* (pp. 125–142). Cambridge, England: Cambridge University Press.

Gold, P. W., Gabry, K. E., Yasuda, M. R., & Chrousos, G. P. (2002). Divergent endocrine abnormalities in melancholic and atypical depression: Clinical and pathophysiologic implications. *Endocrinology and Metabolism Clinics of North America, 31*, 37–62.

Hansen, K. M., Messenger, C. J., Baun, M., & Megel, M. E. (1999). Companion animals alleviating distress in children. *Anthrozöos, 12*, 142–148.

Havener, L., Gentes, L., Thaler, B., Megel, M. E., Baun, M. M., Driscoll, F. A., . . . Agrawal, S. (2001). The effects of a companion animal on distress in children undergoing dental procedures. *Issues in Comprehensive Pediatric Nursing, 24*, 137–152.

Joynt, K. E., Whellan, D. J., & O'Connor, C. M. (2004). Why is depression bad for the failing heart? A review of the mechanistic relationship between depression and heart failure. *Journal of Cardiac Failure, 10*, 258–271.

Kingwell, B. A., Lomdahl, A., & Anderson, W. P. (2001). Presence of a pet dog and human cardiovascular responses to mild mental stress. *Clinical Autonomic Research, 11*, 313–317.

Lindau, S. T., Laumann, E. O., Levinson, W., & Waite, L. J. (2003). Synthesis of scientific disciplines in pursuit of health: The Interactive Biopsychosocial Model. *Perspectives in Biology and Medicine, 46,* S74–S86.

Maas, J. W., Katz, M. M., Koslow, S. H., Swann, A., Davis, J. M., Berman, N., . . . Landis, H. (1994). Adrenomedullary function in depressed patients. *Journal of Psychiatric Research, 28,* 357–367.

McCain, N. L., Gray, D. P., Walter, J. M., & Robins, J. (2005). Implementing a comprehensive approach to the study of health dynamics using the psychoneuroimmunology paradigm. *ANS Advances in Nursing Science, 28,* 320–332.

Motooka, M., Koike, H., Yokoyama, T., & Kennedy, N. L. (2006). Effect of dog-walking on autonomic nervous activity in senior citizens. *Medical Journal of Australia, 184,* 60–63.

Nagengast, S. L., Baun, M., Megel, M. M., & Leibowitz, J. M. (1997). The effects of the presence of a companion animal on physiological arousal and behavioral distress in children during a physical examination. *Journal of Pediatric Nursing, 12,* 323–330.

Odendaal, J. S., & Meintjes, R. A. (2003). Neurophysiological correlates of affiliative behavior between humans and dogs. *Veterinary Journal, 165*(3), 296–301.

Rajack, L. S. (1997). *Pets and human health: The influence of pets on cardiovascular and other aspects of owners' health* (Doctoral dissertation, University of Cambridge, Cambridge, England).

Souter, M. A., & Miller, M. D. (2007). Do animal-assisted activities effectively treat depression? A meta-analysis. *Anthrozoos, 20*(2), 167–180.

Straatman, I., Hanson, E. K. S., Endenburg, N., & Mol, J. A. (1997). The influence of a dog on male students during a stressor. *Anthrozöos, 10,* 191–197.

Thomas, S. A., Chapa, D. W., Friedmann, E., Durden, C., Ross, A., Lee, M. C., & Lee, H-J. (2008). Depression in patients with heart failure: Prevalence, pathophysiological mechanisms, and treatment. *Critical Care Nurse, 28,* 40–55.

Turner, D. C., Rieger, G., & Lorenz, G. (2003). Spouses and cats and their effects on human mood. *Anthrozoos, 16*(3), 213–228.

Watkins, L. L., Blumenthal, J. A., & Carney, R. M. (2002). Association of anxiety with reduced baroreflex cardiac control in patients after acute myocardial infarction. *American Heart Journal, 143,* 460–466.

Wells, D. L. (2005). The effect of videotapes of animals on cardiovascular responses to stress. *Stress and Health, 21,* 209–213.

Wilson, C. C. (1991). The pet as an anxiolytic intervention. *The Journal of Nervous and Mental Disease, 179*(8), 482–489.

Young, E. A., Abelson, J. L., & Cameron, O. G. (2004). Effect of comorbid anxiety disorders on the hypothalamic–pituitary–adrenal axis response to a social stressor in major depression. *Biological Psychiatry, 56,* 113–120.

10

ANIMAL-ASSISTED INTERVENTION IN HEALTH CARE CONTEXTS

REBECCA A. JOHNSON

Over the past 3 decades, considerable interest has grown among the research community, health care practitioners, and the general public in the potential benefits to human health that may occur when humans interact with companion animals in therapeutic contexts. In the 1800s, Florence Nightingale advocated the use of small caged birds or other small pets to cheer her hospitalized patients during their recovery. Although the basic premise remains the same, this form of interaction has been transposed into various forms in current health care environments.

Animal-assisted intervention (AAI) includes several activities in which animals are participants, with the aim of assisting human patients. These activities commonly involve quiet interaction with a dog. This type of interaction is associated with a relaxation effect (Odendaal, 1999) resulting from sensory input involving four senses; namely olfactory, tactile, auditory, and visual. The patient sees and smells the dog, pets and talks to the dog and its handler, listens to the noises made by the dog and hears the handler's interpretation of the dog's behavior, and a decrease in the patient's serum cortisol levels occurs, leading to a decrease in blood pressure and heart and respiratory rates. This relaxation may be the factor making AAI applicable in high-anxiety contexts (Wilson, 1991). Given that anxiety is typically associated with medical and psychotherapeutic treatment, this mechanism may be the main reason that use of AAI has increased so markedly in recent years.

Essentially, two forms of AAI are being used in health care contexts. Animal-assisted activity (AAA) consists of animal visits that are usually conducted by volunteer dog-handler pairs. The hallmark of AAA is spontaneous content of the visits; there are no visit-related treatment goals for the person receiving the visits (Kruger & Serpell, 2006). In contrast, animal-assisted therapy (AAT) is a specific treatment goal-directed activity that is customized for the particular patient. This chapter explores the use of AAI in health care contexts across the lifespan and proposes dog walking as a possible form of AAI.

AAI ACROSS THE LIFE SPAN

Relevance for Children

AAI has been used with patients of all ages, and increasingly, these interventions have become the subject of empirical study. However, the body of research with children is extremely scant. For children, introduction of AAA has occurred in situations commonly associated with high anxiety. However, findings have not been consistently positive; for example, Havener et al. (2001) studied 7- to 11-year-old children (N = 40) undergoing dental procedures and found that the presence of a dog during the procedures yielded no change in either the children's distress or skin temperature (a measure of stress, with decreased skin temperature indicating greater stress levels). Conversely, in another study, investigators identified that behavioral signs of distress observed through videotaping children ages 2 to 6 years during a medical examination were significantly less among 34 children randomly assigned to a treatment group in which a dog was present during the examination. The investigators also studied physiological indicators of blood pressure, heart rate, and fingertip temperature but found no significant differences in these variables (Hansen, Baun, Messinger, & Megel, 1999). Findings from these studies show preliminary evidence supporting the presence of a dog during a stressful experience. However, additional study is needed before we can confidently add a dog as part of pediatric treatment environments.

More recently, a one-time dog visit was associated with decreased pain ratings by 25 children ages 5 to 18 years, 1 to 3 days after surgery (Sobo, Eng, & Kassity-Krich, 2006). The study used a one-group, pretest posttest design, and the children rated their pain and distress using a ruler-like visual rating scale before and after a brief visit with varying degrees of interaction from a therapy dog and its handler. The degrees of interaction with the dog ranged from low (quiet petting) to high (rough play or walking). The small sample size limits generalizability of the findings, as does the lack of a control group. The findings were positive despite a nonstandardized intervention across children, suggesting that we need further knowledge about the varying benefits of the range of children's involvement with a dog in a hospital setting. In addition, we do not know whether children in more pain engaged in less intense interaction, and what degree of interaction was most beneficial.

Martin and Farnum (2002) used a within-participants, repeated-measures design to study AAT with 10 children ranging in age from 3 to 13 years who had autism or other pervasive developmental disorders. Each child experienced each experimental condition (live dog present, stuffed dog or ball present during therapy). When the therapy dog was present, the children were significantly more focused, more playful, and more aware of interactions than in either of the other conditions. Although the goal of therapy is commonly to increase the child's engagement with other individuals, additional research is needed to better delineate how much involvement with a dog during therapy may be most beneficial for these children. Furthermore, it is unclear to what extent the child may have paid more attention to the dog than the therapist. Clearly, individual therapy goals for the children need to enter into the research design or the data interpretation, and such findings need to be replicated in larger samples.

In a completely different context, the effects of hippotherapy (therapeutic horseback riding) were studied in children with spastic cerebral palsy. Fifteen children ranging in age from 4 to 12 years were randomly assigned via a detailed research protocol to either undergo an 8-minute riding session or to sit astride a barrel for 8 minutes while wearing a portable electromyogram (EMG) device. Through EMG readings, the investigators found a significant improvement in the muscle symmetry of the children who had ridden the horse but not those who sat astride a barrel (Benda, McGibbon, & Grant, 2003). The findings indicated that symmetry occurred via reduced activity of overactive muscles and increased activity in underactive muscles on contralateral sides.

These few studies of AAI in children raise questions warranting further investigation. They also raise issues common to all studies of AAI, such as the need for randomized trials with larger samples, the importance of standardized intervention protocols, and the complexity of measuring relevant outcome variables.

RELEVANCE FOR ADULTS

Acute Care Contexts

Stoffel and Braun (2006) conducted a secondary data analysis in which they compared pediatric and adult hospitalized patients. In both categories

(40 pediatric patients and 25 adults), patients reported less pain during and after an animal visit in qualitative testimonials about the experience of AAT. Participants most commonly reported feeling a sense of relaxation in response to AAI. They also reported feeling pain relief and a sense that the dog "took on the pain." In addition, their statements indicated a positive change in affect in response to the AAI and that their breathing and heart rates "matched the dog's" during the AAI, helping them to relax and feel more peaceful. Pediatric patients were significantly more likely to describe the feelings of relaxation than were adults (Stoffel & Braun, 2006). The testimonial data of the participants in this study add richness to our understanding of how AAI may benefit hospitalized patients. It would behoove investigators to include such data collection techniques (testimonials) in future studies to further elucidate quantitative findings.

Including such qualitative data was done by Johnson, Meadows, Haubner, and Sevedge (2008) in a randomized trial of 30 adult patients undergoing radiation therapy for cancer. The patients were randomly assigned to dog-with-handler visits, friendly human visits, or quiet reading sessions for 30 minutes, three times per week for 4 weeks. The investigators found no significant differences in mood or sense of coherence across groups. However, compared with others their age, participants receiving dog visits reported that their health improved during the study period. Participants in each group described their experiences as beneficial and gave advice regarding timing of such experiences for future patients with cancer. The study illustrates the complexities of designing and implementing standardized AAI for research protocols and identification of appropriate control experiences for future randomized trials.

A similar randomized, three-group, repeated-measures design was used with 76 hospitalized adult patients ranging in age from 18 to 80 years and experiencing advanced heart failure (Cole, Gawlinski, Steers, & Kotlerman, 2007). The investigators studied a range of physiological variables, including blood pressure, pulmonary artery pressure, pulmonary capillary wedge pressure, and plasma catecholamine levels (epinephrine and norepinephrine). Patients' self-rated anxiety was also studied. The intervention consisted of one, 12-minute visit with a dog and handler, a human visitor, or a quiet rest period. Patients in the dog/handler group had significant improvements in hemodynamic indicators, decreased catecholamine levels both during and after the intervention, and decreased anxiety levels after AAI. The study used 14 different dogs. It is not reported how many different handlers or human volunteers were used. No attempts were made to standardize conversations in any of the visits. However, the use of biophysiologic indicators with a randomized design make this study a major contribution to the literature on the efficacy of AAI in an acute care setting.

Long-Term Care

There is a growing body of research developing in long-term care settings with older adults. However, in an early study (Kongable, Buckwalter, & Stolley, 1989), investigators found that when a dog was making visits to residents in a nursing home setting, there were more pro-social behaviors among residents and increased interaction among residents and also between residents and staff. The investigators not only tested these outcomes when dogs visited, but after a "washout" period, introduced a resident dog mascot to the nursing home environment. Findings were similar.

Banks and Banks (2002) randomly assigned 45 nursing home residents to receive one 30-minute individual AAI session per week, three 30-minute AAI sessions per week, or no visits, for 6 weeks. They found that both dog visit situations were associated with significantly less loneliness than the no-treatment control situation. Previous pet ownership was associated with a desire to receive AAI.

Subsequently the same investigators compared group versus individual AAI in 37 nursing home residents with loneliness scores indicating that they were lonely. Participants were randomized to receive either individual or group (consisting of 2–4 persons) AAI sessions once per week for 6 weeks. Findings revealed significant beneficial changes in loneliness scores in the individual AAI sessions but not in the group sessions. The authors concluded that the main effects for AAI were associated with interacting with the dog and not the added socialization that occurred between participants in the group AAI sessions (Banks & Banks, 2005).

In another study, Banks, Willoughby, and Banks (2008) compared AAI using a living dog with AAI using AIBO, the robotic dog created by Sony. In 38 nursing home residents receiving one 30-minute session for 8 weeks with either a live dog or AIBO, the investigators found that loneliness scores decreased significantly in both conditions. Attachment to either the live dog or the AIBO was not related to loneliness. The authors concluded that robotic dogs may be beneficial for these older adults. A no-treatment control group was used, but there was no interaction/sham control group to identify whether the attention of having regular visits of any kind may have been of benefit. Furthermore, as is the case in many AAI studies with small samples, the mean values of the dependent variables were used as the basis for statistical analysis. Given the instability of mean values, with small samples, the median values would produce results less vulnerable to extremes.

In a different form of AAI, Edwards and Beck (2002) studied 62 residents of Alzheimer's special care units in a time series design with a non-equivalent control group. The older adults had significant increases in food intake (21%) and weight (1.65 lb) during a treatment period and for 6 weeks afterward while watching fish swim in self-contained aquariums during meal-times. The improvement in nutrition intake resulted in a decreased use of nutritional supplements, resulting in a health care cost savings.

Studies of nursing home residents are the most numerous in the AAI field. Although each of the example studies described here may be viewed as providing preliminary data due to small sample sizes, their designs are robust and their findings worthy of further investigation. They raise important questions that need to be addressed in the same and different contexts.

A DIFFERENT MODEL OF AAI: DOG WALKING

Recently, dog walking has been receiving growing attention as an alternative form of AAI. Although it is commonly viewed as a usual activity associated with proper care of a dog by its owners, dog walking may also be used as an intervention in a variety of contexts. It may be especially relevant for older adults in whom maintaining physical functioning is critical to maintaining independence and preventing nursing home placement. For example, the author has undertaken a three-group, repeated-measures design testing the efficacy of a 12-week (5 day/week) shelter dog walking program for 54 retirement facility residents older than age 65. Participants either walked with a shelter dog and a handler, a human walking companion, or engaged in usual activities (Johnson, McKenney, & McCune, 2009). Participants in the dog walking group lost 2 pounds compared with no weight loss in the other two groups. Participants in the dog walking group significantly increased their mean 6-minute timed walk distances by 28% ($p = .012$), whereas those in the human walking companion group and control group had nonsignificant increases of 6% and 4%, respectively. Walking speed is believed to be an indicator of balance, and for older adults, balance is crucial for preventing falls and maintaining independence.

In another dog walking study using a one-group, repeated-measures design, 13 community-dwelling older adults walked both with and without a therapy dog for 30 minutes on 3 consecutive days. They experienced a significant increase in parasympathetic neural activity while walking with a dog, and this continued to increase during successive walks. The investigators also took the therapy dog to the homes of participants for two, 30-minute free interactions with the dog. They concluded that the dog walking and dog visits were potential buffers to stress given the relaxation responses observed (Motooka, Koike, Yokoyama, & Kennedy, 2006).

If dog walking is to be construed as an intervention to facilitate fitness, reduce stress, and maintain functioning, perhaps the best context for testing this notion is the current obesity and sedentary lifestyle epidemic that is pervasive in the United States and elsewhere. For example, in one study (Kushner, Blatner, Jewell, & Rudloff, 2006) in the United States, 36 obese adult dog owners whose dogs were also obese and 56 overweight or obese people without pets engaged in a prospective weight loss program. Weight loss and an increase in activity levels were similar in both groups; however, in the dog walking group, two thirds of this total physical activity was dog-related activity. The dogs were seen by participants as support sources promoting physical activity.

In another study (Johnson & Meadows, 2010), 26 overweight, sedentary adult residents of public housing were motivated to engage in a graduated dog walking program in which they walked with therapy dogs with a handler. Participants walked 20 minutes, 5 days per week, for either 26 or 50 weeks. Thirteen participants in the 50-week group had a mean adherence rate of 72% and weight loss of 14.4 pounds ($p = .035$). Thirteen participants in the 26-week group had a mean adherence rate of 52% and weight loss of 5 pounds (ns). Participants' most commonly stated reason for participating was that the dogs "need us to walk them." The study demonstrated that commitment to a dog that is not one's own may be a motivator of physical activity.

The notion of commitment to dogs that need their exercise is also a beneficial motivator for exercise among dog owners. For example, Australian dog owners walked 18 minutes per week more than did nonowners and met national physical activity recommendations of 150 minutes per week (Bauman, Russell, Furber, & Dobson, 2000). Similar trends were found in the United States, where adults who walked dogs accumulated at least 30 minutes of walking in bouts of at least 10 minutes daily, meeting governmental recommendations for physical activity (Ham & Epping, 2006). More recently, 142 community-dwelling older adult dog owners who walked their dogs three times per week had faster walking speeds and were more likely to maintain these over a 3-year period than were 252 dog owners who did not walk their dogs, or 2,137 nonowners of dogs (Thorpe et al., 2006). The findings suggest that the walking of their dogs by older adults may be a beneficial activity for maintaining physical function.

ISSUES IN AAI RESEARCH

Although AAI has been used in various health care practice settings for many years and has shown rapid growth during the past decade, the body of research evidence demonstrating its benefits has been slower to grow. To date there has been one meta-analysis conducted in which 49 published studies of AAI were compared (Nimer & Lundahl, 2007). In this synthesis, the authors concluded that AAI is effective for "medical well-being" and behavioral outcomes in adults and for improving the therapy participation of children with autism and autism-related developmental disorders. The investigators found that effect size was not significantly related to rigor in conduct of the studies included in the meta-analysis. They concluded that individual AAI was more beneficial than group AAI and that fewer AAI sessions yielded stronger effect sizes than did studies with greater numbers of AAI sessions. Most studies included in the analysis involved adults, targeted mental health concerns, and involved dogs as the AAI medium. Their findings showed that AAI was as effective as other interventions studied by comparison. They further found no significant differences in effect size between studies using comparison groups and those not doing this.

Another testament to the development of the AAI field of inquiry is a recently published evaluation of the evidence base for AAI (Halm, 2008). The author applied the international classes of clinical evidence to 10 studies that focused on AAI with hospitalized patients and concluded that AAI met the criteria for Classes IIa and IIb, meaning that it is acceptable and useful for this population, based on research evidence that is substantiated by expert opinion.

However, despite the meta-analysis findings and clinical evidence review, the AAI field needs to advance the science rapidly to more beneficially guide practice, rather than continuing to allow practice to lead the field. There exists a critical need to further test AAI to identify what populations may be most likely to benefit (e.g., adults, children, acute care settings, or long-term care), what may be the optimal dose (length of AAI and number of sessions), and means of administration (group vs. individual AAI). Now a robust body of preliminary studies exists from which to ask these questions with more sophisticated designs and methods. In particular, data analysis decisions need to be considered carefully. Investigators have begun to ask these questions in comparing AAI modalities and mechanisms. The evidence has begun to show that AAI is not a one-size-fits-all intervention, thus further study is needed to ascertain the most likely clinical situation in which it will be of benefit. This will help to refute the common belief that AAI is beneficial in all situations with all patients. Clearly, it is time to move the field beyond anthropomorphic-based assumptions that animals used in AAI can address any clinical problem. However, due to the inevitable logistical complexity of the next generation of research (larger-scale randomized trials), larger funding pools are needed if this advancement is to take place. In the last several decades, investigators have been building the body of preliminary evidence using internal or small externally funded grants. The time has come for large, randomized, and perhaps multisite studies to take place. Until investigators and funders make a strong commitment to rigorous scientific studies at a level that can legitimately build an evidence base sufficient to influence clinical practice, it will not be possible to move the AAI field forward enough to make a significant difference toward a clear delineation of acceptable AAI practice.

REFERENCES

Banks, M., & Banks, W. (2002). The effects of animal-assisted therapy on loneliness in an elderly population in long-term care facilities. *Journal of Gerontology: Biological Sciences, 57A,* M428–M432.

Banks, M., & Banks, W. (2005). The effects of group and individual animal-assisted therapy on loneliness in residents of long-term care facilities. *Anthrozoos, 14*(4), 396–406.

Banks, M. R,. Willoughby, L. M., & Banks, W. A. (2008). Animal-assisted therapy and loneliness in nursing homes: Use of robotic versus living dogs. *Journal of the American Medical Directors Association, 9*(3), 173–177.

Bauman, A. E., Russell, S. J., Furber, S. E., & Dobson, A. J. (2000). The epidemiology of dog walking: An unmet need for human and canine health. *Medical Journal of Australia, 175*(11–12), 632–634.

Benda, W., McGibbon, N. H., & Grant, K. L. (2003). Improvements in muscle symmetry in children with cerebral palsy after equine-assisted therapy (hippotherapy). *Journal of Alternative and Complementary Medicine, 9*(6), 817–825.

Cole, K., Gawlinski, A., Steers, N., & Kotlerman, J. (2007). Animal-assisted therapy in patients hospitalized with heart failure. *American Journal of Critical Care, 16,* 575–585.

Edwards, N. E., & Beck, A. M. (2002). Animal assisted therapy and nutrition in Alzheimer's disease. *Western Journal of Nursing Research, 24*(6), 697–712.

Halm, M. A. (2008). The healing power of human-animal connection. Clinical evidence review. *American Journal of Critical Care, 17*(4), 373–376.

Ham, S. A., & Epping, J. (2006). Dog walking and physical activity in the United States. *Preventing Chronic Disease, 3*(2), A47.

Hansen, K. M., Baun, M. M., Messinger, C. J., & Megel, M. (1999). Companion animals alleviating distress in children. *Anthrozoos, 12*(3), 142–148.

Havener, L., Gentes, L., Thaler, B., Megel, M. E., Baun, M. M., Driscoll, F. A., ... Agrawal, S. (2001). The effects of a companion animal on distress in children undergoing dental procedures. *Issues in Comprehensive Pediatric Nursing, 24,* 137–152.

Johnson, R. A., McKenney, C., & McCune, S. (2009). *Walk a hound lose a pound & stay fit for seniors.* Talk through poster presented at the Midwest Nursing Research Society, 33rd Annual Research Conference, Minneapolis, Minnesota, March 27–30, 2009.

Johnson, R. A., & Meadows, R. (2010). Dog-walking: Motivation for adherence to a walking program. *Clinical Nursing Research*. Advance online publication. doi: 10.1177/1054773810373122.

Johnson, R. A., Meadows, R., Haubner, J., & Sevedge, K. (2008). Animal assisted activity with cancer patients: Effects on mood, fatigue, self-perceived health and sense of coherence. *Oncology Nursing Forum, 35*(2), 1–8.

Kongable, L., Buckwalter, K., & Stolley, J. (1989). The effects of pet therapy on the social behavior of institutionalized Alzheimer's clients. *Archives of Psychiatric Nursing, 3*(4), 191–198.

Kruger, K., & Serpell, J. (2006). Animal-assisted interventions in mental health: Definitions and theoretical foundations. In A. Fine (Ed.), *Handbook on animal assisted therapy* (pp 21–38). San Diego, CA: Elsevier, Academic Press.

Kushner, R. F., Blatner, D. J., Jewell, D. E., & Rudloff, K. (2006). The PPET study: People and pets exercising together. *Obesity, 14*(10), 1762–1770.

Martin, F., & Farnum, J. (2002). Animal-assisted therapy for children with pervasive developmental disorders. *Western Journal of Nursing Research, 24*(6), 657–670.

Motooka, M., Koike, H., Yokoyama, T., & Kennedy, N. (2006). Effect of dog-walking on autonomic nervous activity in senior citizens. *Medical Journal of Australia, 184*, 60–63.

Nimer, J., & Lundahl, B. (2007). Animal-assisted therapy: A meta-analysis. *Anthrozoos, 20*(3), 225–238.

Odendaal, J. S. (1999). *A physiological basis for animal-facilitated psychotherapy.* Unpublished doctoral dissertation. University of Pretoria, Faculty of Veterinary Science, Pretoria, South Africa.

Sobo, E. J., Eng, B., & Kassity-Krich, N. (2006). Canine visitation (pet) therapy: Pilot data on decreases in child pain perception. *Journal of Holistic Nursing, 24*, 51–57.

Stoffel, J., & Braun, C. (2006). Animal-assisted therapy: An analysis of patient testimonials. *Journal of Undergraduate Nursing Scholarship, 8*(1). Retrieved August 22, 2007, from http://juns.nursing.arizona.edu/

Thorpe, R., Simonsick, E. M., Brach, J. S., Ayonayon, H., Satterfield, S., Harris, T. B., . . . Kritchevsky, S. B. (2006). Dog ownership, walking behavior, and maintained mobility in late life. *Journal of the American Geriatrics Society, 54*(9), 1419–1424.

Wilson, C. (1991). The pet as an anxiolytic intervention. *Journal of Mental and Nervous Disease, 179*, 482–489.

AFTERWORD: AN AGENDA FOR FUTURE RESEARCH

PEGGY McCARDLE, SANDRA McCUNE, LAYLA ESPOSITO,
VALERIE MAHOLMES, AND LISA FREUND

Pets are a major part of family life in many nations around the world. In some industrialized nations, as many as two thirds of families own pets. In addition, family demographics in many of these nations are changing. For example, as the size of the typical family household in the United States decreases, many children may be more likely to grow up with a pet than with a younger sibling, two parents, or a grandparent in the home. Therefore, it is important for research to examine the effects of these changing demographics on child development and health.

The National Institutes of Health (NIH, 1987) conference "The Health Benefits of Pets" specifically highlighted the need to study the effect of animal interaction on children and their development. Now, more than 20 years later, we reiterate and strengthen that call. To guide and stimulate further study, a research agenda is presented.

Broadly, this research agenda calls for additional work, with a focus on the interaction between human and animal, on human or animal behaviors

The views expressed in this manuscript are those of the authors and do not necessarily represent those of the National Institutes of Health, *Eunice Kennedy Shriver* National Institute of Child Health and Human Development, the U.S. Department of Health and Human Service, or Mars, Incorporated.

that would affect that interaction, and the influence/effect that interaction has. This is addressed in five major segments: (a) research on the interaction itself, which can guide deeper basic understanding, safety for both humans, especially children, and animals, and injury prevention; (b) research on the effect of pets on child development; (c) research on child health; (d) intervention studies, testing the efficacy of human–animal interaction (HAI) as an intervention or adjunct to intervention; and (e) the importance of biomarkers and biobehavioral and genetic data.

THE NATURE OF THE HUMAN–ANIMAL INTERACTION

Research is needed to better understand the nature of interactions between people and various types of animals, including study of the relationships themselves, as well as the contexts and conditions under which they occur. Studies of essential behaviors in both animals (see Chapter 5, this volume, which describes studies of dog behaviors) and humans will help to inform a deeper understanding of HAI and to underpin the development of HAI-based interventions. It is important that we understand HAI aspects that can present safety hazards to minimize danger and prevent problematic interactions that might be harmful either for the human or the pet. The Centers for Disease Control reports that 4.5 million Americans are bitten by dogs each year, and one in five dogs bites results in injuries that require medical attention (Gilchrist, Sacks, White, & Kresnow, 2008). Dog bites are most prevalent among young children, and although the rate of dog bite-related injuries in children has decreased recently (Gilchrist et al., 2008), such injuries remain a serious public health issue. Knowing how and when and under what conditions such injuries occur is crucial to preventing them. In addition, clear descriptions of animal behaviors and what they signal regarding interactions between pets and people is crucial to reducing the risk of injuries (e.g., dog bites, which are more prevalent with preschool children). Research on how and when animals demonstrate fear, aggression, or defensive behaviors can provide a base of information to guide people in their interactions with animals and can guide parents and those advising parents about how and when to let their children have pets of their own and interact with the pets of others.

Studies are needed to address why relationships with pets are more important to some individuals than to others and to explore the quality of human–pet relationships, noting variability of human–animal relationships within a family. For example, it has been noted that abusive individuals often have a history of abusing animals before abusing other humans; however, the presence of a pet may be a solace to a maltreated child or adult (Arkow,

2007). Developmental studies are needed that examine child–pet interactions and relationships as they change over time and within changing family dynamics. Community-level and social benefits of interactions with animals also should be considered, beyond the benefits of the individual pet owner.

HAI AND CHILD DEVELOPMENT

HAI studies can inform us about how interactions between children and pets can influence children's social, emotional, cognitive, and even language development. One interesting question that could be addressed experimentally is whether the presence of pets can mitigate shyness or inhibition in timid children. Is there an optimal or minimal age at which such a relationship or interaction might be most effective? Self-esteem and self-regulation in children, especially in children with ADHD/ADD, might be enhanced via interaction with animals. Pets may play a role in providing solace to children who are grieving the loss of a loved one, and indeed loss of a pet may even represent such a loss to a child. Displaced families, whether displaced by disasters or through seeking shelter from abusive situations, may not be able to keep pets with them, and being deprived of interaction with an animal that has become important in a child's life can have traumatic effects. Studies of grief and loss in children should include the roles of animals in those children's lives.

CHILDREN AND PETS: HEALTH AND PHYSICAL WELL-BEING

There are critical public health issues facing children and youth today for which HAI may have a direct impact, such as activity level and obesity, allergies, attention deficit, depression, and other mental health issues. Anecdotally, most people will agree that animals may have a therapeutic effect, whether informal or formally, on the lives, health, and development of children. Studies suggest pets may affect children's health, either causing or preventing allergies and easing anxiety (Nagengast, Baun, Megel, & Leibowitz, 1997) and encouraging exercise (see Chapter 7, this volume). However, many of the available studies in the literature are based on small samples and stop short of providing answers to key developmental questions (see Introduction and Chapter 2, this volume).

There are many questions about the health effects of HAI that could be answered by well-designed research studies. For example, how important is the timing of children's exposure to pets regarding health? That is, what effect does earlier or later exposure have on the development of allergies and immune function? It is important to know whether HAI can change the perception of pain, other physical symptoms, and sense of well-being in children undergoing painful procedures and in post-treatment situations. This can be particularly important in children with chronic or life-threatening diseases requiring painful or stressful treatments, such as cancer. Therapeutic involvement of animals also addresses both health and development issues in children.

THERAPEUTIC INVOLVEMENT OF ANIMALS

Clinically, the field has not waited for definitive studies of HAI effects to be completed before involving animals in therapeutic settings. Dogs, cats, horses, and even other species such as llamas and monkeys are being trained and involved in assisting those with disabilities and as adjuncts to therapeutic interactions. An increasing number of therapeutic interventions involve HAI, often based on anecdotal evidence and short-term observation. Clearly, clinical studies are needed to demonstrate the efficacy of animal-assisted intervention (AAI) in therapeutic settings for those with specific health or behavior problems or developmental disabilities. How can professional service providers best determine whether, in what context, and with what frequency animals might play a beneficial role in delivering therapeutic services to those who, for example, have experienced traumatic events or have developmental or physical disabilities? Does animal-assisted therapeutic intervention influence the ability of individuals with autism spectrum disorder to engage with and relate to humans? Is the effect of this intervention different for older individuals than it is for children? Does a child with autism spectrum diagnosis react differently when looking at a dog versus a human face or to eye contact with dogs versus that with humans?

Although there is ongoing work on the use of animals in rehabilitation (Barker, Knisely, McCain, Schubert, & Pandurangi, 2010; Macauley, 2006; Wisdom, Saedi, & Green, 2009; Yorke, Adams, & Coady, 2008;), most of this work has been done in adults; more work is needed focused on children and adolescents. In addition, in all ages, it is important to examine for whom animal-assisted therapy is effective in rehabilitation settings (e.g., in the treatment of post-traumatic stress disorder [PTSD]), and under what conditions it is most effective.

Other important questions regarding treatment and rehabilitation also deserve investigation. For example, in children, can companion animals or pets support rehabilitation, both physically (exercise, physiological healing) and cognitively (learning disabilities are a known side effect in many pediatric cancer treatments)? Social and emotional benefits also should be studied. Can a low-cost intervention such as dog walking support rehabilitation after trauma or treatment procedures? Dog walking also may facilitate the benefits afforded by community contacts (a social facilitation effect leading to greater social capital) for those recovering from medical treatment or those with chronic illness.

BIOMARKERS AND BIOBEHAVIORAL AND GENETIC STUDIES

There are several questions about the nature and effect of HAI that can be answered by combining behavioral and biological measures (see Chapter 9, this volume). Specifically, there is a need for biobehavioral and genetic research in both animal models and human studies examining stress and social behavior. There are several questions that mesh well with the more behavioral aspects of HAI, child development, health, and therapeutic intervention issues discussed earlier, which provide examples of studies that might be conducted to address this area. The study of biological/physiological responses to HAI is crucial to our deeper scientific understanding of HAI and its effect on health, including child health and development. For example, are the effects of parental or human caregiver care on epigenetic regulation of hippocampal glucocorticoid receptor expression also seen in companion animals raised in abusive or neglected environments, and when such animals are rescued, can these biological effects be modified? In humans, can a companion animal modify the effect of non-nurturing or abusive experiences on epigenetic regulation of the hypothalamic–pituitary–adrenal (HPA) stress responses?

It is important to examine the neuroendocrine responses of both animals and humans to determine whether they vary during HAI. For example, what is the role of oxytocin and arginine vasopressin in the animal–human bond? Different polymorphisms of the vasopressin 1A receptor gene are linked to pair bonding and found in a variety of species. Is pair bonding between species also linked to this gene? Furthermore, could this gene be useful in the identification of pets for HAI activities?

There is a need to understand how interactions with a companion animal modulate the behavioral and stress response effects of adversity and to examine the interaction with genetic variations of the monoamine oxidase-A (MAOA) gene, the 5-HTT polymorphism, or the vasopressin 1a polymorphism. It would be interesting to examine whether individuals behave and react differently to HAI depending on their variant of these genes.

The canine genome has been available since 2005. Gene-behavior associations relevant to identifying suitable companion dogs have just begun to be investigated (Chapter 5, this volume; Jones, Chase, Martin, Ostrander, & Lark, 2008). Could such investigations be used to identify gene-behavior traits in canines, such as sociability, trainability, and ability to attend to humans?

Given that we have a canine genome and dogs have the potential to model various aspects of human socioemotional behavior, such as attachment, temperament, and self-regulation, could dogs be an appropriate model for understanding human gene-behavior associations? For example, guanylate cyclase (in humans and dogs) has a possible link between loss in early life experiences for children and late depression/anxiety, and the repeat polymorphism of the DRD4 gene, associated with ADHD in humans, is present in certain breeds of dogs exhibiting high activity-impulsivity depending on their environmental conditions. Are there genetic candidates in the dog for studying various social and emotional behaviors expressed by humans?

Finally, studies of animal and human nutrition linked to HAI may be highly informative. For example, it may be interesting to investigate whether nutritional support from sources such as omega 3 has a role in improving human and animal adaptive behaviors. Could there be a synergistic effect of nutritional support and animal-assisted therapy in children with maladaptive behaviors? Can aggressive dogs be managed through nutritional support?

METHODOLOGICAL ISSUES

Several chapters in this volume address research methods and approaches. In addition, as part of the research agenda development, multiple experts working in the field of HAI, conducting clinical work employing animal-assisted therapy techniques, and those from other disciplinary perspectives were asked to consider how best to approach key questions and issues in HAI research. There are several areas in which HAI can be seen as influencing the lives of people, and these influences can take place at multiple levels (individual, family, community), in formal and informal treatment settings, and using various methodological approaches. Some key approaches and methods are highlighted.   .

Clinical Trials

To study the effectiveness of AAIs, a clinical trial approach is recommended, using experimental or quasi-experimental methods, although mixed methods are recommended to understand not only whether an intervention is effective but also why and under what conditions. Although randomized controlled trials are a gold standard for making causal inferences, it is recognized that there may be times when such a design cannot be fully implemented;

where it can be used, it should, and where it cannot, the next most rigorous design should be used. Dose-response issues (such as how much time is required per session or how many sessions may be needed before results begin to be seen in the use of an animal as an adjunct to psychotherapy or behavior therapy) should be carefully targeted in research designs whenever possible. Simple pre- and post-treatment assessment designs, with valid and reliable behavioral measures or language production coding systems, are necessary to support or discount anecdotal beliefs, but moving beyond that, in therapeutic situations, rigorous experimental trials are needed to investigate the potential efficacy of the use of animal-assisted therapies. Both direct measurement and observational data are needed; measures may be physiological (e.g., neuroendocrines, genetic, heart rate, neuroimaging) or behavioral (cognitive, psychosocial, or psychoeducational).

Population-Level Studies of HAI

Large, population-based studies can inform the role of pets in the lives of people, yet such studies are costly and labor intensive. Nonetheless, primary prevention research through population studies is needed, including the development of survey instruments. One possible means of accomplishing this is with adjunct studies that can take advantage of ongoing large-scale projects, although feasibility may be limited by the time constraints faced by large studies, which can ask only so many questions and must limit the burden to respondents. Still, collaborating with population-based studies aimed at studying health and development offers a potentially cost-effective way of gathering important information about pets in the home and community and their effect on health and development for children, adults, and families. Although this information can be useful and informative in cross-sectional population studies, it is also important to gain information longitudinally on the same subjects when possible, with attention given to collaborating with studies that have appropriately diverse samples.

Inclusion of Diverse Samples

In the studies reporting health effects or therapeutic effects of HAI to date, few, if any, have examined the extent to which the relationship between pet ownership and health varies by race or socioeconomic status (SES). Minorities and members of low SES groups consistently exhibit higher rates of negative health behaviors, morbidity, and mortality (Agency for Healthcare Research and Quality, 2007). It is important, as HAI studies are undertaken, for investigators to ensure that their studies have a sufficient number of minorities and variation in SES to bolster our knowledge regarding the role of pets across racial/ethnic and SES groups. These efforts will provide key information necessary for health promoting strategies and interventions that may ultimately lead to policies that help reduce health disparities among these groups.

Protection of Both Human and Animal Research Participants

Ethical considerations must be remembered as HAI research is designed and conducted. HAI research raises ethical considerations for both the human and the animal partners in any interaction. Protection for both parties should be in place for any research conducted on HAI. Gathering information ethically and responsibly from children who are particularly vulnerable and for whom parental consent may be difficult to obtain (e.g., those in foster care) is a challenge that must be carefully addressed. Animal welfare is important and must be considered at all times, especially when animals are working with individuals who are emotionally disturbed or are placed in potentially abusive situations. In general, experienced animal handlers, animal behavior experts, or veterinarians should be considered as partners in HAI research endeavors, when they are not the primary investigators themselves.

Additional Tools and Methods

There is a specific need for tools/methods development to assist the study of HAI. For example, computerized methods of measuring animal–human activity that can be used in both cross-sectional and longitudinal studies are needed. Such methods might also be applicable to the development of behavioral phenotypes. As noted for population-level studies, standard questionnaires on pet ownership/exposure are needed for use in large-scale public health studies and in epigenetic studies and surveys, both prospective and retrospective, in children and adults. In addition, studies of social pair bonding using new methodologies to identify and classify pair bonding between people and pets and social traits in dogs and cats could offer valuable information, and investigations of dog–human eye tracking could help to determine the role of eye contact in the developing relationship between person and pet. Thus, the development and use of new technologies and tools, as well as new applications of existing methods and approaches, are needed.

CONCLUSION

A solid research base is needed at a foundational level to better understand the nature of the interaction between people and animals, including both pets encountered in daily life and the more formal use of animals in therapeutic interactions. Clinical trials of that interaction when used as a treatment itself or an adjunct to treatment will help the field to understand whether, how, and perhaps why such interactions have the effects they do. Given the prevalence of animals in nearly every aspect of our lives, in homes, clinics, schools, and care facilities, it is imperative that we develop a more comprehensive and rigorous research base on HAI and its influence on human health and child development. We hope that basic and applied research on HAI will enrich the broader field of psychology and that the work shared in this volume will mark a step in that direction, as well as entice more researchers to study HAI.

Finally, as the base of scientific evidence in these areas grows, research scientists must conscientiously share their HAI research findings not only with fellow researchers but also with care providers and educators, including those who provide guidance to families and communities and those engaged in the care and treatment of people and animals. Dissemination of findings and communication about effective practices will move us to an evidence-based practice from which individuals, families, and their pets can benefit.

REFERENCES

Agency for Healthcare Research and Quality, U.S. Department of Health and Human Services. (2007). *National healthcare disparities report*. (AHRQ Pub. No. 08-0041). Rockville, MD: Author.

Arkow, P. (2007). Animal maltreatment in the ecology of abused children: Compelling research and responses for prevention, assessment and intervention. *Protecting Children, 22,* 66–79.

Barker, S. B., Knisely, J. S., McCain, N. L., Schubert, C. M., & Pandurangi, A. K. (2010). Exploratory study of stress buffering response patterns from interaction with a therapy dog. *Anthrozoos: A Multidisciplinary Journal of the Interactions of People & Animals, 23*(1), 79–91.

Gilchrist, J., Sacks, J. J., White, D., & Kresnow, M. J. (2008). Dog bites: Still a problem? *Injury Prevention, 14*(5), 296–301.

Jones, P., Chase, K., Martin, A., Ostrander, E. A., & Lark, K. G. (2008). Single-nucleotide-polymorphism-based association mapping of dog stereotypes. *Genetics, 179,* 1,033–1,044.

Macauley, B. L. (2006). Animal–assisted therapy for persons with aplasia: A pilot study. *Journal of Rehabilitation Research and Development, 43,* 357–366.

Nagengast, S. L., Baun, M., Megel, M. M., & Leibowitz, J. M. (1997). The effects of the presence of a companion animal on physiological arousal and behavioral distress in children. *Journal of Pediatric Nursing, 12,* 323–330.

National Institutes of Health. (1987). The health benefits of pets. NIH Technology Assessment Statement Online, 1987 Sep 10–11. Retrieved August 4, 2009, from http://consensus.nih.gov/1987/1987HealthBenefitsPetsta003html.htm

Wisdom, J. P., Saedi, G. A., & Green, C. A. (2009). Another breed of "service" animals: STARS study findings about pet ownership and recovery from serious mental illness. *American Journal of Orthopsychiatry*, *79*(3), 430–436.

Yorke, J., Adams, C., & Coady, N. (2008). Therapeutic value of equine–human bonding in recovery from trauma. *Anthrozoos*, *21*, 17–30.

APPENDIX: A RESOURCE FOR STUDYING HUMAN–ANIMAL INTERACTION

TIM ADAMS

Human–animal interaction (HAI) research is still in its infancy, as evidenced by the fact that one major scientific term for the field—anthrozoology—still requires definition in many circles. Like infant animals and infant humans, this still-nascent field ventures forward in a sometimes bold, always curious, and occasionally vulnerable manner. Students, professionals, and researchers who find themselves interested in a new field often seek a centralized source of literature and information. A website is often a helpful place to begin exploring the literature and getting to know what a field is about.

In 2004, as part of work with an Australian noncommercial information service, Petcare Information and Advisory Service (PIAS),[1] an information management project on HAI research was developed (http://www.anthrozoology.org). To accomplish the website development work for this resource, it was important to understand the context and gain insight into: (a) how the many diverse areas of science that might seek this information perceived HAI, and (b) how these perceptions might be presented under one single banner. Informal background research was undertaken, with a literature review that extended beyond peer-reviewed material to gray literature and commentaries published on and around the topic of HAI. What emerged from this background research were three key themes, which are described here.

THEME 1: HUMAN–ANIMAL INTERACTION IS A YOUNG FIELD OF INVESTIGATION

Changes in attitudes to pet-keeping in the 1960s spurred interest in the role companion animals or pets play in human lives,[2] with the earliest formal studies of HAI occurring in the 1960s.[3] Interest in the field has grown considerably since that time, championed particularly by the Delta Society, a pioneering HAI organization.[4]

---

[1]http://www.petnet.com.au.
[2]Franklin, A. (1999). *Animals in modern culture—A sociology of human–animal relations in modernity.* Thousand Oaks, CA: Sage Publications.
[3]Levinson, B. (1962). The dog as "co-therapist." *Mental Hygiene, 46,* 59–65.
[4]Hines, L. (2003). Historical perspectives on the human–animal bond. *American Behavioral Scientist, 47(1),* 7–15.

TABLE A.1
Examples of the Use of the Term "Anthrozoology"
in Tertiary Institutions in the Last Two Decades

University	Use of the Term "Anthrozoology"
Azabu University, Japan	The Educational Research Center for Anthrozoology
Azabu University, Japan	*Journal of Anthrozoology,* Japan; published by IPEC Inc. Tokyo
University of Cambridge, UK	Centre for Animal Welfare and Anthrozoology
University of Chester, UK	Chester Centre for Stress Research, Anthrozoology Unit
Liverpool Hope University, UK	Psychology offers a course in Anthrozoology
Monash University, Australia	Anthrozoology Research Group
Norwegian University of Life Sciences, Norway	Center of Anthrozoology
University of Southampton, UK	Anthrozoology Institute
University of Wales, Lampeter, UK	Department of Archaeology and Anthropology offers an MA Anthrozoology
University of Wales, Lampeter, UK	Anthrozoology Society
Western Illinois University, U.S.	Sociology and Anthropology Department offers a course in Anthrozoology

The first HAI journal, *Anthrozoös*, had its first edition published in 1987, followed shortly thereafter by the creation of the term "anthrozoology."[5] Organizational interest in the field grew soon after, with the creation of two new groups: (a) an academically oriented organization, the International Society for Anthrozoology (ISAZ),[6] founded in 1990 after a Waltham Symposium on "Pets, Benefits and Practice" and (b) the more practitioner-oriented International Association of Human Animal Interaction Organisations (IAHAIO),[7] founded in 1990 at the Leicester Hospice in the United Kingdom (and incorporated in 1992 in Renton, Washington). During the past two decades, many smaller groups and organizations with an interest in HAI also have formed.

The term *anthrozoology* is used most notably by the ISAZ, although several tertiary institutions and special interest research groups also use the term (Table A.1).

---

[5]Personal Communication. (November 2001) Anthony Podberscek quoting correspondence with Andrew Rowan and ISAZ Newsletter November.
[6]http://www.isaz.net.
[7]http://www.iahaio.org.

THEME 2: THE DIVERSITY OF THE FIELD CAN BE BOTH A STRENGTH AND A WEAKNESS

In 1998 Wilson[8] provided a sound overview of a field still coming to grips with scientific diversity. She listed a series of issues that complicated the study of human animal relationships, such as the selection of conceptual framework(s), management of projects, professional credibility, methodological issues, political and professional considerations, and training and funding. She makes the pragmatic observation that the complexities listed will be "both the strength and the weakness of the continued development of the field."

A considerable number of disciplines are represented in the literature that encompasses HAI (see Table A.2), and there are an equally broad array of schools with some form of offering in anthrozoology, including schools of arts; animal welfare and ethics; medicine; nursing; psychology; sociology and anthropology; social and cultural studies; social work; and veterinary science.

THEME 3: DEFINITIONS, SEARCH TERMS, AND KEYWORDS ARE SOMEWHAT FLUID

Targeted searches for literature in anthrozoology can at times be challenging because contributions to the literature come from many different fields. There are two international journals dedicated to publishing material relating to the interactions of humans and animals: *Anthrozoos*, published quarterly by Berg Publishers (Oxford, United Kingdom), and *Society and Animals*, published quarterly by Brill Academic Publishers (Leiden, The Netherlands). In addition, there are more than 200 other journal titles from around the world in more than a dozen broad fields that carry articles on HAI. (See Table A.2.)

With consideration of the three themes, the anthrozoology.org project was able to develop the following objectives:

- to provide freely available high-quality information on HAI;
- to encompasses the diverse HAI field;
- to identify multiple disciplines and group them together under a single "banner"; and
- to give further context and substance to the term *anthrozoology*.

---

[8]Wilson, C., & Turner, D. (Eds). (1998) *Companion animals in human health*. Sage Publications.

TABLE A.2
Journals With One or More Abstracts Appearing
on Anthrozoology.org

Discipline	Journal
Animal Sciences	*Indian Journal of Animal Sciences*
	Institute for Laboratory Animal Research (ILAR) Journal
Anthrozoology	*Anthrozoös*
	Society and Animals
	People–Animals–Environment
	Journal of Anthrozoology, Japan
Behavioral Science	*Ethics & Behavior*
	Ethology
	Evolution and Human Behaviour
	Journal of Behavioral Medicine
	Physiology & Behavior
	The American Behavioral Scientist
	Animal Behaviour
	Applied Animal Behaviour Science
	Behavioural Processes
	Developmental Psychobiology
Child Development	*Child and Youth Care Forum*
	Child Development
	Child: Care, Health and Development
	China Children's Centre Psychological Development and Education
Education	*Teaching Tolerance*
	Health Education
Environment	*Environmental Education Research*
	Alternatives Journal
	Children, Youth and Environments
Medicine	*Journal of Gerontology*
	Journal of the American Geriatrics Society
	Contemporary Pediatrics
	Current Allergy and Asthma Reports
	East African Medical Journal
	Emerging Infectious Diseases
	Environmental Research
	Epidemiology and Infection
	Expert Opinion on Biological Therapy
	Gerontology
	Headache
	Hypertension
	International Journal for Parasitology
	Japanese Journal of Geriatrics
	Journal of Applied Gerontology
	Journal of Clinical Microbiology
	Journal of Communicable Diseases
	Journal of ECT
	Journal of Nutrition for the Elderly
	Journal of Reproduction & Fertility
	Journal of the American Medical Association

Discipline	Journal
	Journal of the Royal Society of Medicine
	Acta Medica Mediterranea
	Respiratory Medicine
	Journals of Gerontology Series A—Biological Sciences & Medical Sciences
	Medical Hypotheses
	Medical Journal of Australia
	Neurology
	New York State Journal of Medicine
	Nippon Ronen Igakkai Zasshi (Japanese Journal of Geriatrics)
	Occupational Medicine
	Palliative Medicine
	Pediatric Allergy and Immunology
	Prevention
	Preventive Medicine
	Psychiatric Journal of the University of Ottawa
	Psychiatric Services
	Revista Alergia Mexico (Tecamachalco, Puebla, Mexico) [*Rev Alerg Mex*]
	Saudi Medical Journal
	Seizure
	Southern Medical Journal
	The Physician and Sportsmedicine
	Thorax
	Tropical Biomedicine
	Allergie et Immunologie [*Allerg Immunol (Paris)*]
	Allergy: European Journal of Allergy and Clinical Immunology
	American Family Physician
	American Journal of Alzheimer's Disease & Other Dementias
	American Journal of Cardiology
	American Journal of Geriatric Psychiatry
	American Journal of Infection Control
	American Journal of Preventative Medicine
	American Journal of Respiratory and Critical Care Medicine
	American Surgeon
	Annales Medico-Psychologiques [*Ann Med Psychol (Paris)*]
	Anticancer Research
	Archives of Gerontology and Geriatrics
	Archives of Internal Medicine
	British Journal of Psychiatry
	British Medical Journal

(continues)

Discipline	Journal
Multidiscipline	*Chest*
	Children's Health Care
	Clinical and Experimental Allergy
	Clinical Geriatrics
	European Respiratory Journal
	Journal of Allergy & Clinical Immunology
	The Annals, Academy of Medicine, Singapore
	Focus on Autistic Behavior
	Journal of Nervous & Mental Disease
	Psychosomatic Medicine
	Human Biology
	International Journal of Aging & Human Development
	Current Science. Indian Academy of Sciences, Bangalore, India
	Journal of Azabu University
	Journal of Hospital Infection
	Journal of Medical Speech–Language Pathology
	Journal of Occupational Health Psychology
	Obesity Research. North American Association for the Study of Obesity
	Psychotherapy and Psychosomatics
	Science [NLM - MEDLINE]
	Clinical Rehabilitation
	Ergotherapie und Rehabilitation
Nursing	*Clinical Nurse Specialist*
	Clinical Nursing Research
	College of Nursing and Health Science, George Mason University
	Critical Care Nurse
	Geriatric Nursing
	Holistic Nursing Practice
	Home Healthcare Nurse
	Image—The Journal of Nursing Scholarship
	Journal of Advanced Nursing
	Journal of Child & Adolescent Psychiatric Nursing
	Journal of Clinical Nursing
	Journal of Gerontological Nursing
	Journal of Holistic Nursing
	Journal of Psychosocial Nursing & Mental Health Services
	Nursing Research
	Nursing Spectrum
	Perspectives in Psychiatric Care
	Public Health Nursing
	Spinal Cord Injury (SCI) Nursing
	Western Journal of Nursing Research
	AACN Clinical Issues (American Association of Critical-Care Nurses)

TABLE A.2
Journals With One or More Abstracts Appearing
on Anthrozoology.org   *(Continued)*

Discipline	Journal
	Archives of Psychiatric Nursing
	AORN Journal (Association of periOperative Registered Nurses)
	Canadian Oncology Nursing Journal
	Critical Care Nursing Clinics of North America
	Journal of Clinical Nursing
	Journal of Pediatric Nursing
	Nursing Clinics of North America
Occupational Therapy	*Journal of Geriatric Physical Therapy*
	OT Practice
	Activities, Adaptation & Aging
	American Journal of Occupational Therapy
	Revue Canadienne d'Ergotherapie (*Canadian Journal of Occupational Therapy*)
Other	*Acta Biologica Hungarica*
	Journal of Leisure Research
	Journal of Park & Recreation Administration
	Journal of Pastoral Care
	The Journal of Death and Dying
	Death Studies
	American Zoologist
Psychology/Sociomedicine	*Current Directions in Psychological Science*
	Family Relations
	Journal of Children and Adolescent Group Therapy
	Journal of Personality & Social Psychology
	Journal of Psychosomatic Research
	Journal of Social Psychology
	Journal of Social Indicators Research
	Aggression and Violent Behavior
	Anxiety, Stress and Coping
	Focus on Autistic Behavior
	Stress, Trauma and Crisis
	Professional Psychology—Research & Practice
	Psychology & Aging
	Chinese Mental Health Journal
	Journal of Psychology
	Psychological Reports
	AIDS Care
	Behaviour Change
	Behaviour Research & Therapy
	British Journal of Psychology
Public Health	*International Journal of Behavioral Nutrition and Physical Activity 2008*
	Nippon Koshu Eisei Zasshi (*Japanese Journal of Public Health*)
	Public Health Reports
	Reviews on Environmental Health

(continues)

TABLE A.2
Journals With One or More Abstracts Appearing
on Anthrozoology.org *(Continued)*

Discipline	Journal
	Revista de Saude Publica (*School of Public Health, University of São Paulo*)
	American Journal of Public Health
	Annali dell Istituto Superiore di Sanita
	Annual Review of Public Health
	Health & Place
	Health Promotion Journal of Australia
	Journal of Physical Activity and Health
	Science and Medicine
Social Science(s)	*Social Indicators Research*
	Social Work in Health Care
	Symbolic Interaction
	American Behavioral Scientist
	Australian Social Monitor
	Journal of Family Social Work
	Social Work
Speech Therapy	*Seminars in Speech and Language,* journal
	Seminars in Speech and Language
	ASHA Leader (American Speech–Language–Hearing Association)
Veterinary Science	*Compendium Continuing Education for Veterinarians*
	Dipartimento di Scienze Sperimentali Veterinarie
	European Journal of Companion Animal Practice
	Journal of American Veterinary Medical Association
	Journal of Veterinary Behavior: Clinical Applications and Research
	Journal of Veterinary Medical Education
	Journal of Wildlife Diseases
	Preventive Veterinary Medicine
	Problems in Veterinary Medicine
	Small Ruminant Research
	The Veterinary Journal
	The Veterinary Quarterly
	Tieraerztliche Umschau
	Veterinary Clinics of North America: Small Animal Practice
	Veterinary Record
	Wiener Tierarztliche Monatsschrift
	Yamaguchi Journal of Veterinary Medicine
	Zentralbl Veterinarmed A
	Avian Diseases
	Acta Veterinaria Brno
	Acta Veterinaria Scandinavica
	American Journal of Veterinary Research
	Archives of Veterinary Science
	Australian Veterinary Journal

TABLE A.2
Journals With One or More Abstracts Appearing
on Anthrozoology.org *(Continued)*

Discipline	Journal
	Canadian Veterinary Journal
	Journal of the American Veterinary Medical Association
	Journal of the South African Veterinary Association
	Veterinary Research
Welfare Science	*Journal of Applied Animal Welfare Science*
	Animal Welfare

Organizing information logically was vital, as was the desire to be inclusive, rather than exclusive. The following sections discuss features of anthrozoology.org, as well as tips for using the website.

HOW ABSTRACTS ARE SELECTED FOR INCLUSION IN ANTHROZOOLOGY.ORG

When approaching a literature search in anthrozoology, it is important to recognize that there is a lack of common search terms. Differing search terms and definitions can return a similar set of results. There appear to be several terms commonly used to describe the field itself, including human–animal interaction, human–animal bond(s), human–companion-animal bond, human–pet bond, and people and pet relationships. When reviewing the literature, one must be prepared to interchange synonyms (e.g., human or people, animal or pet, interaction or relationship) to ensure a comprehensive search. In addition, the variable use of punctuation (e.g., *human–animal* or *human animal*) can make character-sensitive searches challenging.

Thanks to modern information technology, automated searches can increase the efficiency of literature research. However, with the need to use top level search terms, such as "human" and "animal," the requirement for researchers to manually filter their results remains high.

The boundary defining the field of anthrozoology appears to be rather porous. Bearing this in mind, the anthrozoology.org project applies two layers of filtration to abstracts before they appear on the database. The first layer consists of several crude automated searches using the broad (and interchangeable) keywords such as "human" and "animal." The second filter requires human input, whereby the content of an article is compared against a set of selection criteria intended to be still rather broad, yet able to be clearly articulated. These broad selection terms appear in Table A.3.

TABLE A.3
Terms Used as Selection Criteria for Abstracts for Anthrozoology.org

Terms	Example Paper
Animal effects on human physiology, health, and quality of life	Friedmann, E., Thomas, S. A., Cook, L. K., Tsai, C. C., & Picot, S. J. (2007). A friendly dog as potential moderator of cardiovascular response to speech in older hypertensives. *Anthrozoos, 20*(1), 51–63.
The influence of humans on animal physiology, health, and quality of life	Hennessy, M. B., Williams, M. T., Miller, D. D., Douglas, C. W., & Voith, V. L. (1998). Influence of male and female petters on plasma cortisol and behaviour: Can human interaction reduce the stress of dogs in a public animal shelter? *Applied Animal Behaviour Science, 61*(1), 63–77.
The influence of animals on human behavior, including social interaction, learning, and empathy	Daly, B., & Morton, L. L. (2006). An investigation of human–animal interactions and empathy as related to pet preference, ownership, attachment, and attitudes in children. *Anthrozoos, 19*(2), 113–127.
The influence of humans on animal behavior	Takeuchi, Y., Houpt, K. A., & Scarlett, J. M. (2000). Evaluation of treatments for separation anxiety in dogs. *Journal of the American Veterinary Medical Association, 217*(3), 342–345.
Animals harming humans	Sudarshan, M. K., Mahendra, B. J., Madhusudana, S. N., Ashwoath Narayana, D. H., Rahman, A., Rao, N. S., …Gangaboraiah. (2006). An epidemiological study of animal bites in India: Results of a WHO-sponsored national multi-centric rabies survey. *Journal of Communicable Diseases,38*(1), 32–39.
Humans harming animals	Ascione, F. R., Friedrich, W. N., Heath, J., & Hayashi, K. (2003). Cruelty to animals in normative, sexually abused, and outpatient psychiatric samples of 6- to 12-year-old children. *Anthrozoos, 16,* 194–212.
Social, cultural, historical attitudes to animals	Franklin, A. (1999). *Animals & modern cultures: A sociology of human–animal relations in modernity.* Thousand Oaks, CA: Sage Publications.
The psychology of the human–animal relationship	Zasloff, R. L. (1996, April). Measuring attachment to companion animals: A dog is not a cat is not a bird. *Applied Animal Behaviour Science, 47*(1–2), 43–48.
Human relations with, and attitudes to, the wider natural world	Lundgren, K. (2004). Nature-based therapy: its potential as a complimentary approach to treating communication disorders. *Seminars in Speech and Language, 25*(2), 121–131.
Animals in a therapeutic setting	Orlandi, M., Trangeled, K., Mambrini, A., Tagliani, M., Ferrarini, A., & Zanetti, L. (2007). Pet therapy effects on oncological day hospital patients undergoing chemotherapy treatment. *Anticancer Research, International Institute of Anticancer Research, Attiki, Greece, 27*(6C), 4301–4304.

HOW TO FIND ARTICLES IN ANTHROZOOLOGY.ORG

Anthrozoology.org has a broad audience that may include nonscientists (e.g., journalists, practitioners, students, and industry groups). Accordingly, a customized approach has been used to sort articles in the database. A system of topic headings or "categories" is used to enable easy sorting by area of user interest (e.g., "pets and children"). These categories can be used to locate articles of interest (in addition to the more common terms of author, journal, year, and title), and the category system, at least in part, addresses the difficulties encountered in a cross-disciplinary field. The system has been designed to ensure that each abstract is permitted to fall within multiple categories, thus ensuring flexible access to data. In addition, a search engine enabling simple Boolean logic is built into the site, enabling searches of all text content on the site, including author, journal, year, and title.

OTHER FEATURES OF ANTHROZOOLOGY.ORG

Additional supportive features on the site include a section for listing scientific events such as conferences and meetings, a media section for articles relating to research that appear in the popular press, and listings of tertiary institutions conducting research or offering course material in anthrozoology. The home page of the site also provides links to the most recent abstracts added to the site.

CURRENT USAGE AND STATUS OF THE WEBSITE

An anecdotal evaluation of the website shows it has achieved steady growth in visitors, receiving more than 3,000 unique visitors per month at the close of 2008. It has also received an industry award[9] (Australian Web Designers Network) in the categories of graphics, artwork, layout, navigability, functionality, and originality.

Ongoing site maintenance chiefly requires the addition of new scientific abstracts and when they are published. Abstracts are located through automated search, filtered manually by applying the terms outlined in Table A.3, and loaded to the site.

---

[9]Australian Web Designers Network, Gold Award, 2006; http://www.webdesigners.net.au/gold_website_awards.php

LIMITATIONS

The dominant language of the anthrozoology.org website is English, which has the potential to create a cultural bias on the site.

To develop the anthrozoology.org project, an informal review of available literature was undertaken. Although the author devoted considerable time to exploring the subject matter and seeking advice from those working as researchers in the field, the historical and contextual interpretations in the field of anthrozoology that apply to the development of the website are those of the author and have not been tested.

Because this project was undertaken outside of the university system, formal review of the resultant product (http://www.anthrozoology.org) has not occurred, chiefly due to resourcing. The content (scientific abstracts) has been provided on the site in good faith. Further opportunity exists to seek peer input on how material on the site is presented (e.g., rank, priority setting, categorization), an action that would require collaboration with a university or professional group.

Capacity for more exhaustive searches among published literature always exists. Additional available and established search tools such as PubMed[10] are recommended to augment all literature searches undertaken in anthrozoology.

---

[10]http://www.ncbi.nlm.nih.gov/pubmed/.

INDEX

AAA. *See* Animal-assisted activity
AAE (animal-assisted education), 18
AAI. *See* Animal-assisted interaction;
    Animal-assisted intervention
AATs. *See* Animal-assisted therapies
ACE (angiotensin-converting enzyme),
    172–174
Achenbach-Connors Quay Behavior
    Checklist (ACQ), 119, 120
ACTH. *See* Adrenocorticotrophic
    hormone
Acute care, 185–186
Acute stress, 169–174
Adolescent obesity. *See* Childhood
    obesity
Adolescents, 37–38, 144–145
Adrenal cortex, 64–66
Adrenocorticotrophic hormone
    (ACTH), 56, 61, 66–67
Adults, 19–20, 185–188
Affordances, perceptual, 15–16
Age, 96
Aggression, in dogs, 108
AIBO (robotic dog), 187
Allen, K., 145, 172
Allen, K. M., 174
Alzheimer's patients, 187–188
Ambiguous samples, 40
American Pet Products Manufacturers
    Association (APPMA), 14
Amico, J. A., 71
Anderson, G. M., 72
Anecdotal reports, 163
Angiotensin-converting enzyme (ACE),
    172–174
Animal abuse, 117–130
    assessment instruments, 119–120
    definition of, 118–119, 129
    developments in assessment of,
        121–126
    exposure to, 124–126
    future research directions, 129–130
Animal-assisted activity (AAA), 7,
    184–185

Animal-assisted education (AAE), 18
Animal-assisted interaction (AAI), 175,
    177–179
Animal-assisted intervention (AAI),
    183–191
    for adults, 185–188
    for children, 35, 184–185
    clinical trials, 198–199
    defined, 7
    dog walking model, 188–189
    in health care contexts, 183–184
    research issues, 189–191
    in therapeutic settings, 196
Animal-assisted therapies (AATs),
    35–50
    in child psychotherapy, 36–39
    defined, 6–7
    in health care contexts, 184
    methodological problems with
        research, 39–45
    questions for guiding treatments,
        47–49
    and relationship development, 18
    research design options, 45–47
Animal cruelty, 118–119, 129
Animals. *See also specific headings*
    in animal-assisted interaction
        research, 179
    animated/cartoon, 92–93
    attentional bias toward, 96
    and children, 14
    children's attention to, 87–88
    companion. *See* Companion animals
    and cultural vocabulary, 28
    human attention to, 87–88
    in human history, 85–86
    infant interactions with, 15–16,
        88–92, 95
    oxytocin levels in, 57–59
    presence of, 19, 26–27, 166–174
    in research design, 42–43
    sexual acting out with, 120–121
    socially valued, 122
    species of. *See* Species of animals
    static/dynamic features of, 94–95

Bond, human–canine, 105–107
Bonnett, B., 154
Boys, 123
BP levels. *See* Blood pressure levels
Brain, oxytocin levels in, 58–59, 64–65
Braun, C., 185
Breast-feeding, 59–62
Breeds, dog, 22, 105, 108–109
Bronfenbrenner, U., 26
Brown, S. G., 149
Bryant, B. K., 19
Buff, H., 88
Buffering hypothesis, 27
Bullying, 127
Burt, C., 119

CAAI (Children and Animals Assessment Instrument), 121–122
CABTA. *See* Children's Attitudes and Behavior Toward Animals
CAI (Children and Animals Inventory), 122–124
Call, J., 104
Cancer, 186
Canine genome, 197–198
Cardiovascular disease (CVD), 140
Cardiovascular stress responses, 171–172
Carter, C. S., 73
Cartoons, 93
Cats, 14, 15, 91, 108, 145, 159, 160, 172, 178, 196, 200
Causality, 42, 156–157
CBCL. *See* Child Behavior Checklist
CEDV (Children's Exposure to Domestic Violence Scale), 126
Cerebral palsy, 185
Change, 39, 42, 48–49
Characteristics, species-specific, 23–24
Chatterton, M., 71
Chemistry, hormone, 54–55
CHI (child-human interactions), 24–26
Child abuse, 128
Child–animal relationships, 26–27
Child Behavior Checklist (CBCL), 119, 120

Child development, 85–96
    animate-monitoring hypothesis, 87–88
    biophilia concept in, 86–87
    cruelty in, 130
    and human–animal interaction, 15–21, 195
    journals, 206
    pet ownership in, 4, 14–15
    research findings, 93–96
    visual attention to animals in infants, 88–93
Childhood obesity, 139–149
    and dog walking, 145–147
    future research directions, 147–149
    health and health behaviors, 140–142
    and pet ownership, 142–145
    and physical activity, 142–145
    rates and risk factors, 140
Childhood Trust Survey on Animal Related Experiences, 121
Child-human interactions (CHI), 24–26
Child maltreatment, 128
Child–pet interactions, 194–195
Child psychotherapy, 36–39
Children
    animal abuse by, 119–124
    animal-assisted interventions for, 35, 184–185
    antisocial behavior in, 119
    and attention to animals, 87–88
    behavior toward dogs by, 109–110
    diverse relationships of, 25
    as dog owners, 144–145
    and dogs in household, 101–102
    dogs socialized to presence of, 107
    and dog walking, 149
    effects of companion animal presence on, 26–27, 169–170
    evidence-based psychotherapies for, 49
    health and physical well-being in, 195–196
    in health care contexts, 184–185
    individual differences of, 22
    methods adapted for use with, 110–111
    and naturally occurring contexts, 13
    obesity in. *See* Childhood obesity

Development
  child. *See* Child development
  cognitive, 16
  human, 4
  of interventions, 148–149
  of language, 19–20
  moral, 20–21, 28
  perceptual, 15–16
  of relationships, 18
  social–emotional, 17–19
Developmental niches, 13
Developmental processes, 107
Developmental psychopathology,
    117–118
*Diagnostic and Statistical Manual of Mental
    Disorders (DSM-III-R)*, 119
Diagnostic Interview Scale for Children
    (DISC)-IV, 120
Distress, psychosocial, 164–165
Diverse samples, 39, 199–200
Dog aggression, 108
Dog bites, 102, 108–109, 194
Dog breeds, 22, 105, 108–109
Dog-caused fatalities, 102, 108
Dog owners
  children as, 107–108, 144–145
  cortisol levels in, 61, 63–64
  in development of interventions,
    148–149
  nonowners vs., 158–159
  oxytocin levels in, 102
  and physical activity of children,
    142–143
  weight status of, 146–147
Dogs, 101–111
  behavior variations of, 22
  canine genome, 197–198
  effect of blood pressure levels,
    169–174
  hormone levels in, 61, 63–64
  hormone measurement in, 67–68
  human-compatible behaviors in,
    105–107
  interactions with children,
    107–110
  interactions with humans, 102–104
  obese, 149, 189
  playing with, 143–144
  robotic, 187
  sensitivity to human actions in, 106

Dog walking
  and childhood obesity, 145–147
  in children, 144–145
  effect on heart rate variability, 167
  factors that support/restrict, 149
  by families, 143–145, 147
  model for animal-assisted inter-
    ventions, 188–189
  and physical activity recommenda-
    tions, 142
Domestic dogs. *See* Dogs
Domestic violence, 25, 126–128
Dominic Interactive, 120
Dorey, N. R., 106
Dose effects, 179
*DSM-III-R (Diagnostic and Statistical
    Manual of Mental Disorders)*, 119
Duffy, D. L., 109
Duncan, A., 128
Dynamic features, 94–95

EAA (exposure to animal abuse),
    124–126
Ecological niches, 27, 101
Ecological systems, 13
Economic benefits, 159
Education journals, 206
Edwards, N. E., 187
EIA. *See* Enzyme immunoassay
ELISA (enzyme-linked immuno-
    absorbent assay), 69
Elliot, O., 105
Emotion, 26–27
Emotional health, 141–142
Emotional responses, 89–90
Empathy, 108, 127
Endocrinologic measurement, 62–70
Environmental experiences, 107
Environmental risk factors, 109
Environmental specificity, 24
Environment journals, 206
Enzyme immunoassay (EIA),
    68–69, 73
Enzyme-linked immunoabsorbent assay
    (ELISA), 69
Estrogen, 67–68
Esveldt-Dawson, K., 120
Etiology, 42
Evidence-based psychotherapies, 37

Hormone research, 53–74
  on cortisol levels, 61
  effects of hormones, 61, 63–64
  endocrinologic measurement,
    62–70
  on oxytocin levels, 55–60, 70–73
  peptide hormones, 55
  release profiles of hormones, 66
  steroid hormones, 54–55
Horseback riding, 185
Horvat-Gordon, M., 73
Hospitalized patients, 185–186
HPA (hypothalmic-pituitary-
    adrenocortical), 164–165
HR. *See* Heart rate
HRV. *See* Heart rate variability
Hsu, Y., 109
Human–animal interaction (HAI),
    193–198. *See also specific
    headings*
  biobehavioral and genetic studies,
    197–198
  and child development, 15–21, 195.
    See also Child development
  of children with pets, 195–196
  defined, 6
  early humans, 85–86
  in health context, 164–166
  hormone levels in, 61, 63–64
  nature of, 194–195
  therapeutic involvement of animals,
    196–197
Human–animal interaction research,
    3–7, 13–28
  challenges of, 5–6
  child development in, 15–21
  contextual research in, 13–15
  contributions of, 4–5
  controls in, 176
  cultural meanings of, 27–28
  definitions/search terms/keywords
    for, 205, 211–212
  individual differences, 21–24
  interpersonal interactions and
    relationships, 24–26
  levels of analysis in, 24
  literature searches in, 211–212
  measures of stress indicators in,
    176–177
  methodological issues in, 198–200

multidimensionality in child–animal
    relationships, 26–27
  as new field, 203
  protection of participants in, 200
  quantification of, 176
  scientific diversity in, 205
  terminology for, 6–7
Human–canine bond, 105–107
Human cues, 102
Human gestures, 103
Human history, 85–87
Human perceptions, 24
Hypothalmic–pituitary–adrenocortical
    (HPA) system, 164–165

IAHAIO (International Association of
    Human Animal Interaction
    Organisations), 204
Inagaki, K., 16
Inanimate objects, 88–91, 93
Incarcerated men, 125
Individual differences, 21–24
Infants, 88–96
  biological motion preference, 88
  early vocabularies of, 86
  preference for animals, 95
  recognition of animals by, 91–92
  response to animals by, 15–16
  visual attention to animals, 88–93
Interaction(s)
  animal-assisted. *See* Animal-assisted
    interaction
  child-human, 24–26
  child–pet, 194–195
  of children with dogs, 107–110
  with companion animal, 174–177
  human–animal. *See* human–animal
    interaction
  human–dog, 102–104
  of infants with animals, 15–16,
    88–92, 95
  interpersonal, 24–26
  with siblings, 17–18
International Association of Human
    Animal Interaction
    Organisations (IAHAIO), 204
International Society for Anthrozoology
    (ISAZ), 204
Interpersonal interactions, 24–26

Motooka, M., 160, 167, 174, 175
Movement, animate, 90
Multidimensionality, 26–27
Myers, G., 16, 22

Nagasawa, M., 72
Nagengast, S. L., 169
National health costs, 159–160
National Institutes of Health (NIH), 193
Nationally representative surveys, 153–154
Natural landscapes, 87
Natural world, 86–87
Neighborhoods, 145
Nested ecological systems, 13
Neuroendocrine responses, 197
New, J., 87
Newborns, 88
Niches. *See* Ecological niches
Nielsen, J. A., 16
Nightingale, Florence, 183
NIH (National Institutes of Health), 193
Nimer, J., 5
Nissen, E., 62
Nonviolent crimes, 124, 125
Nucleus of the tractus solitaries (NTS), 58
Nursing homes, 187–188
Nursing journals, 208–209
Nutrition, 198

Obesity
  childhood. *See* Childhood obesity
  in dogs, 149, 189
  and dog walking, 188–189
Objects
  animated, 92–93
  inanimate, 88–91, 93
Occupational therapy journals, 209
Odendaal, J. S., 70
Offenders, juvenile, 124
Ohta, M., 72
Onaka, T., 72
Ontogeny, 106
Outcome Questionnaires, 44
Overweight children. *See* Childhood obesity

Oxytocin
  in animals, 57–59
  in blood samples, 58–59, 70
  collection of samples, 66–67
  in dog owners, 61, 63–64, 102
  in dogs, 61, 63–64
  and estrogen, 67
  hormone research on, 55–60, 70–73
  in human–animal interactions, 53–54
  in humans, 59–62
  measurement of, 64–66, 68–70
  in saliva, 73
  and sensory stimulation, 57–60
  in urine, 70–72

Pagani, C., 125
Pain, 184–186
Paraventricular nuclei (PVN), 55
Parker, J. G., 17
Patients, hospitalized, 185–186
Paul, E. S., 107
Pearse, V., 121
Pellino, T., 24
Peptide hormones, 55, 68–70
Perceptions, human, 24
Perceptual affordances, 15–16
Perceptual development, 15–16
Person characteristics, 23
Pervasive developmental disorders, 185
PET (Physical and Emotional Tormenting Against Animals Scale), 125
Pet ownership, 153–160. *See also* Dog owners
  and blood pressure levels, 166–177
  causal direction in research on, 156–157
  changes in attitudes toward, 203
  in child development, 4, 14–15
  and child health/physical well-being, 195–196
  and childhood obesity, 142–145
  emotional and physical health benefits of, 141–142
  and heart rate, 164–165, 167, 171–172, 174–176
  and human health/development, 4
  magnitude of health effects, 157–159

ABOUT THE EDITORS

Photo by Ian Smythe

Peggy McCardle, PhD, MPH, is chief of the Child Development and Behavior Branch at the *Eunice Kennedy Shriver* National Institute of Child Health and Human Development (NICHD) of the National Institutes of Health. At NICHD, in addition to her oversight of the branch, Dr. McCardle directs the research program on language, bilingualism, and biliteracy and developed the branch programs in adolescent and adult literacy. As branch chief, Dr. McCardle oversaw the development of a new program of research on the influence of interactions with animals on child health and development, for both pets in the home and in psychological and medical therapeutic settings, and she is committed to promoting evidence-based practice in the field of human–animal interaction. She is lead editor of the volumes *The Voice of Evidence in Reading Research* (2004); *Childhood Bilingualism* (2006) and *Infant Pathways to Language: Methods, Models, and Research Directions* (2008); lead author of *Reading Research in Action: A Teacher's Guide for Student Success* (2008); and has served as guest editor of thematic journal issues on reading, bilingualism, and English-language learner research.

Sandra McCune, PhD, heads up the research program on human–animal interaction at the Waltham Centre for Pet Nutrition in the United Kingdom. Her background is in ethology, and she has studied a range of topics in cat and dog behavior for many years, including aspects of temperament, social behavior, feeding behavior, cognition, and age-related changes in behavior. The practical experience she gained while a veterinary nurse informed much of her doctoral study assessment of individual variation in the temperament of cats and its impact on their welfare when confined. She also has extensive experience studying what happens when cat and dog behavior interacts with human behavior in a variety of contexts.

James A. Griffin, PhD, is the deputy chief of the Child Development and Behavior Branch at the *Eunice Kennedy Shriver* National Institute of Child Health and Human Development (NICHD) of the National Institutes of Health and the director of the early learning and school readiness program. Before his work at NICHD, Dr. Griffin served as a senior research analyst in the Institute of Education Sciences at the U.S. Department of Education; as the assistant director for the Social, Behavioral, and Education Sciences in the White House Office of Science and Technology Policy; and as a research analyst at the Administration on Children, Youth and Families.

Valerie Maholmes, PhD, CAS, directs the research program in social and affective development/child maltreatment and violence in the Child Development and Behavior Branch at the *Eunice Kennedy Shriver* National Institute of Child Health and Human Development of the National Institutes of Health. Dr. Maholmes received a doctorate in educational psychology from Howard University in Washington, DC, and a 6-year degree with advanced study in school psychology, with a concentration in neuropsychological and psychosocial assessments from Fairfield University in Connecticut. Her research and clinical work have focused on the psychosocial, cultural, and environmental factors that influence children's learning and development, particularly low-income minority children. She held a faculty position at the Yale University Child Study Center in New Haven, CT, where she served in numerous capacities, including the director of research and policy for the school development program and the Irving B. Harris assistant professor of child psychiatry, an endowed professorial chair for social policy.